DUFF BAKES

ALSO BY DUFF GOLDMAN
(WITH WILLIE GOLDMAN)

Ace of Cakes

WILLIAM MORROW

An Imprint of HarperCollinsPublishers

DUFF BAKES

THINK AND BAKE LIKE A PRO AT HOME

DUFF GOLDMAN
AND SARA GONZALES

PHOTOGRAPHY BY CAREN ALPERT

HarperCollins books may be purchased for educational, business, or sales promotional use. For information please e-mail the Special Markets Department at SPsales@harpercollins.com.

FIRST EDITION

Designer: Shannon Nicole Plunkett
Photographer: Caren Alpert
Prop stylist: Robin Turk
Food stylist: Hannah Canvasser
Photographer's assistant: William Bradford

Library of Congress Cataloging-in-Publication Data has been applied for.

ISBN 978-0-06-234980-4

15 16 17 18 19   OV/QGT   10 9 8 7 6 5 4 3 2

TO CHEF CINDY WOLF,
WHO CHANGED MY LIFE BY MAKING ME
BAKE CORNBREAD AND BISCUITS
FOR TWO YEARS STRAIGHT

CONTENTS

INTRODUCTION

BY DUFF GOLDMAN

Originally I wanted to call this book *Bake Awesome*. It's one of the things I write when I sign an autograph. I know that sounds really lame, but hear me out. Most people I meet tell me how they love to cook and they love watching me bake, but they just can't do it. They can't bake. Too much measuring, too much science—it seems like this impenetrable fortress of knowledge that one can only gain access to by laying culinary siege to it for many, many years, or by being a grandmother.

I try to explain to people that baking is the kind of thing that you can be successful at the first time you try it and spend the rest of your life learning about. Baking is science, yes. Baking is math, physics, chemistry, and measuring. But baking is also feeling, smelling, loving, and intuition. Baking is something you dance with. It's a slow dance, though, not a mosh pit. It's a measured pace of placing every foot and every hand in just the right spot at just the right time and moving with, not at, your partner. You feel when the cake is done. You smell when the cookies are perfect. You listen to the bread when it crackles as it cools and you know that crust is going to be delicious.

Baking is just like playing music. I've always found a striking relation between playing music and baking in that they both require harmony to have quality. Music is constructed in such a way that certain notes sound good coming before or after other notes. Baking observes these same rules. There are steps you take that come before other steps to make sure the muffin is good. What I want everyone to understand is that baking isn't this cold, rigid "science" that you need a PhD for; it's a craft like any other that you discover for yourself every time you do it. It's the perpetual excitement at seeing what you bake when it comes out of the oven. It never ceases to be magic, and it only becomes more fascinating the more you do it.

Sara and I want to give people our view of baking as professional bakers, but we want to do it in a language that everyone can understand. We want to explain the shorthand and make it accessible. And we really, really want you to bake.

INTRODUCTION

BY SARA GONZALES

WHO IS SARA GONZALES?

I'm going to write the intro to the intro of Sara Gonzales.
I want Sara to tell you about herself, but first, let me tell you about Sara.
Sara Gonzales is the most naturally gifted baker I've ever worked with.
When you're fortunate enough to witness anyone doing the thing that they
were born to do in your presence, cherish it. There's nothing as beautiful as
watching someone create with so much skill it seems effortless. That's how
Sara bakes. She bakes from the heart, and I know that sounds clichéd,
but when you taste the love in everything she bakes, you understand the
true meaning of it. Take it away, Sara. —Duff

ell, shucks, Duff, thank you for that lovely intro to my intro. So who am I? I'm simply a young lady who likes to create things that make people smile, and I happen to have a knack for baking. People love to ask me if I always wanted to bake, if I sought a career in it, if I studied and went to school to learn and perfect my baking. The answer is actually no, not at all.

I've always loved baking as a hobby. My mom taught me how to make pie crust around the age of six or so, and quick breads and cookies not long after that, and later the hobby really blossomed into an after-school activity to pass the time with my best friend when we didn't want to go to swim team practice that day. I went on to get a degree in health education (ironic, I know), and in college I was lucky enough to have friends around me who relished cooking and baking as much as I did, so the skill set, the confidence, and the hands-on experience grew in the space of my own kitchen as the years went by.

My first professional job baking in a kitchen was a happy accident. I happened to find a baking assistant position that I considered a temporary gig until I could find something more in line with my degree. And wouldn't you know, I fell in love with it. The feeling of the dough stuck to my fingers, the sound of the mixer whirring to combine a seemingly random assembly of ingredients into the most decadent brownie batter, and the smells of fresh baked goods—oh, the smells!

Baking lets my creative side flourish—a side of myself that six years ago I had little idea even existed. Now I have the coolest damn job! Duff says, "Hey, Sara, what if we make this pie that has this and that in it? Can you do that?" and I get to respond with "I have no idea! Let's try it, plus we can add this!" This is what I do now—I experiment, I create, I develop my skills and experience new things daily, and the best part about it is that I'm just getting started. I love baking—it's a wonderful thing—and I hope this book helps you to feel that way, too.

PHILOSOPHY AT 375 DEGREES

In baking, as in life, always ask "why?" It's important for two reasons: The first is that when you know *why*, you gain a deeper understanding of the thing you're attempting to learn. The second is that when you ask someone "why?" and they don't know, and you go off and find the answer yourself, it's a spectacular way to learn lots of other stuff in the process.

I always ask "why?" when I bake (and in general), and not just because I have a degree in philosophy. I enjoy knowing "why" because it helps me create something better than I would have if I didn't know. Say the recipe says, "Don't overmix." Okay, why? Well, overmixing creates stronger protein strands, which make a chewier texture, and I like my cake tender, not hard like a bagel. There, you just learned a "why." When I say, "Scrape down the sides of the bowl," ask me "why?" Funny you should ask—I'll tell you. When you're mixing a batter, ingredients will often get stuck to the sides of the bowl. What if that includes all the salt in a recipe? Well, then most of your cookies will be real flat-tasting, while *one* cookie will be salty, which will of course be the cookie I sell to a food blogger, who will then tell the entire world that I bake salty cookies.

Our philosophy at Charm City Cakes is relatively simple: Make awesome stuff, be nice to people and each other, and have fun while we do it. It's so glaringly obvious when someone enjoys what they do. You can see it. You see it in the details. You see it in the (almost) (wink, wink) flawless execution of a project. We laugh a lot. We enjoy our customers and joke around with them. We have funny pictures of cats all over the bakery. But we make incredible cakes. I've worked in a lot of kitchens, and I can tell you that when there's no joy in a kitchen, it can be very difficult to achieve excellence. But in a kitchen like mine, where laughter and silliness are the rule, it's so much easier to get the best work done.

It should be the same in your kitchen. It should be a place of joy, not dread. Bake fearlessly. Bake knowing that nothing, and I mean nothing, makes a kid happier than a fresh-baked cookie, and nothing can make you happier than knowing you made a kid happy. We do what we do at Charm City Cakes because of the look on our customers' faces when they see their cake for the first time . . . and then again when they taste it. Having fun and caring deeply about what you're doing are not mutually exclusive concepts. In some professions, such as being a surgeon, I can imagine that it's very important to be serious and focused. We're bakers, though, and a certain amount of frivolity is not only tolerated, but expected.

Another idea we prescribe to is one of innovation. This is important—pay attention. We wouldn't be who we are if we didn't take what the rest of the world says—"This is how it is"—and then turn it around by saying, "What about this and this and this?" It's the same thing with this book—I want you take these recipes and instructions and make them your own. If I give you an apple pie, make a pear pie. If I give you a pecan muffin, make it with walnuts. If I give you a seven-grain bread, give me back a honey-wheat loaf. I guess what I'm trying to say is that baking is a craft like any other that is based on rules and methods. But those rules and methods are like a building. You need walls, floors, stairs, a roof, hopefully some windows, and electricity to have a functional building, but what people do inside that building is what makes it special. Maybe it's an art studio, maybe a call center, or maybe it's a church (the building that Charm City Cakes is in has been all those things). The building itself is necessary, yes, but it's just a building until you fill it with endeavor and creativity. I was told when I first started Charm City Cakes back in 2002 that cakes were round. I was told in 2004 not to hire my friends. I was told when I went to my first competition in 2005 that nobody uses power tools in cake decorating. I was told in 2007 that nobody would want to watch my friends and me make cakes on television. I'm told almost daily what won't work, and I keep doing it anyway. And it does work.

Here's the bottom line: You can be awesome at this and still laugh while you do it. You can bake excellent things . . . and I give you permission to enjoy doing so.

INGREDIENTS

If you walk down the baking aisle in your grocery store, you'll see dozens of different flours. What do you do with them all? Baking soda—that's the same as baking powder, right? What do you mean, honey is sweeter than sugar? These are confusing things, I know, and the store really doesn't help you understand it all, so I will. It's actually pretty simple.

Okay, let's talk about flour for a second. Now, I could get all nerdy and really break down the chemical composition of flour and explain why different varieties are grown at different times of the year, and what ash content is and all that, but I won't. That's like if you ask me what time it is and I tell you how to build a clock.

There are different flours for different baked goods, and the distinctions are pretty easy. The most important thing that you need to know about flour is how much protein is in each variety. Bagels are not made with the same flour as cakes. Cakes are tender, while you can play hockey with a bagel.

Before we get into different kinds of flour, I want to draw your attention to a few words on flour packages that seem innocuous but are actually very important.

Bleached flour is chemically treated to make it whiter, and it has less protein. Sometimes you'll see it listed as "maida" flour. Bleached flour may or may not be naturally bleached (so read the package carefully), but either version is a much finer flour than bread flour or unbleached all-purpose flour. When flour is unbleached, it naturally gets lighter in color over time, but will always be a creamier color than bleached flour, and "creamier" just looks and sounds more delicious than "bleached." Some say that bleached flour is better for waffles, crêpes, and cookies. I think it's best to use flour that has been treated gently and one with a naturally lower protein content, such as a 50/50 mixture of pastry flour and unbleached all-purpose flour.

Bromated flour has had potassium bromate added to it to strengthen the protein by oxidizing it more quickly. Try to find flour that doesn't have potassium bromate in it and just mix your dough longer to strengthen the protein. Again, gently treated flour is the best flour.

Stone-milled flour is simply flour that's been milled slowly between two stones. It's not some hipster fad or some trick to get you to spend more on flour. Stone-milled flour is better for a number of reasons, but I'll spare you the dissertation. Basically, stone-milled flour makes better baked goods because the milling process doesn't heat up the flour and cook off the protein and nutrients. With stone-milled flour, the first time the gluten is activated is when *you* decide to activate it. Also, stone-milled flour tastes better. It has more of the bits of the wheat kernel in it, and "white" stone-milled flour is actually kind of tan. What's the rule? Color is flavor. Stone-milled flour is gently treated flour.

Organic flour is grown from pesticide-free grain in naturally fertilized soil. Also, once the wheat has been harvested, it hasn't been kept in fumigated conditions. It's good to buy organic whenever possible. It's better for you, it's better for the planet, and it's better for your cookies. I think organic flour really does taste better. I'm not trying to be precious about flour. It's just the most ubiquitous element in my life; I think about it all the time.

Those are the words you should be paying attention to on the package of your flour when you shop. As always, making good choices at the grocery store is the most important step in making good choices for yourself. Now, let's get into the different types of flour.

All-purpose or AP flour isn't really "all" purpose. It's more like "most" purpose. While AP flour can be used to make everything from delicate pastries and cakes to crusty French bread, it certainly has a sweet spot. AP flour is really great for baked goods that need to be held together because they have a high fat content and a more robust texture. AP flour is best for quick breads, cookies, muffins, and most pie and tart doughs. Also, AP flour can be mixed with other flours to either strengthen or weaken the proteins in them. A lot of recipes will say to use so much cake flour and so much AP flour. This will help you get the texture you want. Yes, you can make bread with AP flour, but it's best to use a higher-protein flour, usually called bread flour.

Bread flour is used for . . . that's right! Bread! It has a higher protein content than AP flour and makes good, chewy bread with a thick, crusty crust. Bread flour is also good for New York–style pizza dough. Some breads, like chapatti or focaccia, are better with a weaker flour; I like big, fluffy focaccia with lots of olive oil in the dough. But for bread that requires neck muscles to tear through, use bread flour. There are even stronger flours out there, called (funnily enough) strong flour or high-gluten flour. They're used more on the industrial side of baking, and are for really chewy things like bagels.

Cake flour has the ideal protein content (8 to 10 percent) for the specific texture of American high-ratio cakes (which have roughly an equal amount by weight of sugar to flour and use much more butter than a French genoise or angel food cake) and some soft kinds of cookies. Cake flour in the United States is typically very finely milled and bleached; if you want an unbleached flour with a similar protein count, use pastry flour.

Pastry flour has a bit more protein than cake flour but a similar texture, while it is weaker than AP flour and more finely milled. Pastry flour is great for most fine pastries, in which a delicate texture is desired.

Self-rising flour is weird, and I don't ever use it. It's about equivalent to a weak AP flour in gluten, but has the salt and baking powder already in it. If you want salt in something, put it in there. If you want baking powder in your recipe, add it. I don't need no flour telling me what's in my flour. I want flour in my flour! (Okay, I'm not that mad at self-rising flour. There are actually some really good old-school grandma recipes that call for it, and if you're going to learn how to bake, it's best to learn from old-school grandmas.)

Whole-wheat flour contains every part of the wheat grain: the bran, the germ, and the endosperm. I know, big words, but basically, the bran is the wrapper (and a great source of fiber), the germ is like the yolk of the wheat berry (where the oils and plant embryo are stored), and the endosperm is the starchy part of the kernel (the food the germ eats to grow up into a big ol' wheat stalk). Baking with whole wheat is fun and challenging in that you get nuttier flavors, but you really have to pay attention. Because of the oils and bran found in whole-wheat flour, it doesn't rise as high as white flour and might spoil more quickly if not properly stored. But use it right and your little baked yummlies will be that much more yummly.

Graham flour is whole-wheat flour that's milled so that the starch is ground very fine but the germ and the bran are left coarse. You use it to make graham crackers. You can certainly use regular whole-wheat flour for graham crackers, but don't let me catch you. I'll call you out!

White whole-wheat flour is real whole-wheat flour. No tricks. Whole-wheat flour that's brown is milled from red (or sometimes golden) wheat. White whole-wheat flour is made from hard white spring wheat. The most important difference is that white whole-wheat flour has much less protein and also tastes more like white flour. It doesn't have the earthy flavors of whole-grain red wheat flour.

In essence, the chewier you want your product to be, the higher the protein content you want in the flour. The more tender and delicate (like me), the less protein. And never forget—color is flavor. Now let's get into leavening agents, which make things rise. There are three types of leavening that I want to discuss:

Chemical leavening agents are most commonly baking soda and baking powder. Baking soda (sodium bicarbonate), as we all know from playing with vinegar, makes bubbles when you combine it with an acid. Baking powder is baking soda plus cornstarch and a powdered acid, usually cream of tartar. If you have a recipe that calls for baking soda *and* cream of tartar, don't ignore the cream of tartar or your cookies won't rise and they'll taste of nickels. Many recipes call for both baking powder and baking soda. This is when a smaller ratio of cream of tartar is needed and there's enough other acid in the recipe to neutralize the sodium bicarbonate. Double-acting baking powder has two acids in it; one that reacts in a batter when it's wet and one that reacts to the heat in the oven.

You need to know this because if your baking soda isn't reacting with anything or you have too much in your cookies, they really will taste like nickels. If this happens, check your recipe and see if you forgot something (or the recipe writer forgot something), and also check the date on the can of baking powder. It slowly reacts with air over time and becomes weaker, and baking powder has a habit of sitting in your pantry for years. Also, make sure you mix the batter properly and scrape down the sides of the bowl to ensure that the batter is homogeneous.

Biological leavening agents are yeasts. Dry yeast, fresh yeast, brewer's yeast, and sourdough starter—all yeast. You have to love your yeast—it's a living organism, and when you treat it right, keep it warm, and feed it, it does what it's supposed to do—it eats and farts and pees. Yeast eats sugar and starch, farts out CO_2, and pees out alcohol. The CO_2 expands and makes the bread rise, and the alcohol adds flavor. Yummy!

Mechanical leavening is making things rise using air and steam. You can whip air into your batter, which expands in the oven and makes your cake rise (it's how French people make genoise); you can make a laminated dough like puff pastry, in which the moisture in the dough steams between layers of butter and flour and rises that way; and you can also add yeast to a laminated dough and make danishes! A lot of leavening is actually a combination of mechanical and biological or chemical. In cookies, for example, you cream the butter and sugar together until it's nice and fluffy, then add baking soda or baking powder, and the action of the air plus the action of the CO_2 make the cookies rise.

Now let's talk about some of the ingredients that can be confusing to a new baker, or even someone who has been using these ingredients for a while. I've been cooking since I was fourteen, and it wasn't until four months into culinary school that one of my teachers caught on that I thought "zest" was a fancy word for "juice." I had no idea you could eat the lemon peel! Let's start with the letter Z, shall we?

Zest is the outermost layer of a citrus fruit (lemon, lime, orange, and so on), also known by the fancy word "exocarp." Sounds like a Swedish black metal band, right? Anyway, the essential oils that give a citrus fruit its taste and smell are found in abundance on the outside of the fruit, but only the very outer layer. (The white pith—mesocarp—just underneath the zest is really bitter, and you can candy it, but don't eat it raw.) Zesting a fruit is a great way to get all that good natural flavor out of the fruit without using an extract or an artificial flavoring. You can use a zester or a paring knife to remove the zest and use it however you see fit.

Buttermilk is the liquid that is left over after butter is made from cream. You'll find buttermilk in a lot of baking recipes because it's very acidic and will be sure to react with all the baking soda in your product so it doesn't taste like nickels when it's done. Some people drink buttermilk, especially in the South. Fun fact: I've never even tasted buttermilk on its own, only in things I've baked it into. I have no idea what buttermilk tastes like solo.

Gelatin is an animal by-product used to thicken some creams, custards, and candies. Marshmallows are basically whipped gelatin with sugar, vanilla, and egg whites. In professional kitchens, gelatin comes in sheets and is soaked in cold water before being added to a warm mixture. Sheets are uncommon at the grocery store, however, so look for powdered gelatin, which usually comes in ¼-ounce packets. You bloom all gelatin the same way, though—soak it in cold water until it's rubbery, then add it to something warm. When that warm thing cools down, it'll be thicker than it was before. Magical!

Cornstarch is exactly that—the starch derived from corn. It's every baker's best friend. It's great for thinning out flour and creating a crispy crust, and it makes crispier deep-fried foods than flour. At the bakery, we use it to keep fondant from sticking to things. And the best thing about cornstarch is that when you're running around the kitchen all day and you start to get chafed, you know, down there, a handful of cornstarch on the irritated parts provides instant relief! In the professional cooking world, we call it "monkey butt." When you go to a restaurant and you see a box of cornstarch in the restroom, that's why.

Arrowroot is similar to cornstarch but more akin to potato starch in that it comes from the rootstock of low-lying warm-weather plants. You'll find arrowroot used in a lot of gluten-free recipes, but it is not a 1:1 flour replacer—it still needs something to bind it together. It's great for making jellies and other soft candies.

Xanthan gum is used to hold together gluten-free flours in the absence of that protein. It's a tricky little ingredient; it's very potent and a little goes a long way. Just for fun, you should look up how it's made.

Semolina is not fine cornmeal, as a lot of people think. It is durum wheat flour, and it's naturally yellow. It's used in Cream of Wheat, pasta, couscous, and semolina puddings. Outside of Italy, semolina is usually served sweet with some kind of berry, currant, or raisin.

Cornmeal is milled dried corn. It's the base for cornbread, but it's also used in bread production as a buffer between a hot surface and a sticky dough. A lot of times you'll find cornmeal on the bottom of a loaf of focaccia, and it adds a nice crunch to the bite.

Rye flour is a staple of Northern and Eastern Europe. It's a very hardy grass related to wheat that makes a delicious, nutty, dark flour and bread. It doesn't develop protein as white flour does and makes a much denser bread. It's usually very moist, makes great sandwiches and toast, and in the hands of the right baker, makes the most delicious sourdough on the planet. Try my recipe for sourdough on page 130, but use rye for your starter and substitute rye for half the flour in the recipe and you'll make your mouth happy.

Rice flour (*komeko* in Japanese) can be either white or brown. In Asian cuisine, it's used in a variety of ways, including baking and thickening soups and sauces. In the United States, rice flour is also used in gluten-free baking. It's not easy to work with and can get clumpy quickly, but learn how to bake with rice flour and you'll be rewarded with really awesome textures.

Butter isn't unfamiliar to anyone, but there are still a few things you need to know. Cheap butter is cheap because it contains a lot of water. When you bake with cheap butter, the water boils off and you're left with a product that's drier than intended because the fat percentage has gone down. Don't skimp. Also, besides tasting like butter, organic butter tastes like the grass the cows were eating when they were milked. This is great for spreading on warm toast, but most of that flavor is usually lost when you bake with it. I'm not saying don't buy organic butter—you should—but don't expect a banana-cranberry loaf to taste like the California hillside those cows were grazing on.

Brown butter (*beurre noisette* in French) is butter that has been slowly melted until the milk solids separate from the butterfat, sink to the bottom of the pan, and get nice and brown. While it's hot, it's great for sauces (a little brown butter and sage on fresh linguini . . . mmm!), but in baking you can make large quantities and keep it in the fridge. Brown butter has a very distinct flavor, very nutty, and will up your baking game considerably. Check out the blondies on page 85 to see brown butter in action.

Nuts should be kept in the fridge or freezer. They have a high amount of fat and can turn rancid quickly. When baking with nuts, toast them a bit in a dry pan over low heat before adding them to a wet batter—they'll stay crunchier and will release more oils as they bake, giving your product a richer nut flavor.

Eggs are one of the most important ingredients you'll use. All these recipes call for extra-large eggs—don't buy the less expensive "large" ones. Extra-large eggs (not to be confused with "jumbo" eggs) are what most recipes are based on, so traditionally, as recipes got passed around over the ages, they are the standard. There's about a three-ounce difference in weight between a dozen "large" and a dozen "extra-large" eggs, and since baking recipes are based on ratios, a three-ounce difference can really affect your end product. When you're baking with eggs, pull them out of the fridge and let them come to room temperature. Cold eggs resist mixing and make you mix longer—the longer you mix, the tougher your muffins will be. I'm the only tough muffin you need! And if you're making a meringue, choose older eggs; an egg aged a week or so has lost some of its moisture, so the egg whites will have a higher concentration of albumen, the protein in egg whites that traps air. Egg whites start out as 98 percent water, so the more water that has evaporated, the more albumen you'll have and the stronger your meringue will be. The best way to "age" your eggs is to either buy the oldest eggs in the case (they all have a "sell-by" date) or buy them ahead of time and mark the package so nobody makes an omelet with your special meringue eggs. The way to test an egg's age is to float it in a glass of water. If the egg barely breaks the surface, it's very fresh; the more egg that shows above the water, the older the egg. If the egg smells like, well, rotten eggs, don't use it. The smell test is the best test for eggs.

Vanilla is the second-most expensive flavor next to saffron, and it's in almost everything in this book! Fresh vanilla from the vanilla bean is always wonderful, but not exactly realistic—the beans are on the pricey side. When you do use fresh vanilla beans, however, be sure to steep the pod after you scrape it in whatever liquid you're baking with, or keep a jar of sugar special and add the scraped vanilla pods to it so you'll always have some vanilla sugar on hand. There's a ton of flavor in that pod, and it's a real shame to waste it. Vanilla extracts are much easier to use, but *please* make sure to use pure vanilla and not imitation vanilla. Imitation vanilla tastes like cheap birthday cake, and unless you're baking cheap birthday cake, use the good stuff—it's worth it.

Okay, so I have a strong opinion about spices. If you bake a lot and are any kind of baking snob, buy a bunch of mini coffee grinders and label each one with a particular spice. Once you grind nutmeg in a particular machine, you can't use it for anything else. Grind your spices fresh when you're baking. Spices that are pre-ground "die," and the difference is astronomical. If you don't bake that much but care enough to make me happy, buy a Microplane and shave your spices directly into the bowl. I promise, freshly ground spices are not an affectation—they really make a difference.

Amaranth grain has been cultivated for around 8,000 years as a major staple crop of the ancient Aztecs, until it was outlawed by the Spanish *conquistadores*, who were generally just all-around jerks who would outlaw things like growing amaranth. It's been making a bit of a comeback since the 1970s, as it's very nutritious and also naturally gluten-free. Fun fact: Amaranth is still used in Mexican cuisine as a staple ingredient and in a candy bar that mixes amaranth, honey, and sometimes pumpkin seeds made especially around Día de Los Muertos.

Spelt goes back as far as 5000 BC and is in the same family as modern wheat, but it's sort of like wheat's tough dad—it has old-man strength. It's a hardier grain, higher in fiber, and with a molecular structure that allows it to be easily integrated into food and a gluten structure that's more water-soluble and thus more digestible than common wheat. Spelt flour can be substituted 1:1 for whole wheat flour in anything from bread to pasta to cookies to waffles (just be ready for variations in texture) and can be found at most specialty and health food stores.

Garbanzo bean or **chickpea flour** (*farina di ceci* in Italian) is not only awesome in taste, but loaded with protein and fiber. Flour made from these beans is naturally gluten-free, so it makes a great wheat flour substitute, along with rice flour or another gluten-free starch. Aside from baking, chickpea flour is often used in Middle Eastern cuisine in falafel, hummus, and so on.

CHOCOLATE

All right, I'm 99 percent sure that the majority of people reading this book are aware that not all chocolate is the same. There is milk chocolate, dark chocolate, white chocolate, sweet chocolate, not-so-sweet chocolate—heck, it even comes in a powder that you can use to make chocolate milk (that's instant hot cocoa mix—which is *not* cocoa powder, something I learned at like six years old!). When following a recipe, it's important to use the type of chocolate the recipe calls for, so that your final product tastes as good as possible. So let's do a quick breakdown of the types of chocolate:

White chocolate contains cocoa butter (the fat part of the cocoa bean) but no solid parts, leaving it a pale color. It's mixed with vanilla, an emulsifier, and a sweetener and is, on the whole, rather sweet and mild in flavor.

Milk chocolate contains cocoa butter but also 15 to 20 percent cocoa bean solids, lending a brown color. It's mixed with sugar and milk (usually some form of powdered dairy product), so it has a creamy, sweet flavor. Milk chocolate typically isn't used in baking, but for bribing children to get them to do stuff like clean their room or eat their greens.

Semisweet chocolate is a subcategory of dark chocolate, classically used for baking cakes, cookies, and brownies. It contains up to 65 percent cocoa solids, sugar, and no milk solids.

Bittersweet chocolate is a rich, dark chocolate that contains less sugar than semisweet chocolate but is just as good to bake with. A quality bittersweet chocolate typically contains anywhere from 60 to 85 percent cocoa solids. The higher the percentage, the less sweet and more rich and bitter it tastes.

Unsweetened chocolate, also known as "baking" or "cooking" chocolate, is pure cocoa solids and fat, but no sugar. So don't eat it by itself—it's gross—and when baking with it, better not forget the sugar!

I'm going to keep this as simple as possible: **Cocoa powder** in general is ultra-pulverized cocoa beans with nearly all of the cocoa butter removed from it. Now, there are two kinds of cocoa powders—natural cocoa powder and Dutch-processed or "Dutched" cocoa powder—and there's a noticeable difference between them when it comes to baking.

Natural cocoa powder is lighter in color and more acidic than Dutch-processed. When baking with natural cocoa powder, the recipe will call for baking soda, because the metallic taste of the baking soda and the acidity of the cocoa powder will neutralize each other.

Dutch-processed cocoa powder goes through an additional processing step; it's treated with an alkaline substance to neutralize its acidity. Stripped of much of its acid, this cocoa powder is noticeably darker in color but has a milder taste than natural cocoa powder. It's more often associated with baking powder recipes, because baking powder is baking soda that contains its own acid and doesn't need the extra acidity to make CO_2.

So there you have a quick guide to chocolates and cocoa!

Simple syrup is simply equal parts water and sugar. If you need it right away, you can cook it on the stove and it will be ready in a few minutes. If you find that you use a lot of it or know you want it tomorrow, mix the water and sugar in a bowl and cover it. The sugar will dissolve overnight.

Most baking recipes don't call for too much oil, so in that sense any oils will provide a similar texture in the finished product. But keep in mind the flavor and the smoke point. If an oil has a bold flavor (think peanut or sesame oil), you'll taste it in your finished product. An oil's smoke point is important because at that temperature the oil begins to break down, losing flavor and nutrients and releasing free radicals. Canola oil, vegetable oil, coconut oil, almond and walnut oils, and many others have a smoke point of 400°F or higher, so they're pretty safe to bake with. Olive oil has a lower smoke point than some of these other oils, but most baking occurs at lower temperatures anyway.

Cooking spray. There are like, three hundred brands of cooking and baking spray out there. You will need it, so it's important to know what's on the market and what you're looking for. There's a popular cooking spray with flour in it called baking spray, but, believe it or not, I have never used it so I can't speak to whether it works. Some home bakers swear by it, and if you want to give it a shot, I say go for it. All the spray I call for in this book is 100 percent natural vegetable oil, nonhydrogenated. We use a brand called Vegalene in my bakeries, which is an industry standard and is sold retail but only online. The big commercial ones are fine to use, but can sometimes contain more lecithin and fewer releasing agents than the 100 percent natural sprays. The best ones to use are usually available in a regular grocery store, just not as prominently placed as Pam. Also, anything from Whole Foods is going to be exactly what you want. That being said, if your grandma taught you to always butter and flour the pan, and that's how you like to bake, then you butter and flour that pan! No school like the old school.

EQUIPMENT

There are few pieces of equipment that I want to briefly mention, either because they're important (or useless) or because I just find them to be fascinating. A lot of this list will be familiar to most of you, but there are little details about certain baking implements that are important to understand.

Candy thermometer: This is used to very precisely measure the temperature of hot sugar. It's designed to be easily read and can withstand very high temperatures. Most also have a guide printed on them, so instead of having to know the precise physical and chemical make-up of sugar at any given temperature, it just says on the thermometer "hard crack" or "soft ball" or whatever stage you're going for. Most recipes will call for not only the target temperature, but also the name of the stage of that sugar as it cooks.

Just a quick note on sugar so this makes sense: Sugar changes as it gets hotter. As it heats up, its physical properties change, so that if you heat it to 235°F and then cool it, the sugar will be gummy like clay when it cools. If you heat it to 300°F and then cool it, it will be hard and brittle, like a lollipop.

Cookie scoop: Basically, a small ice cream scoop. They come in various sizes, from a third of an ounce to half a pound. Restaurant scoops are usually referred to as "disher scoops" and have color-coded handles that are industry standard. You might see a recipe somewhere that says "one purple scoop" or "three red scoops." This was a recipe taken directly from a professional kitchen.

Stand mixer: A whisk or a spoon is great for mixing, but saving some time and energy when mixing batter, whipping cream, or combining dough is an awesome thing. Mixer attachments like the whisk, paddle, and dough hook will make a baker's life 100 percent easier. It's important that a simple physical task doesn't defeat you. I can hand-whisk a 2:3 ratio meringue, but I can also bench-press 315. Use a KitchenAid for your meringue.

Rubber spatula: Used for scraping down the sides of a mixing bowl, folding ingredients, and ensuring that every last drop of batter is scraped out of your bowl, a heat-resistant rubber or silicone spatula is a baker's best friend. I always make sure to have plenty on hand. They aren't expensive, and it's good to have a bunch so you aren't stopping to wash every time you use one. The commercial ones with the red handle are more stiff and heat resistant. The ones with the white handle are not heat resistant but are more flexible.

Metal spatula: There are so many things in the kitchen that are called a spatula. Metal spatulas for baking and pastry are long and thin and are either straight or offset. They're used for icing cakes, lifting soft pieces of dough, and removing cookies from a tray.

Plastic taping knife: These are meant for use for drywall and plastering and can be as narrow as 1 inch or as wide as 18 inches. They're great for icing tall cakes, and they're super cheap at the hardware store.

Propane blowtorch: I use the big self-igniting kind from the hardware store. Those little torches you buy in kitchen catalogs are fun, but for real baking, get the big blue bottle. Don't buy the red bottle or the yellow bottle! The red bottle is oxygen and the yellow bottle is MAP gas. They burn way too hot and are a super fire hazard in your house. They also make your food taste like crap. Propane is more than capable of heating a bowl of buttercream or crisping a brûlée.

Measuring cups and spoons: Baking is a damn science! Once you're super comfortable with baking, you can eyeball *some* amounts, but until then . . . measure your baking powder and baking soda. It's important. Try measuring out ingredients with teaspoons and tablespoons and then putting them into your palm. You'll get used to what they look like, and soon you'll be able to measure by pouring ingredients into your hand. Also, when measuring dry ingredients, use a "dry" measuring cup, and when measuring wet ingredients, use a "liquid" measuring cup. They are designed differently so you get the most accurate reading possible for whichever ingredient you are using. Dry measuring cups have flat, even tops (no spouts) so you can run the back of a knife over the top to get exact amounts of dry ingredients.

Thermometer: Having an instant-read kitchen thermometer is especially essential to find that perfect temperature of milk to activate yeast or of oil to fry the perfect doughnut. If you don't have a thermometer, you can always toss a bit of dough into the fryer and see if the oil is too hot or cold, but it takes a little experience to really gauge it by eye. Also, it's a good idea to have an oven thermometer inside your oven. The dial on your oven can be off by 30 to 40 degrees, which is a huge difference.

Microplane: This long, fine grater on a handle is great for harvesting citrus zest or grating spices such as cinnamon sticks or nutmeg.

Digital kitchen scale: Sooner or later, you'll come across recipes asking for ingredients in either grams or ounces. Have a reliable kitchen scale that measures in both units and you'll be prepared.

Rolling pins: I enjoy a heavy, solid wooden pin with no handles. Rolling pins with handles are one of the most useless and frustrating inventions known to man. When you roll dough with a rolling pin with handles, you don't have a feel for the dough the way you do with a simple rolling pin. You need to be one with your dough. It's the difference between driving stick versus automatic. Also, when you roll with a handled pin, it has to be large enough so you don't drag your knuckles through your dough like some baking troglodyte, and a big, fat rolling pin is hard to control. A simple, semi-thick, non-tapered rolling pin gets you in touch with your dough.

Bench knife or bench scraper: I love using the bench knife for gently cutting off portions of butter, dough, and other ingredients. It also works great for smoothing the sides of cakes when icing and decorating.

Baking sheets and pans: These are also called cookie sheets or sheet pans. It's important to have nice, flat sheet pans. If you can bend it with your hands, it won't last one bake in the oven. It will warp and be stupid and ruin your perfectly executed cookies and gingerbread. Test it before you buy it; if it feels cheap, it is.

Kitchen towels: Clean, dry kitchen rags are suitable replacements for oven mitts, potholders, and many other kitchen items. But always remember that a wet towel can burn you!

Pastry brush: Some recipes will ask you to brush your baked item with an egg wash or other type of glaze. I like pastry brushes with artificial bristles. The brushes are food safe, and if one comes off and sticks to the top of a biscuit or something, it turns very dark in the oven so you can see it and remove it before you serve it. Also, use a specific brush just for pastry. If you have a brush that's been basting a squab or sitting in garlic butter, your scones will taste like something you don't want them to.

Liquid measuring cups: Get accurate with your liquids and know how much you're using. Liquid measuring cups should be translucent and made of either plastic or Pyrex and should have a spout for clean and easy pouring. I am personally not a fan of glass in my kitchen, ever, so I recommend a trip to the commercial kitchen store to buy the plastic kind. They have great handles and will never let you down.

Pastry bags: I like the big, plastic, disposable piping bags. The heavier cloth reusable pastry bags are tricky to wash and keep from mildewing, and the plastic pastry bags feel better in your hands. Also, with transparent plastic piping bags, you can see what you're piping—you'll know if it's melting or lumpy or otherwise problematic.

Cake wheel: A cake wheel is that lazy Susan–looking thing that you use to rotate cakes as you decorate them. It's essential for decorating cakes, but also is a very useful item to have (they're great for lots of crafts, and for at-home pu-pu platter consumption) and I wouldn't consider it extravagant to have one in your house even if you make only a couple of cakes per year.

Pizza cutter: Dough is delicate. When cutting dough, is it better to drag a questionably sharp knife along the dough, pulling at it and snagging it and making a mess? Or do you let a pizza cutter roll along the dough, with all the pressure going straight down instead of lengthwise? It's physics, guys. It matters. (See what I did there?)

TECHNIQUES

The trick to baking well is understanding some of the basic techniques used in creating delicious baked goods. I could write a three-volume set on baking and pastry techniques, but here are a few possibly unfamiliar terms and techniques that you'll find in this book. This list is from my own experience growing as a baker and how I learned to do things right. Understand these techniques and how they can go wrong, and you've taken a huge stride toward baking awesome.

Folding is carefully assimilating two or more delicate preparations into one homogenous mass. I think mousse is the best example (and angel food cake is a close second). To make a fantastic chocolate mousse with a pillowy, light texture is not difficult, but it must be done right. First, you melt a bunch of chocolate on the stove with some butter. Next you whip some cream. Then you whip air into egg yolks until they're light and fluffy. Next you whip egg whites until a meringue is formed. Now, you have three light, air-filled preparations and one dense chocolate ganache. The correct way to make these four completely different blops get along is to fold them together. If you dump them all in a bowl and just stir it with a spoon, you'll end up with a thick, dense, fatty chocolate mass that might taste good, but it won't have the desired light and fluffy texture.

This is why we fold. With a large rubber spatula, place the three fluffy ingredients in a big bowl. Begin gently lifting up the bottom of the mixture and folding it over onto itself. With your other hand (or enlisting the help of a friend), slowly drizzle the chocolate into the mixture while you fold. Count each fold to help you mix slowly and keep focused and aware of how much you're mixing. You have a bunch of air whipped into unstable elements and it wants to escape, which it does when it's beaten out of the mixture. Raise your spatula from the bottom and lay it down. Repeat. Count. Keep going until the mixture is just combined, but no more. Visualize the air in the mixture and how it will feel in your mouth. The more air you save, the lighter and more sublime the mousse will be. Mix with a heavy hand and your mousse will be dense and worthy of French scorn!

Macerating is a technique used to soften fruits without cooking. Basically it means tossing fruit with a small amount of sugar and a little salt to allow the liquid in the fruit to pass through the semi-permeable membrane of the cell walls the wrong way and break those walls down. Let's use raspberries as an example. Look closely at a raspberry and you'll see that it's made up of hundreds of tiny spheres. Each one of those spheres has a skin that lets water in but not out. When you add a hydroscopic element like sugar or salt, it attracts that moisture and forces it to move the wrong way through the skin of the fruit. This is a gentle way of breaking the fruit down without damaging the texture and fiber. As an experiment, take a few fresh raspberries, toss them in sugar, and walk away for an hour. When you come back, you'll find that you have three completely whole raspberries that have been deflated and are sitting in a puddle of raspberry juice.

A water bath or bain marie refers to both a technique and the equipment used. A water bath is an ingeniously simple method of gently heating sensitive ingredients without burning, scorching, or curdling them. The way it works is that you use steam or water to surround a vessel you're cooking in. On the stovetop, you place a bowl over a slightly smaller pot of simmering water to, say, melt chocolate or whip egg yolks. If you did this over direct heat, the chocolate would burn and the eggs would scramble. In the oven, you put water in a large baking pan and place a smaller vessel or vessels in the pan. We do this a lot for custards. When baking a crème brûlée, you place the ramekin with the liquid custard into a large pan and fill the pan with water to less than the height of the ramekin. The water conducts the heat from the oven very evenly and gently and allows your custard to cook much more slowly. This allows the long strands of protein in the custard to gently unravel and lengthen rather than tear themselves apart. This is why sometimes you get a crème brûlée that's silky and velvety and sometimes you get one that's chunky. If a crème brûlée is chunky, it means no water bath was used, or it was baked too hot and fast. Crème brûlée is always my little test of another pastry chef.

Melting chocolate is as easy as you think it is, but can go very wrong if you aren't careful. Chocolate is very fickle. The gentlest way to melt chocolate is in the top section of a double boiler or bain marie. Put about 2 inches of water in a small saucepan. Use a glass or stainless steel bowl that's larger than the pot so the rim of the bowl extends beyond the rim of the pot. You don't want the bowl sitting in or touching the water, and you don't want any water getting into your chocolate. If you get a tiny amount of water into your chocolate as it melts, the chocolate can "seize," a disaster in which the fats and solids separate from each other and create a disgusting brown mess that you have to throw away.

Turn the flame on medium-low and allow the steam from the water in the pot to warm the bowl gently. You don't have to stir, just let the chocolate warm for about 7 minutes or so, depending on how much chocolate you're melting. As you look at the chocolate in the bowl, you'll see the chocolate on the bottom has liquefied and the chocolate on top has become very shiny.

Now give it a stir with a rubber spatula or a wooden spoon; it should be completely melted. Carefully remove it from the heat and wipe any excess water off the bottom of the bowl to ensure that none of it ends up in your chocolate.

You probably have a microwave in your house, and a lot of people use a microwave to melt chocolate. I don't know how, and I don't trust invisible death rays to be gentle with my chocolate. Feel free to experiment with the microwave, but I recommend the analog method, using steam as an indirect heat source.

Creaming refers to the process of combining sugar and butter and mixing on high speed until the sugar is partly dissolved and a good quantity of air has been whipped into the butter, making it very light and loose and pale in color. Creaming butter and sugar happens a lot in baking cookies and quick breads and butter-based cakes. The air you whip into the butter helps the product rise in the oven as it expands in the heat, and it also makes the entire mixture lighter and easier for the leavening agent to elevate.

Proofing is any length of time in a yeast-baking process during which you step back and allow the dough to rise. This can happen two or three times during the process and can take anywhere from a half hour to a full day. Proofing dough overnight in the fridge is called "retarding" the dough and is highly desirable in bread baking. When you get a good, crusty loaf of bread, look closely at the crust. If it has little tiny light-colored bubbles baked into it, that bread was retarded overnight. This does a couple of things. One, it allows the bread to rise more slowly and gives you a bigger, more mature flavor, as the yeast was able to produce more alcohol during the fermenting process. Two, it makes the crust thicker, flakier, and crustier because while the dough retards, there's a secondary fermentation going on in the skin of the loaf that makes all those little bubbles and gives the crust more body to bake later. Basically, proofing means letting the dough do its thing. It's the point in baking a yeast product when you leave it alone and let the yeast and flour and water and sugar work. There's no shortcut in proofing—it's done when it's done. Deal with it.

Blooming can refer to two very different things. One is a useful technique, and one is a bad thing. The good kind of blooming refers to activating an ingredient, usually gelatin or yeast. Gelatin is always dry, so to use it in baking, you have to soften, or "bloom," it in cold water. Yeast can be either fresh or dry, and some recipes call for the yeast to be added directly to the dough. That's fine, but I like to give my yeast a head start by mixing it with a little warm water and sugar first. This lets the yeast wake up, get going, and be active as soon as you begin the mixing, like stretching before a run. The bad kind of blooming is when the fat or the sugar in chocolate separates from the cocoa solids. Have you ever opened a chocolate bar and noticed that it looked dusty? It has bloomed. It is perfectly safe to eat, but you get a texture on the surface that's less than awesome, and it just looks kinda old. If you're using chocolate in baking, however, it doesn't matter—once the chocolate melts you'll never know the difference. Chocolate is expensive—don't throw it away!

Meringue is any combination of whipped egg whites and sugar, and there are a few techniques involved in making a sturdy, robust meringue. Let's explore three types of whipped meringues: French, Swiss, and Italian.

A French, or "cold," meringue is a meringue that starts with whipping egg whites and slowly adding sugar until the meringue is whipped to how you want it to be. This is the easiest but least stable of the three.

In a Swiss meringue, you slowly heat the egg whites and sugar over the stove just until the sugar is dissolved, and then you whip the mixture to the desired stiffness. This method produces a meringue that is more stable than the French style, but with the extra heating step.

An Italian meringue is the most stable of the three but also requires the most effort and is a bit dangerous. (Hence, "Italian.") The method is to cook sugar to the soft-ball stage (237°F) and add it slowly to the whipping egg whites.

There are a few things to know that will help your meringue be all it can be. First, adding some kind of acid to a meringue as it's beaten makes the bonds of protein stronger and will help keep your meringue stable. This is called "acidulating." Any acid works—lemon juice, cream of tartar, even a bit of vinegar (it's such a small amount, nobody will taste it). It's also important to understand how we describe the "doneness" of a meringue. This is the "peaks and beaks" method. Stick a whisk straight down into the meringue, pull it out, and stick it straight up into the air. If the little point stays up, that is a "stiff peak." If it flops over but keeps its shape, that is a "soft peak." If it flops over and goes gooey, keep whipping. Another term you'll see is a "sparrow's beak." Stick the whisk in, pull it out, and hold it sideways. If the little point on the end holds its shape and stays in a small triangle, that's a sparrow's beak. If it droops like a proboscis monkey, it's not done.

Steeping is a process of naturally extracting the flavor out of a whole food (as opposed to using an extract or artificial flavor). If I want to make a banana custard, for example, I would steep the bananas in hot cream for a few hours instead of just adding a few drops of banana flavoring. Of course it takes more time, but if you were worried about something taking too long, you probably wouldn't be baking in the first place. This works really well for spices and vanilla, too.

Rolling any dough like pie dough or puff pastry is a skill that needs to be practiced. It's very important to roll dough gently. You're not going to get a ball of dough to the exact thickness you want on the first pass. Persuade the dough, a little at a time. Also, make sure the dough is the correct temperature for rolling. If it's too cold, the fat in the dough will be solid and break apart, and if it's too warm, the fat can separate out and make the dough very hard to work with. When that happens, novices tend to add more flour to the dough to make it stiff while it's warm. Huge mistake—adding flour will cause it to shrink rapidly as it bakes and will make it too tough. You should use a little flour on your work surface and rolling pin when you're rolling out dough, but use it sparingly—you don't need that much to keep your dough workable.

Resting dough after you've mixed it or rolled it out is also very important. You don't want to go to the gym directly after a massage, because your muscles have been worked and kneaded and need time to relax. Muscles are protein, just like gluten in dough. If you work dough without letting it rest, it will tear and shrink and generally be unhelpful. If you're blind baking a pie or tart shell (see opposite), roll out the slightly cold dough, form it into the pan, then let it rest for at least 20 minutes in the fridge before you bake it. If you put it directly in the oven, I promise the dough will shrink and warp and not have the texture you intended.

Blind baking is baking a dough before it's filled, for one of two reasons. First, in order to have a baked vessel for an unbaked filling. Sometimes you want to bake a tart shell or vol-au-vent all the way so you can add a sweet or savory filling, such as a mushroom stuffing or fresh fruit. You want the fruit to stay fresh and raw, but the tart shell has to be brown and crispy. Second, sometimes you want to start the baking process before filling and baking further. Some pie fillings don't take very long to bake, and blind baking allows the longer-baking pie shell and the shorter-baking pie filling to finish at the same time.

When blind baking, it's usually a good idea to cover your pie or tart shell with a layer of parchment paper and then fill it with uncooked rice or dried beans. The rice or beans fill the shell cavity and keep it in its proper shape while it bakes. If you're blind baking to a finished stage, you'll generally remove the rice or beans halfway through the baking so the tart shell gets brown on top as well.

Egg wash may sound like a good time, but in baking all it means is brushing an egg mixture over a dough that won't have much color on top otherwise. Biscuits are a good example: Without an egg wash, they'll be too blond on top, and you might end up baking them too long in an effort to get some nice color on them. Using an egg wash actually does several things: It keeps the biscuits moister by forming a skin and keeping moisture from escaping; it gives a nice, thin, crunchy texture to the top of your biscuits; and it makes your biscuits shiny and golden brown. My usual egg wash is a few eggs cracked in a bowl with a bit of sugar added to it and beaten with a fork so the mixture becomes liquid. The sugar breaks down the proteins and turn the eggs into a true homogeneous liquid. Some people add a bit of salt or cream as well—no harm there. You can even make your wash sweeter if you're into that sort of thing, or flavor it with herbs and spices.

CHAPTER 1

PASTRY DOUGH
(& SOME OTHER RANDOM STUFF)

Baking is a pyramid. We start with some very basic ingredients (flour, butter, sugar, eggs) and then we mix them in different quantities and different ways and end up with different products. Well, much like a fractal, this also works on the general body of knowledge that baking requires. We can start with some very basic recipes that do very important things and then use those recipes in a variety of ways as ingredients in other recipes to make an even wider variety of things.

This chapter is basically a go-to reference of some very useful doughs and batters that can be used in a multitude of ways to bake almost anything you can think of. See, some baking requires precise measuring and some doesn't. For example, in this chapter is a recipe for crisp. Crisp is a crunchy, spicy topping that can go on top of almost anything you can think of. Apple crisp comes to mind, but you can use it for pears, strawberry and rhubarb, peaches, curds, custards—you name it. Once you find that you can play with fruit and you don't need some mechanical textbook to tell you what to do with it, you'll find that baking is *so* not as rigid as you might think. I just thought of the idea of a layered chocolate and orange custard crisp while I was writing that sentence. I've never heard of that before, but now I want to go make it. And because I can make a crisp in my sleep (sometimes I do, is that weird?), I can probably make that entire dish without looking at a recipe . . . *just like grilling a steak*! Once you get them down pat, the recipes in this chapter will give you that same ability. Yes, you should still measure your ingredients, but you'll come to find that baking can be just as spontaneous as cooking.

These are the basic dough recipes I use, and they work. Add stuff to them like spices or cocoa or both. Use them in ways I haven't thought of. Make a savory gingerbread house starting with the savory pastry dough recipe and decorate it with bacon and gravy and fill it with Brunswick stew, for all I care! Go bananas and you'll soon understand that baking isn't that difficult—and it's a lot more fun than most people realize.

SWEET ALL-PURPOSE PASTRY DOUGH

You can use this great all-purpose pastry dough for almost any tart or pie or anything that requires a shell, like mini-desserts for a party or even sweet "chips" to dip into a mousse. It's a vehicle to convey sweet stuff to your mouth . . . but it's also good to keep around for cookie projects with the kids! Make some shapes, bake them off, and decorate with sprinkles and frosting and chocolate and gummies and anything else you can find. Better than video games! —*Duff*

Makes about 2 pounds of dough; enough for three 9-inch tart shells

3 extra-large egg yolks

¼ cup whole milk or cream, plus more as needed

¼ teaspoon pure vanilla extract

2 cups all-purpose flour

1 cup pastry or cake flour

½ cup sugar

Pinch of kosher salt

2 sticks (1 cup) butter, softened

MIXING THE DOUGH

1. Get two big bowls. In one, put everything wet except the butter. In the other, put everything dry plus the butter. Whisk all the wet stuff so it looks like it's one color and use clean, bare hands to mix up all the dry stuff, massaging the butter into the flour.

2. Pour the wet stuff into the dry stuff and use your hands to gently work everything together until it forms a ball of dough. Keep to the side some extra flour and milk or even water. If your dough is too wet and won't come off your hands, work in more flour. If it's too dry, work in a bit more liquid.

3. Once you have a nice consistent ball that isn't overmixed, gently press it flat onto a piece of plastic wrap, then wrap it up, squeeze out the air, and chill it in the fridge for at least 1 hour or freeze it for later. (This is one of those things you can do in March that will make Thanksgiving or Christmas easier.)

USING THE DOUGH

1. When rolling out this dough, you want it colder than the room you're in but warmer than the fridge. The butter needs to be pliable, but not liquid, so don't knead the dough, just pull it out of the fridge and let it warm up until you can make a dent in it with your finger.

2. Preheat the oven to 350°F.

3. Lightly flour a surface and very gently knead the dough just two or three times to get it used to the idea that it is going to be moving. Use a rolling pin to roll it into a 14-inch round, then put it into a tart shell according to your recipe.

4. If the recipe calls for blind baking, first look at the tart shell. If the sides of the tart shell are on the high side, blind bake with parchment paper and dry rice or beans (see page 29) for half the baking time, but if it's a shallow tart pan, just dock the dough (poke holes in it with a fork) and keep an eye on it while it's in the oven. If the dough makes a big bubble, just poke a hole in it and push it down.

5. Bake for 30 to 40 minutes, or until golden brown. Let cool in the pan on a wire rack for 20 minutes, then remove the tart shell from the pan so it doesn't get soft.

KINDA-SWEET TART DOUGH

This good, hardy tart dough is great for rustic tarts, hand-held folded pastries, and even sweet break-fast tarts. It's awesome with fruit, jams and jelly, and even chocolate. The best thing about this dough is that it takes a beating, so the kids can play with it and make their own Pop-Tarts! It freezes great, too; you can keep it for at least six months. —*Duff*

Makes about 2 pounds of dough; enough for three 9-inch tart shells

2½ cups all-purpose flour

5 tablespoons sugar

1 teaspoon kosher salt

2 sticks (1 cup) cold butter, cubed

2 extra-large eggs

2 tablespoons whole milk or cream

2 teaspoons pure vanilla extract

1. In a big bowl, combine the flour, sugar, and salt with a wooden spoon or your clean hands. Toss in the cold, cubed butter and massage it into the mixture until you have a sandy texture with some butter chunks in there. Pile the flour mixture into the center of the bowl and use your finger to make a well, like a sweet little volcano.

2. In a medium bowl, whisk together the eggs, milk, and vanilla until the mixture is all one color.

3. Pour the liquid into the center of the volcano and use a fork to mix the wet and the dry until the mixture clumps into a ball. Slowly add ½ cup cold water, tablespoon by tablespoon, until the dough forms a firm ball (you might not use all the water). Put some extra flour on your hands and gently pat the ball together to make a workable dough.

4. Wrap the dough in plastic, squeeze out the air, and chill it in the fridge for at least 1 hour before use, or freeze it for a rainy day.

Options: This dough can be used for almost any pastry that requires a sweet, crunchy shell to hold it together. Feel free to play with it and add spices such as cinnamon or cardamom or even little bits of dried fruit. Raisins, dried apricots, and even dried apples will give this dough a surprising texture that will make all your friends think you're a pastry chef star.

ALL-PURPOSE SAVORY TART DOUGH

This is a killer dough to keep in your freezer all year long so you always have a quick, savory dough on hand for quiches and savory tarts. Don't get scared—it's basically a fancy pizza dough without the yeast. You can take this super-versatile dough in a thousand different directions—you can even grease it up with some butter, herbs, and cheese and bake some crunchety cheesy bread-cracker things for an appetizer! *—Duff*

Makes about 1½ pounds of dough; enough for two 9-inch tart shells or 3 dozen cheesy crackers

2½ cups all-purpose flour, plus more as needed

1 teaspoon kosher salt

2 sticks (1 cup) cold butter, cubed

1. In a bowl, mix up the flour and salt.

2. Massage in the cold butter, leaving some streaks. The streakier the butter, the flakier the crust. If you want a solid, cracker-like dough, mix the butter all the way in.

3. Slowly add ½ cup cold water, tablespoon by tablespoon (you might not use all the water), and gently work the dough until it's not sticking to your hands. Keep some extra flour out just in case. If your dough is too wet and won't come off your hands, work in more flour. If it's too dry, work in a bit more liquid.

4. Wrap the dough tightly in plastic wrap and chill it in the fridge for at least 1 hour or freeze until ready to use.

Options: Like I said, you can do almost anything with this dough. I almost always add a pinch of cayenne just because I like to bring out the flavor of anything I make. You can add chopped fresh herbs, cheese, little bits of bacon, bits of dried mushrooms, or anything you want; baking isn't nearly as rigid as you might think.

PIE DOUGH

This here is my pie dough recipe that I've been using for almost twenty years. It's super-basic, super-adaptable, and helps me make awesome pie! You can goof around with it and add flavor and spice and stuff, but the ratios are good, I promise. Also, there's vinegar in this dough, which keeps the gluten from forming and helps make your dough flaky and tender. If you don't have vinegar, just squeeze a lemon into the water. If the pie calls for a top and bottom crust, double this recipe. *—Duff*

*Makes enough for one
9-inch single pie crust*

2¼ cups all-purpose flour

Pinch of kosher salt

Big pinch of sugar

1 to 1½ sticks (½ to ¾ cup) cold butter, cubed (1 stick will make prettier pie crust, 1½ will make butterier, more delicious pies)

1 tablespoon vinegar (nothing distinct like balsamic, but rice wine or distilled white are totally cool) or lemon juice

1. In a big bowl, combine the flour, salt, and sugar and make a claw with your hand to mix it up real good. Toss in the cold butter cubes and massage them into the flour mixture so you get nice big chunks.

2. Combine the vinegar with ½ cup cold water (this is called acidulating, which just means adding acid to something . . . usually water). Stir the acidulated water into the flour mixture and gently work the dough until a ball is formed.

3. Wrap the dough in plastic, squeeze out the air, and chill it in the fridge for at least 1 hour. This also freezes awesome for up to a year.

QUICK PUFF PASTRY

Many times I've found myself in need of puff pastry and I realize that I don't have the time to make it or any back-up in the freezer, so I keep this little gem from culinary school and it has made me some absolutely stunning puffs that have made everyone happy, 'specially my boss. It still takes time and practice, but follow the directions and I promise you will be so stoked and amazed at your own baking prowess you'll think you went to pastry Hogwarts or something. —*Duff*

Makes about 1¼ pounds of dough

2 cups all-purpose flour, plus more as needed

Big pinch of sugar

Big pinch of kosher salt

2½ sticks (1¼ cups) cold butter, cubed

1. In a big bowl, mix together the flour, sugar, and salt. Massage a small handful of the butter cubes into the flour mixture until it's dry but sandy textured.

2. Toss the remaining butter cubes into the bowl and coat them with flour, but don't work them in—leave them nice and whole. Add ½ cup cold water to the mixture and ever so gently fold the mixture so the dough forms around the butter pieces but doesn't smash them.

3. Flour the table, turn out the dough onto the table, and lightly flour the top of the dough. Using your hands, shape the dough into a thick rectangle.

4. Roll the dough out to about ½ inch thick, but keep it as a rectangle.

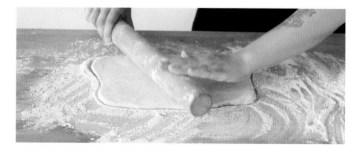

5. Fold one third of the dough toward the middle.

6. Then fold the remaining third over that. You should now have a rectangle roughly the size of the one you started out with. Cover with plastic wrap and refrigerate it for 6 minutes.

7. Repeat the rolling and folding steps.

8. Repeat the rolling and folding steps again.

9. Now you have quick-puff. Chill it for at least 1 hour before you use it (or freeze it for later)—the dough needs to relax.

HOW TO USE

Use this dough for any puff pastry application. The trick is to shape the dough, then chill it before baking so the butter doesn't leak out in the oven. Always use an egg wash (page 29) on the exposed bits so the dough gets nice and golden and shiny, and bake this stuff *hot*! Like 450°F. Puff pastry uses a physical reaction (mechanical leavening of steam) that needs high heat to work.

COBBLER BATTER

Cobbler rules. It's a super-easy from-scratch baking project that you can make awesome the first time you do it and spend the rest of your life perfecting. It uses basic ingredients and all the fruit you have in your fridge that you don't know what to with. Some cobblers have what's basically biscuit dough on top, and those are totally fine (I'm not trying to insult anyone's grandma here), but this batter is loose. I like this batter because it becomes one with the fruit and there is no distinct line where the cobbler crust begins and the fruit ends. This recipe is generic for the batter; the fruit is up to you, and I'll give you some ideas at the end. Mmmkay? —*Duff*

Makes enough batter for one 9 x 13-inch baking pan or eight 6-ounce ramekins of cobbler

Cooking spray

1½ cups whole milk or cream, at room temperature

1 extra-large egg

1 tablespoon pure vanilla extract

1½ cups plus 2 tablespoons sugar

1 tablespoon baking powder

Big pinch of kosher salt

1 teaspoon ground cinnamon

2 cups plus 2 tablespoons all-purpose flour

1 stick (½ cup) butter, melted

4 cups chopped fruit (your choice)

1. Preheat the oven to 350°F and lightly spray a large casserole dish or eight 6-ounce ramekins (if you're feeling fancy) with cooking spray.

2. In a big bowl, whisk together the milk, egg, vanilla, 1½ cups of the sugar, the baking powder, salt, and cinnamon. Gently whisk in 1½ cups of the flour until incorporated, then whisk in the melted butter.

3. Toss the chopped-up fruit in the remaining 2 tablespoons sugar and 2 tablespoons flour.

4. Pour half the batter into the dish(es), then spoon in the fruit mixture, then top with the rest of the batter. Don't overfill the dish(es). Leave some room for the cobbler batter to rise, about ½ inch. If you have leftover batter, heat up some oil to 425°F and make funnel cakes or something (see page 215).

5. Bake for 40 minutes, or until golden blond on top, then at 400°F for 5 minutes to brown the cobbler.

6. Serve with something cold and creamy, like whipped cream or ice cream.

Options: Look around in your pantry and see if you have any old dried fruits that you can toss in with your fresh fruits. The juice from your fresh fruit will invade the dried fruits and you'll end up with a whole new layer of flavor in your cobbler. Osmosis is your friend.

- Not all fruits are the best choice for cobblers. Tree fruits like pears and apples, stone fruits like apricots and peaches, and berries typically work best. Stay away from citrus fruits (except as a minor ingredient for flavor) and bananas.
- And don't forget about nuts! Chopped walnuts and pecans or anything else add a nice texture and flavor that are unexpected in a cobbler.

STREUSEL

You know that crunchy, sweet, spiced topping you find on muffins, pies, and coffee cakes? Yeah, that. As a professional pastry chef, I always kept a bucket of streusel in the fridge and used it all the time to jazz up practically everything. You can even bake it by itself and use it as a textured garnish for plated desserts. Everyone should know how to make streusel, and even if you're making muffins from a mix, top them with streusel and you are just gonna be that much cooler. —*Duff*

Makes enough streusel for 2 dozen large muffins, 3 or 4 quick-bread loaves, or 1 huge baked apple thing

½ cup granulated sugar

½ cup lightly packed brown sugar

1 stick (½ cup) butter, softened

1 tablespoon pure vanilla extract

Pinch of ground cinnamon

Pinch of ground nutmeg

Tiny pinch of ground cloves

1 cup all-purpose flour

1. With a wooden spoon in a big bowl, cream the sugars, butter, vanilla, and spices until the mixture is all one color.

2. Add the flour and stir until crumbly. If the streusel gets doughy instead of crumbly, add more flour until it looks like wet sand. Cover and refrigerate for up to 10 days, or freeze till whenever.

Options: *Two things:* One, you can use all brown or all white sugar—it's totally cool. Two, use any spices you want! If you're putting this on top of a caramel or butterscotch something, add a little cayenne. Try cardamom, or Chinese five-spice, or poppy seeds. Don't be limited by the recipe, man. You're the boss of the streusel—you make it taste however you want. It'll be awesome. Maybe not on top of curry chicken, but you know what I mean.

APPLE CRISP

Apple crisp may be one of the most delicious things on the whole planet. It's good year-round, solo, or with some ice cream. As a professional pastry chef, it's one of those go-to things that I know I can bake and make three hundred people real happy.

This recipe calls for apples, but don't be shy—think about pears, berries, peaches, and so on. Crisp is that blurry line between cobbler and streusel. —*Duff*

Makes one 9 x 13-inch pan or eight 6-ounce ramekins

FILLING

7 to 8 apples, peeled and chopped (I prefer Fujis, Granny Smiths, or Honeycrisps)

1 cup golden raisins

⅓ cup canned crushed pineapple, drained

1 cup chopped pecans

½ cup honey

¼ cup all-purpose flour

TOPPING

2 cups all-purpose flour

1½ cups granulated or light brown sugar

1 tablespoon ground cinnamon

Big pinch of kosher salt

2 extra-large eggs

½ stick (¼ cup) butter, melted

Cooking spray

1. Preheat the oven to 375°F.

2. To make the filling: In a big bowl, combine all the fruit, nuts, and honey. Let it sit for a few minutes to get juicy, then stir in the flour.

3. To make the topping: In another bowl, combine all the dry ingredients. Mix in the eggs until smooth, but don't overbeat. When the mixture is smooth, mix in the butter.

4. Spray a 9 x 13-inch pan (or eight 6-ounce ramekins) lightly with cooking spray. Spoon in the fruit mixture, then spoon the crisp topping on top. Spread it out. The more surface area that gets baked, the crispier it'll be.

5. Bake for 30 minutes (22 to 25 minutes if using ramekins). If it isn't bubbling or golden brown, give it a few more minutes. You want the fruit to boil so you know the flour is cooked off and thick. It can look a little messy!

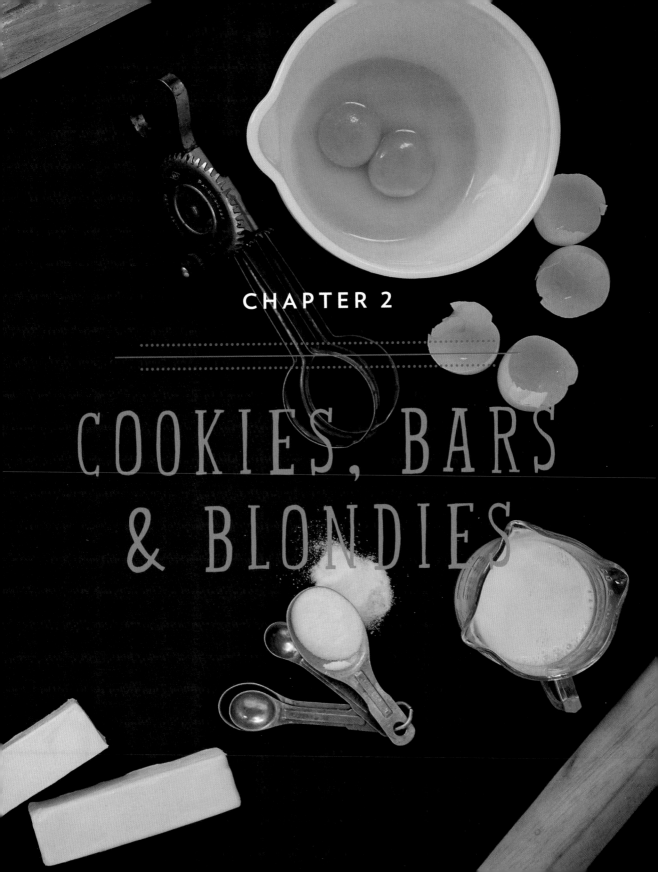

CHAPTER 2

COOKIES, BARS
& BLONDIES

ookies are magical. There's no hurt to the human body or mind or heart that cookies don't help. Keanu Reeves eats a cookie after he finds out he isn't the Matrix messiah and he feels better. Cookies are like karma currency. If you roll with cookies and always have one to give to someone who *obviously* needs a cookie, you'll be repaid a thousandfold in cool points. If you spend a lot of time around children, make sure you always have cookies, unless you can do magic tricks. If you can do magic tricks, that should get you out of any kid-related quandary, but if you can't, learn how to bake.

Cookies and bars, while certainly cute and simple and sweet, can be little devils. Cookies and bars are not easy and truly take practice, patience, and mindfulness. They need to be mixed just right and baked just right; they're much less forgiving than, say, quick breads or pies. Cookies don't bake for very long, usually, and they continue to bake for a while after you pull them out of the oven. You might do everything right for a perfect, gooey brownie or a buttery, crispy chocolate chip cookie, but bake them for a minute or two too long and you'll be mad. That's okay, though. You'll do it right the next time. Cookies really take lots of practice and when someone gives you a truly divine cookie, make sure you appreciate the amount of cookie-baking experience it took to get to that point.

That being said, don't be scared of cookies! Listen to the cookies; be gentle with the cookies. Cookies are the greatest way to get butter and sugar into your mouth. Let's make that experience the best and most memorable it can be. And remember, if you don't like cookies, you hate freedom.

Blondies. I've always had a special relationship with blondies. My love for blondies came rather later in life than is to be expected (I think I was twenty when I had my first one), like my ability to read, and I think that's why I cherish them all the more.

I don't know if you've noticed, but it's terribly difficult to find a good blondie recipe. All the blondies in this chapter are Sara's recipes, not mine, but I wanted to introduce them to you because they mean so much to me. Blondies represent the first time I asked Sara to bake something for me and she knocked me on my duff by how amazing of a baker she really is. I was asked to do a restaurant takeover, and for dessert I had this idea of some plated blondie thing (I forget what the dish was). I asked Sara to bake me some pecan blondies and she was like, "Okay, cool." Very cavalier, I thought. She took a couple of days and then came by Charm City Cakes to share her blondies. I later found out she'd baked like four or five different batches before deciding on one she liked. She tried versions with raw pecans, toasted pecans, regular butter, brown butter, pastry flour, all-purpose flour. After much trial and error, she finally made the blondie she wanted. Everybody at the bakery crowded around the table, and we inhaled an entire pan of them in under a minute. If you were looking in from outside, you would have thought it was a pride of lions feasting on a wildebeest!

I was able to lift myself from the blondie-induced euphoria for long enough to realize that the reaction we were all having to these amazing treats was because Sara is truly an exceptional baker. Here's why she's something special. Really good bakers understand that baking is a process of experimentation. Bakers in the industry don't call recipes "recipes." We call them "formulas." Not because we're gilding the lily—we just think about the things we do differently from how savory cooks think about stew. Sara tinkered away at her blondies, making small adjustments. She knew that each batch would take an hour or two, and she had the patience to wait for the result and evaluate the product, knowing that the quality of a change in step 1 would be revealed in step 30. That's an amazing baker—and believe me, it's humbling.

Now, blondies are basically big fat giant chocolate chip cookies baked in a brownie pan. The best ones are just this side of raw in the middle. Blondies should be chewy, moist, and reminiscent of their darker brownie cousins. This chapter is about blondies, yes. But I also wanted to illustrate a very small but important quirk in baking, and that is when you take the time and bake with brown butter, everybody will think you're a wizard robot baker from the future. They'll chomp away, in awe of the miraculous alchemy that's happened in your magical oven. They won't understand why you're one step higher on the evolutionary chain than they are, but they'll know that you, like Superman, stand for truth, justice, and the American way.

MAPLE-PECAN SQUARES

These bars are super easy to make but make the baker look super talented. (Maybe this is why Duff thinks I'm such a good baker. He loves these things.) They're like little bites of pecan pie, and the additional flavor of maple really evokes the feeling of fall (though I suggest eating them year round). —*Sara*

Makes one 9 x 13-inch pan

CRUST

1½ sticks (¾ cup) butter, softened

1 cup granulated sugar

1 teaspoon kosher salt

3 cups all-purpose flour

TOPPING

2 sticks (1 cup) butter

⅔ cup lightly packed brown sugar

1 tablespoon dark corn syrup

⅓ cup good-quality maple syrup

¼ cup heavy cream

1 teaspoon kosher salt

2 cups pecan "halves and pieces" (not "chopped" pecans)

2 teaspoons pure vanilla extract

1. Preheat the oven to 375°F and heavily grease a 9 x 13-inch pan—and might I recommend laying some parchment paper on top and greasing that, too.

2. To make the crust: In a big bowl, cream the butter and sugar until light and fluffy. Mix in the salt and then gradually mix in the flour until incorporated.

3. Crumble the mixture into the bottom of the pan, then press it firmly into the pan with your fingers.

4. Bake the crust for 12 to 15 or so minutes, or until it is a very pale gold. Set aside.

5. To make the topping: In a medium saucepan over medium heat, melt the butter with the brown sugar, corn syrup, maple syrup, cream, and salt. Bring to a boil and cook, stirring constantly, until the sugar is dissolved, 1 minute or so. Remove from the heat and stir in the pecans and vanilla.

6. While the topping is still hot, pour it over the crust. Bake for 10 to 12 minutes, or until the top is just starting to bubble, then set aside to let it cool completely.

7. Run a knife around the edges and invert the entire baking pan to remove the block instead of trying to pry the squares out of the pan. Flip the block so it's right-side up and cut the squares as you will.

THE BROWNIE

This is not a brownie recipe. This is THE brownie recipe. Brownies can come in so many different flavors that it's hard to choose a favorite. Sometimes you want a salted caramel swirl in there, sometimes you want the brownie to be frosted, other times peanut butter chips are absolutely necessary, and other times you just want a warm chocolate brownie. What people *do* often have a preference about, however, is the texture of their favorite brownie. There are those in the "fudgy" brownie camp, who prefer that ooey-gooey center and a super-bold, rich chocolate flavor. Then there are the "cakey" brownie people. In my opinion, they should just skip to the cake chapter and make some chocolate cake. So, with that said, here's the best fudgy brownie recipe. This one has walnuts, because the Gonzales family won't eat a brownie without some walnuts in there, whereas the Goldmans like their funk uncut, all brownie, no nuts. —*Sara*

*Makes one 8-inch or
9-inch square pan*

1½ sticks (¾ cup) butter

9 ounces bittersweet
  baking chocolate,
  chopped

1½ cups granulated sugar

¾ cup plus 2 tablespoons
  lightly packed brown
  sugar

3 extra-large eggs plus
  2 egg yolks

¾ teaspoon kosher salt

1 teaspoon pure vanilla
  extract

1 cup all-purpose flour

1 cup semisweet chocolate
  chips or chunks
  (optional)

1 cup chopped toasted
  walnuts (toast for
  15 minutes at 375°F)
  (optional)

1. Preheat the oven to 350°F and grease an 8-inch or 9-inch square pan. Lining it with parchment paper is helpful as well.

2. In a double boiler or a heatproof bowl set over a small saucepan of simmering water, melt the butter and bittersweet chocolate together, stirring often to avoid scorching. Set it aside off the heat.

3. In a big bowl, whisk together the sugars, eggs, and egg yolks. Whisk in the salt and vanilla. Add the melted butter and chocolate to the egg mixture and whisk just to combine.

4. Gradually stir in the flour and mix until everything is combined and smooth. Stir in the chocolate chips and walnuts, if using.

5. Scrape the batter into the prepared pan and bake for 35 to 45 minutes, or until a toothpick inserted into the middle displays as much goo on it as you want to see in the middle of those brownies!

6. Let cool in the pan on a wire rack for about 45 minutes. Brownies need time to set, and if you try to cut them while they are too warm, they will fall apart and ruin your day. Slice them at room temp or colder, and if you want them warm, just put them in a hot oven for minute or two.

7. Serve the brownies with ice cream, duh!

BROWN BUTTER–BUTTERSCOTCH KRISPY BARS

One of the very first things a kid learns to make in the kitchen is the sticky, buttery, gooey crispiness that is a Rice Krispies treat. It's the tried and true almost-instant dessert snack that you know exactly how it will taste before even biting in. It's beautifully simple, but it's so very easy to spice it up a bit! You can use different cereal, adding some other fancy flavors or mix-ins, or even throw some frosting on top.

This take on the classic has a rich flavor thanks to the simple act of browning the butter first and adding a couple little extras. —*Sara*

Makes one 9 x 13-inch pan

1 stick (½ cup) butter

½ teaspoon kosher salt

4 cups mini marshmallows

1½ cups butterscotch chips

½ teaspoon ground cinnamon

6 cups crispy rice cereal

2 tablespoons milk or cream

1. Butter a 9 x 13-inch pan with your hands or line it with wax paper.

2. Brown the butter in a large saucepan over medium heat. Keep a close eye on it and don't let it get too dark! When just golden brown, add the salt, marshmallows, ½ cup of the butterscotch chips, and the cinnamon. Stir until everything is all melty and it smells awesome.

3. Remove the pan from the heat and add the cereal. Start to stir very gently to coat the cereal.

4. Press the mixture into the prepared pan. Let it cool for 20 minutes. Meanwhile, in a double boiler or a heatproof bowl set over a small saucepan of simmering water, melt the remaining 1 cup butterscotch chips with the cream. Stir until smooth, then use a spoon to drizzle the butterscotch over the bars like Jackson Pollock.

BLUEBERRY CHEESECAKE BARS

Looking to impress? With these bars, it's hard to decide whether they look or taste better. They're super easy to make, too, so it's really a win-win-win! —*Sara*

Makes one 9 x 13-inch pan

1 (11-ounce) box vanilla wafer cookies

1 stick (½ cup) butter, melted

2 cups frozen blueberries, thawed

⅓ cup plus 2 tablespoons sugar

2 (8-ounce) packages cream cheese, at room temperature

2 extra-large eggs plus 2 egg yolks

1 tablespoon lemon zest

1. Preheat the oven to 350°F and grease a 9 x 13-inch baking pan.

2. Pulse the cookies in a food processor until they're ground pretty fine.

3. In a big bowl, mix the cookie crumbs and melted butter until well incorporated. Press the mixture into the bottom of the baking pan so that it's packed firm and solid.

4. Blind bake the crust for 10 minutes, then set it aside to cool. (You don't need the baking beans to blind bake this crust; *au naturel* is totally cool.)

5. Reduce the oven temp to 250°F.

6. In the food processor, puree 1 cup of the frozen blueberries with 2 tablespoons of the sugar. Set aside.

7. In the bowl of a stand mixer fitted with the paddle attachment, cream the remaining ⅓ cup sugar with the cream cheese. Add the eggs and egg yolks one at a time, beating and scraping the sides of the bowl after each addition. When the mixture is combined and smooth, gently fold in the remaining 1 cup of blueberries and the zest.

8. Smooth the cream cheese mixture over the cooled vanilla cookie crust. Drop small amounts of the blueberry puree all over the top of the cream cheese mixture. Using a toothpick or a butter knife, swirl the blueberry puree into the cream cheese to create a marbled effect.

9. Bake for 70 to 80 minutes, or until it's set and a very pale light brown around the edges (don't let the top brown). Let cool completely and refrigerate, covered, for at least 1 or 2 hours before cutting and serving.

LEMON BARS

Everybody needs a good lemon bar recipe. Lemons are cheap, almost everybody loves lemon bars, and these are basically what the offspring would look like if brownies fell in love with lemonade. This is a flour crust, but you can use any graham cracker crust from this book if you're more into the lemon curd pie thing. —*Sara*

Makes one 9 x 13-inch pan

CRUST

3 cups all-purpose flour

¾ cup powdered sugar

½ teaspoon kosher salt

2 sticks (1 cup) plus
    2 tablespoons butter,
    softened

FILLING

3 extra-large eggs and
    3 egg yolks

3 cups sugar

1½ cups fresh lemon juice

2 tablespoons lemon zest

½ cup all-purpose flour

¼ teaspoon kosher salt

TOPPING

1½ cups powdered sugar

Lemon Bars are pictured on page 60.

1. Preheat the oven to 350°F and grease a 9 x 13-inch pan.

2. To make the crust: In a big bowl, mix together the flour, powdered sugar, and salt. Add the butter and mix until you have a crumbly texture. Press the mixture evenly and firmly into the bottom of the pan. Bake for about 18 minutes, or until blond and lightly golden.

3. Meanwhile, to make the filling: Whisk all the filling ingredients together until well combined.

4. When the crust comes out of the oven and is still hot, pour all the filling on top and spread it evenly over the crust. Cover with foil.

5. Bake for 20 minutes. Remove the foil and bake for 20 to 25 minutes more, or until lightly browned on top.

6. Let the bars cool for 10 minutes, then, using a wire-mesh strainer, sift the powdered sugar evenly over the top.

7. Let the bars cool completely before cutting so that they set up and hold their shape. Store these in the fridge to get the most out of the lemony goodness. The crust might soften a bit in the fridge, but it's worth it for fresh, cold lemon bars.

Top row, left to right: Easy Six-Layer Bars, Date Bars (page 62), Lemon Bars (page 59)

EASY SIX-LAYER BARS

Combining six (well, seven) delicious ingredients into one delicious treat. —*Sara*

Makes one 9 x 13-inch pan

1½ sticks (¾ cup) butter

1¾ cups graham cracker crumbs (packaged, or see page 82; you can grind the crackers in a food processor pretty easily)

1¼ cups semisweet chocolate chips

1¼ cups butterscotch chips

1½ cups sweetened shredded coconut

¾ cup chopped pecans

1 (14-ounce) can sweetened condensed milk

1. Preheat the oven to 350°F. Melt the butter in a 9 x 13-inch pan and spread it evenly over the bottom.

2. Sprinkle the graham cracker crumbs evenly over the butter. Layer the chocolate, butterscotch, coconut, and pecans the same way.

3. Pour the sweetened condensed milk over all of it.

4. Bake for 30 minutes, until browned on top. Let it cool, then cut into bars.

DATE BARS

When I was a little kid, my mom would make date bars. They were so good, with their crispy crust, crumbled topping, and unique flavor. But they were actually from a box mix. Add some water and presto! Date bars! I'd completely forgotten about those bars—they were taken off the market shelves years ago—so I decided to figure out how to make them from scratch. I've also come to think of dates as having a California soul. Next time you're in the Coachella Valley, stop and get a date shake—you won't be mad. —Sara

Makes one 9 x 13-inch pan

Cooking spray

CRUST

2 sticks (1 cup) butter, softened

½ cup granulated sugar

½ teaspoon kosher salt

2 cups all-purpose flour

FILLING

3 cups pitted chopped Medjool dates

2 tablespoons honey

1 teaspoon pure vanilla extract

⅓ cup packed light brown sugar

1 cup old-fashioned rolled oats (not instant)

Date Bars are pictured on page 60.

1. Preheat the oven to 375°F. Prepare a 9 x 13-inch pan: Cut strips of parchment paper 1 inch wider than the sides of your pan. Spray the pan with cooking spray, then adhere the strips to the sides of the pan, then spray the strips again. This will keep the sticky dates from sticking to the sides of the pan.

2. To make the crust: In a big bowl, cream together the butter and granulated sugar. Add the salt. Gradually add the flour, mixing as you go. The mixture will be slightly crumbly.

3. Spread half the mixture evenly over the bottom of the pan. Use your clean hands to press the mixture in an even layer over the bottom. Set aside the remaining mixture for topping.

4. Bake the crust (see page 29) for 10 minutes. Set aside to cool.

5. Meanwhile, to make the filling: Place the dates, honey, vanilla, brown sugar, and ¾ cup room-temperature water in a medium saucepan and cook over medium heat, stirring often, until thickened, about 10 minutes. Let cool for 10 minutes.

6. Add the oats to the remainder of the topping mixture and stir to combine.

7. Spread the date filling evenly over the partially baked bottom crust. Sprinkle the oat topping evenly over the filling, but not super thick—½ inch thick is plenty (you might not use all the remaining topping).

8. Bake for 25 to 30 minutes, or until light brown. Let cool, but I suggest cutting and enjoying while still a bit warm.

OLD-SCHOOL SUGAR COOKIES

This is the sugar cookie recipe I always use when I have cookies to decorate or I'm decorating with a bunch of kids. It's a super-easy recipe that makes delicious cookies for any time of the year. Bust out the royal icing and the sprinkles—Santa is gonna want these! —*Duff*

Makes 3 dozen cookies

6 sticks (3 cups) butter, softened

2 cups sugar

1 teaspoon kosher salt

Pinch of ground cinnamon

1 teaspoon pure vanilla extract

2 teaspoons baking powder

4 extra-large eggs plus 1 egg yolk

3 cups all-purpose flour

2 cups cake flour

Royal Icing (page 291), or your favorite frosting

Your favorite sprinkles and other edible decorations

1. In a big bowl, combine the butter, sugar, salt, cinnamon, and vanilla and mix until smooth and fluffy. Stir in the baking powder, taking care to mix well. Add the eggs and egg yolk and stir well. Add the flours and gently stir until a smooth ball forms. Wrap the dough in plastic and put it in the fridge for at least 1 hour.

2. Preheat the oven to 375°F and line a baking sheet (or sheets) with parchment paper (no cooking spray).

3. On a floured surface, roll out tennis ball–size pieces of dough to about ¼ inch thick and cut out the shapes you want. Lay them on the prepared baking sheet, leaving at least ¼ inch between each cookie.

4. Bake for 8 minutes, or until lightly golden.

5. Let the cookies cool on a wire rack, then decorate them however you like!

SNICKERDOODLES

Snickerdoodles aren't just for the holidays. These cookies are good all year long, and in the heat of summer can remind us that winter is coming, so stop complaining and enjoy the sun while it lasts. That said, these cinnamon cookies treat you right after a snow day of sledding and pond hockey. —*Duff*

Makes 2 dozen cookies

¾ cup sugar

1 stick (½ cup) butter

1 extra-large egg

1⅓ cups all-purpose flour

1 teaspoon cream of tartar

½ teaspoon baking soda

⅛ teaspoon kosher salt

Cinnamon sugar: ¼ cup sugar and 1 tablespoon cinnamon

1. Preheat the oven to 350°F and line a baking sheet or sheets with parchment paper.

2. With a stand or hand mixer, cream the sugar and butter until fluffy. Add the egg and mix well.

3. In a medium bowl, mix the flour, cream of tartar, baking soda, and salt.

4. Add the dry mixture to the butter mixture and mix until a well-incorporated dough forms.

5. Use your clean hands to roll the dough into 1- to 2-inch balls. Roll the balls in the cinnamon sugar to coat them thoroughly.

6. Place on the prepared baking sheet(s) and lightly press the tops down so that the cookies bake a little bit thinner.

7. Bake for 15 to 18 minutes, or until lightly golden. Let cool on a wire rack.

ELVIS COOKIES

The King deserves a cookie, and being in an Elvis tribute band myself (I play stand-up bass), I'm the one to create it for him. The King was known for his love of peanut butter and bananas. That's a winning combo, but I added a few extra goodies that I think the King would approve of. Go buy some bananas now so that they can start ripening, and let's take care of business. —*Duff*

Makes about 30 cookies

Cooking spray

3 cups sugar

2 sticks (1 cup) butter, softened

1 cup peanut butter (crunchy or smooth, your call)

2 tablespoons molasses

1 tablespoon pure vanilla extract

Big pinch of baking powder*

1 garlic clove, minced**

2 teaspoons kosher salt

3 *very* ripe bananas

2½ cups all-purpose flour

1¼ cups chocolate chips

5 ounces hard pretzels, smashed (about ¾ cup pretzel crumbs)

10 bacon strips, cooked crisp and chopped fine

1. Preheat the oven to 350°F and spray a baking sheet or sheets with cooking spray.

2. In a big bowl, mix the sugar, butter, peanut butter, molasses, vanilla, baking powder, garlic, and salt until it's all one color. Add the bananas and mash them up real good in there.

3. Add the flour and gently mix until incorporated, with no lumps.

4. Fold in the chocolate chips, pretzel pieces, and bacon.

5. Using two spoons, form balls about the size of a large walnut and drop them on the prepared baking sheet(s) at least 2 inches apart. Place the sheet(s) in the fridge to chill for 10 minutes.

6. Bake for 12 minutes, or until golden on the outside and super gooey in the middle, just like the King would want them. Let cool on a wire rack off the baking sheet.

* Yes, I said a big pinch of baking powder. Get over it.

** This is optional, but just so you know, the garlic isn't weird. There's a long tradition of putting garlic in chocolate chip cookies. Maybe to keep the vampires from eating your treats. Who knows, but look it up if you want to. I know what I'm talking about.

CHOCOLATE CHIP COOKIES
(THIN & CRISPY)

Crisp and buttery, packed with chocolate chips, flat in shape but not flavor, these cookies are delicious. Duff likes his chocolate chip cookies crispy. I like them soft and gooey in the center, only crisp on the very outer edge. To each their own, I guess (except that I'm right). That said, these are damn good cookies. —Sara

Makes about 18 large cookies

1 cup plus 2 tablespoons
    all-purpose flour

¾ teaspoon kosher salt

¼ teaspoon baking soda

1¾ sticks (½ cup plus
    6 tablespoons) butter,
    softened (brown butter
    works really here)

1 cup lightly packed light
    brown sugar

¾ cup granulated sugar

1 extra-large egg plus
    1 egg yolk

2 teaspoons pure vanilla
    extract

2 cups semisweet
    chocolate chips

1. In a medium bowl, mix together the flour, salt, and baking soda. Set aside.

2. In the bowl of a stand mixer fitted with the paddle attachment, cream the butter with both sugars until light and fluffy. Add the egg, egg yolk, and vanilla and beat well. Mix in ⅓ cup room-temperature water.

3. Mix in the flour mixture until well combined, then stir in the chocolate chips.

4. Scoop the dough into balls slightly smaller than a golf ball onto a parchment-lined baking sheet (you'll need a second sheet for baking). Since the dough is rather wet, use a 1.5-ounce kitchen or ice cream scoop if you have one. The cookies can be placed close together on this sheet because they're just going to set up in the freezer for a while. Chill the cookies in the freezer for 30 minutes to 1 hour.

5. Preheat the oven to 325°F. Line another baking sheet with parchment paper.

6. Take the cookies off the frozen baking sheet and place them at least 3 inches apart on the new sheet. Let them warm up just enough so you can squish them. Pressing with your palm or the flat bottom of a glass, gently flatten each cookie to about ¼ inch thick. This is superthin, but there is a huge difference between ½ inch and ¼ inch thick. These would be two VERY different cookies.

7. Bake for 20 to 25 minutes, or until kinda dark golden brown. Let cool on the baking sheet on a wire rack for 15 minutes.

CHOCOLATE CHIP COOKIES (FAT & CHEWY)

The king of the cookie kingdom has to be chocolate chip. When someone says the word "cookie," chances are it's what pops into your head. When you give a mouse a cookie, it'd better be chocolate chip, and he'll want that glass of milk to go with it. It's what you make for a friend to say *thank you*. It's what you make your kid to say *feel better*. It's what you make that cute boy next door to let him know you can bake.

Everyone has an opinion about the perfect chocolate chip cookie, but in the end, the cookie is going to make someone smile. This recipe might make them smile a little wider. Remember, the art of the perfect fat chocolate chip cookie is knowing when to take it out of the oven. The rest of this nonsense is just details. —*Sara*

Makes about 2 dozen cookies

2¼ cups all-purpose flour

1 teaspoon baking soda

1 teaspoon kosher salt

2 sticks (1 cup) butter, softened

¾ cup granulated sugar

¾ cup lightly packed light brown sugar

2 extra-large eggs

1 teaspoon pure vanilla extract

2 cups semisweet chocolate chips

1. Preheat the oven to 375°F.

2. In a medium bowl, mix together the flour, baking soda, and salt.

3. In the bowl of a stand mixer fitted with the paddle attachment, cream the butter and both sugars until light and fluffy. Mix in the eggs and vanilla.

4. Add the flour mixture and mix until well combined. Stir in the chocolate chips.

5. Eat a bunch of the cookie dough.

6. Scoop what's left of the cookie dough onto an ungreased baking sheet (I like to line mine with parchment paper for easy clean-up).

7. Bake the cookies for 8 to 12 minutes, depending on how gooey you want those centers to be.

8. Let cool for 5 minutes, then transfer the cookies to a wire rack. You'll probably eat them all before they cool because they're so good.

ATHA'S PEANUT BUTTER COOKIES

Atha was my grandmother's housekeeper, and she helped raise my mom and then my brother and me when we were little in Wichita, Kansas. Atha could bake. If I have to say what pushed me into baking at an early age, it was the joy that Atha brought us by making her peanut butter cookies every time we visited my grandma. She would make a whole tin of them, and they'd be gone in a day and she'd have to make more. That's how we kept them fresh. Here's my adaptation of her recipe. I can't make them as good as hers, but I've been told that mine are amazing. Maybe it's just eating a cookie made by somebody who loves you that makes them taste so good. —*Duff*

Makes about 16 cookies

2 sticks (1 cup) butter, softened

2 cups sugar, plus more for rolling

2 tablespoons molasses

1¼ cups crunchy peanut butter

1 tablespoon pure vanilla extract

2 extra-large eggs

1 teaspoon baking powder

1 teaspoon baking soda

Pinch of kosher salt

2½ cups all-purpose flour

1. In the bowl of a stand mixer fitted with the paddle attachment, cream the butter, sugar, and molasses until fluffy. Add the peanut butter, vanilla, and eggs and mix until well combined.

2. Stir in the baking powder, baking soda, and salt. Mix really well. Add the flour and mix gently until you have a sticky ball. Taste it. *Amiright???*

3. Cover and chill in the fridge for 45 minutes.

4. Preheat the oven to 375°F and prepare a baking sheet with parchment paper but no cooking spray. Fill a small saucer with sugar.

5. Roll the dough into balls just smaller than a golf ball. Drop each ball into the sugar, then place it on the baking sheet, sugar-side down.

6. Using a fork, press the cookie down, making a criss-cross pattern, but leave the cookies kind of thick. You want them gooey in the middle.

7. Bake for 10 minutes. Don't let them get too brown. Let them cool right on the baking sheet so the bottoms get a bit more done than the tops and they hold the cookie together. Boom, done. Enjoy with milk!

CRANBERRY-WALNUT OATMEAL COOKIES

This variation on a normal ol' oatmeal raisin cookie is my personal favorite. If you're a raisin lover, feel free to use those instead of cranberries . . . or in addition to them! If you aren't a fan of cookies with nuts, substitute white chocolate chips or butterscotch. —Sara

Makes about 30 cookies

Cooking spray

2 sticks (1 cup) butter, softened

1½ cups lightly packed dark brown sugar

1 teaspoon pure vanilla extract

1 extra-large egg

1½ cups all-purpose flour

1 teaspoon ground cinnamon

2 cups old-fashioned rolled oats (not instant)

1 teaspoon baking soda

¼ teaspoon kosher salt

1½ cups dried cranberries

1½ cups chopped walnuts

1. Preheat the oven to 375°F and lightly spray a baking sheet with cooking spray.

2. In a big bowl, cream the butter and sugar until fluffy. Add the vanilla and egg and mix well.

3. In a medium bowl, mix the flour, cinnamon, oats, baking soda, and salt.

4. Add the flour mixture to the butter mixture and mix until combined, but don't overmix.

5. Mix in the cranberries and walnuts.

6. Roll the dough into balls of about 2 tablespoons each and place them 2 inches apart on the prepared baking sheet.

7. Bake for 20 to 22 minutes if you want your cookies on the softer, chewier side; 25 to 28 minutes if you like them a little more firm. IMHO, make them chewy. Let cool on the baking sheet for 15 to 20 minutes.

PRALINES

Every time I'm in New Orleans, I eat one praline. Just one. I don't eat them anywhere else, just because I know when I get a praline, I'm in New Orleans. They're very special to me because I associate them with a particular geographical location. It's like every time I come to Baltimore, I don't feel like I'm home until I see the Baltimore skyline from the highway just outside the city. Baking and baked goods are funny like that; they really carry emotional and sentimental weight. Okay, I'll sneak one when I make them for other people, but that's it. The only pralines I'll eat are mine and the ones from New Orleans. Yeah, I'm a snob. That's why I'm writing a book—I have opinions and I know my stuff.

Now, seriously, you need a candy thermometer for this recipe because you have to cook the sugar to a very specific temperature or the texture will be all messed up. Read the whole recipe before you start, get prepared, and you'll do great. *Laissez les bon temps rouler! —Duff*

Makes about 30 pralines

1½ cups granulated sugar

¾ cup lightly packed
   light brown sugar

1 teaspoon kosher salt,
   plus another teaspoon
   IF you want to sprinkle
   some on top for a saltier
   experience

1½ cups chopped roasted
   pecans

½ cup skim milk (the fat
   comes from the butter,
   not the milk)

1 stick (½ cup) butter

2 teaspoons bourbon

1 teaspoon pure vanilla
   extract

SPECIAL EQUIPMENT

Candy thermometer

1. Place a large piece of parchment paper on a flat surface, preferably granite or wood.

2. Put all the ingredients in a large pot and attach a candy thermometer to the side. You need to be sure the thermometer goes deep into the mixture. Turn the heat to medium-high.

3. Fill a bowl that's larger than the pot halfway with cold water and set it aside.

4. Stir the mixture with a wooden spoon. When everything has melted together, start checking the temperature. When the thermometer reaches *exactly* 236°F, remove the pot from the heat and stick it in the bowl of cold water to stop the cooking process. Stir for 45 seconds while the pot is in the ice bath to evenly cool the entire mixture.

5. With a large spoon, start dropping puddles of batter onto the parchment. Make sure you're getting some pecans in every cookie. If you feel like it, sprinkle just a bit of salt on the tops. Let them cool all the way. If you're in a humid environment, they might stay sticky, but put them in front of a fan and they should get dry.

6. Store them carefully in a tin, and don't stack them very high— three layers max, separated by wax paper.

ANDES MINT COOKIES

I love the combination of chocolate and mint. Mint chip ice cream, Junior Mints candy, those tasty mint Girl Scout cookies . . . all of them. This cookie recipe is yet another delicious way to combine the two flavors. —*Sara*

Makes 2 dozen cookies

Cooking spray

2½ cups all-purpose flour

¾ cup unsweetened natural cocoa powder

1 teaspoon baking soda

½ teaspoon kosher salt

2 sticks (1 cup) plus 2 tablespoons butter, softened

1 cup granulated sugar

1 cup lightly packed light brown sugar

2 extra-large eggs

1 teaspoon pure vanilla extract

1 teaspoon peppermint extract

1 cup chocolate chips

1 cup mint chips (or chopped-up Andes Chocolate Mints . . . my favorite)

1. Preheat the oven to 350°F and lightly spray a baking sheet with cooking spray.

2. Sift the flour, cocoa powder, baking soda, and salt into a medium bowl and set aside.

3. With a hand or stand mixer, cream the butter and both sugars until fluffy. Add the eggs, vanilla, and peppermint extract and mix well.

4. Add the dry mixture to the butter mixture and mix well. Stir in the chocolate chips and mint chips.

5. Roll the batter into 1½-inch balls and place them on the prepared baking sheet. With two fingers, press the cookies down to about 1 inch thick, keeping the cookies about 2 inches apart.

6. Bake for 15 to 18 minutes, or until not glossy (don't cook 'em too much). Let the cookies cool on a wire rack.

BUCKEYES

It doesn't get more American than a buckeye. From Ohio, the Buckeye State, these little gems are meant to look like the nuts that grow on trees in Ohio and across the Midwest. Forgive me, but I use coating chocolate for this recipe, as I don't think anyone wants to temper chocolate when making such a piece of Americana. Coating chocolate is chocolate that has had the cocoa butter replaced with palm oil so it doesn't bloom. It's much easier to work with, especially in a home kitchen. This recipe is super easy and super delicious. Make plenty, because they go fast! —*Duff*

Makes about 100 buckeyes

2 sticks (1 cup) butter, softened

1½ cups crunchy peanut butter*

2 tablespoons light corn syrup

5 cups powdered sugar

Big ol' pinch of kosher salt

1 teaspoon pure vanilla extract

2 pounds dark coating chocolate

1. In the bowl of a stand mixer fitted with the paddle attachment, mix the butter, peanut butter, corn syrup, powdered sugar, salt, and vanilla until smooth. Don't beat too much air into the mixture. Refrigerate the bowl for 20 minutes.

2. Lay a sheet of parchment paper on a baking sheet. Scoop out 1-inch balls of dough, use your clean hands to quickly roll them into smooth balls, and place them on the sheet.

3. Stick a toothpick in each ball and set the baking sheet in the fridge.

4. Melt the chocolate in the top of a double boiler or in a glass or metal bowl set over simmering water (see page 25).

5. Holding it by the toothpick, set a ball into the chocolate, coating most but not all of it. You have to leave the buckeye poking out!

* It's traditional to use creamy peanut butter; I just prefer chunky. They're *your* Buckeyes—you make 'em how you want! But what do I know, I'm from Baltimore! ;)

6. Shake off any extra chocolate into the bowl and place the buckeye back on the baking sheet. Repeat to coat the rest of the balls, then return the sheet to the fridge.

7. Keep the buckeyes cold and store them in a sealed container. You can stack them, but keep wax paper between the layers.

GRAHAM CRACKERS

It's said that graham crackers were invented to subdue lust. Silly Victorians—in the words of Jeff Gold-blum, "Life always finds a way." In this way, we added a bunch of cinnamon and sugar to a whole wheat cracker. Boom! If you're suddenly randy after eating these crackers, well, mazel tov. —Duff

Makes about twenty 3-inch crackers

1 stick (½ cup) butter, softened

¼ cup lightly packed dark brown sugar

½ cup granulated sugar

Pinch of kosher salt

1 teaspoon pure vanilla extract

1 teaspoon ground cinnamon

Tiny pinch of ground nutmeg

1½ cups graham flour (preferred) or whole wheat flour

1½ cups all-purpose flour

Pinch of baking soda

1 teaspoon baking powder

¼ cup heavy cream, plus extra for brushing

Cinnamon sugar: ¼ cup granulated sugar mixed with 1 tablespoon ground cinnamon

1. In the bowl of a stand mixer fitted with the paddle attachment, mix the butter, sugars, salt, vanilla, cinnamon, and nutmeg until creamy and smooth.

2. In a medium bowl, whisk together the flours, baking soda, and baking powder. With the mixer running, add the dry mixture to the butter mixture in stages, alternating with the cream. Wrap the dough tightly in plastic wrap and chill in the fridge for at least 30 minutes.

3. Preheat the oven to 375°F.

4. Arrange a little bowl of cinnamon sugar, a little bowl of cream, and a pastry brush on a work surface.

5. On a floured surface, roll half the dough out to ⅛ inch thick and just larger than your baking sheet. Cut it into a large rectangle that will fit whole onto the baking sheet. Transfer the dough to the baking sheet, score the rectangle into even 3-inch squares, and dock (prick) the dough evenly with a fork so it really looks like packaged graham crackers. Brush the whole surface of the dough with cream, then sprinkle the cinnamon sugar all over it.

6. Bake for 8 minutes—10 minutes tops—until no longer glossy. Let the graham sheet cool completely, then separate it into crackers along the knife cuts. Repeat the rolling and baking for the remaining dough.

7. Store at room temperature in a sealed container. Nobody will believe you didn't buy them!

SCOTTISH SHORTBREAD

Seriously the easiest recipe you could possibly make. Don't be fooled, though—this is the right way to make shortbread. Anything fancier and the wrath of the highlands will be upon ye, ya silk-wearin' buttercup! —*Sara*

Makes one 9 x 13-inch pan

4 sticks (2 cups) butter

1 cup sugar

5 cups all-purpose flour

1 teaspoon kosher salt

1. Preheat the oven to 325°F.

2. In the bowl of a stand mixer fitted with the paddle attachment, cream the butter and sugar together until creamy. Add the flour and salt and mix thoroughly.

3. Press the dough evenly into a 9 x 13-inch pan with your hands.

4. Prick the dough all over with a fork, making sure the fork hits the pan below. If you're looking to impress with these shortbreads, try using a wooden skewer to prick the dough and make sure to do straight rows of pricks of the same number, so that when you cut the shortbread each one looks uniform.

5. Bake for 1 hour; the dough should be very light gold.

6. Let it cool for 3 minutes, cut it into bars in the pan, and let cool completely in the pan.

Variations: This is a very plain shortbread, but you can use is as a base to get creative. Add lemon zest. Add minced thyme. Add ground cinnamon. Add espresso powder. My suggestion? Ground cardamom and finely chopped pistachios. So good. Plain shortbread is a blank canvas—use some creativity and come up with a flavor combination that you enjoy!

GINGERBREAD COOKIES (OR GINGERBREAD HOUSE WALLS!)

'Tis the season to be baking cookies! This iconic cookie tastes about a billion times better when you make it from scratch at home. The deep flavor of molasses with the spicy bite of ginger makes for a truly perfect holiday cookie. And what's a Christmas without a gingerbread house?! Plus, you get to decorate them however the heck you want to! Get creative and have fun with this recipe—the possibilities are endless with this one! —Sara

Makes enough for 1 small house or 2 brownstones or 30 cookies

Cooking spray

2 cups all-purpose flour

2 teaspoons ground ginger

1½ teaspoons ground cinnamon

½ teaspoon ground nutmeg

¼ teaspoon ground cloves

¼ teaspoon kosher salt

¼ teaspoon baking soda

1 stick (½ cup) butter, softened

⅓ cup lightly packed dark brown sugar

⅓ cup molasses

1 extra-large egg

Royal Icing (page 291), for decorating

1. Preheat the oven to 350°F and line a baking sheet with parchment paper. Lightly spray the paper with cooking spray.

2. In a medium bowl, combine the flour, spices, salt, and baking soda.

3. In a big bowl, beat the butter and sugar together with a wooden spoon or a hand mixer.

4. Mix in the molasses and egg until smooth, then add the flour mixture and mix until well combined.

5. Wrap the dough in plastic wrap and refrigerate for 1 to 2 hours.

6. On a floured surface, roll out the dough to about ⅛ inch thickness. Freeze it flat on a baking sheet for 20 to 30 minutes.

7. Use your preferred cookie cutters to stamp out shapes, or use a paring knife and architect the gingerbread home of your dreams, then transfer the shapes to the prepared baking sheet.

8. Bake for 18 to 20 minutes, or until the dough isn't shiny. Let it cool on the sheet for 10 minutes, then transfer the cookies to a wire rack to cool completely.

9. Decorate with royal icing when cool!

BROWN-BUTTER BLONDIES

This recipe is the jam. One day I asked Sara to bake me some blondies, and this is the recipe she came up with (the one I mentioned at the beginning of the chapter). I have to say that all other blondies pale in comparison. We use it for our blondies at all of my bakeries. —*Duff*

Makes one 9 x 13-inch pan

3 sticks (1½ cups) butter

3 cups lightly packed light brown sugar

3 extra-large eggs

1½ teaspoons pure vanilla extract

3 cups all-purpose flour

1 tablespoon baking powder

½ teaspoon kosher salt

Brown-Butter Blondies are pictured on page 89.

1. First, brown the butter. Place it in a medium saucepan over low heat to cook. Check it after about 10 minutes; it should be a medium-brown color, not too light, not too burned. Once it reaches that color, take it off the heat and let it cool.

2. Preheat the oven to 350°F and grease a 9 x 13-inch pan.

3. In a the bowl of a stand mixer fitted with the paddle attachment, beat the cooled brown butter and brown sugar until creamy. Add the eggs and vanilla and mix, scraping the sides of the bowl. Add the flour, baking powder, and salt and mix until combined.

4. Press the mixture evenly into the prepared pan.

5. Bake the blondies for about 35 minutes, or until a toothpick inserted into the center comes out with only a few crumbs stuck to it. (I like these blondies gooey, so I go with a little less time). Let cool completely on a wire rack, then cut them and wrap them individually in plastic wrap so the sides don't dry out. Store in the freezer or at room temperature.

Options: Add up to ¾ cup of your own ingredients, like pecans, chocolate chips, shredded coconut, butterscotch chips, peanut butter chips, or chopped dried cherries and white chocolate chips. Anything goes.

STRAWBERRY-LEMON BLONDIES

Craving a lemon bar, a piece of cake, and a glass of strawberry lemonade all at the same time?! Well, look what we have here. It has the bright flavors of lemon and strawberry, with the comfort of a delicious baked good. I see nothing wrong with this picture. —*Sara*

Makes one 9-inch square pan

STRAWBERRY SWIRL

½ cup frozen strawberries, thawed and drained well

1 teaspoon sugar

BLONDIES

Cooking spray

1½ cups all-purpose flour

1 teaspoon kosher salt

½ teaspoon baking powder

2 sticks (1 cup) butter, softened

1½ cups sugar

1 tablespoon lemon zest

4 extra-large eggs

2 tablespoons freshly squeezed lemon juice

1. To make the strawberry swirl: Puree the strawberries and sugar in a blender or food processor until smooth. Set aside.

2. To make the blondies: Preheat the oven to 350°F and grease a 9-inch square pan with butter or cooking spray.

3. In a medium bowl, stir together the flour, salt, and baking powder.

4. Using an electric mixer, cream the butter, sugar, and lemon zest at medium speed until light and fluffy. Add the eggs, 1 at a time, beating well after each addition. Mix in the lemon juice.

5. Reduce the speed to low and add the flour mixture, mixing until incorporated.

6. Spread the batter into the prepared pan. Drop spoonfuls of the strawberry swirl onto the batter and use an offset spatula or butter knife to swirl the puree into the batter, making a marbled effect throughout the blondies.

7. Bake for 35 to 40 minutes, or until a toothpick inserted into the center comes out clean. Let cool on a wire rack to room temperature before cutting. Store in the freezer or at room temperature, wrapped in plastic.

Option: If you want to feel cool and British, add about ½ cup chopped candied lemon peel. It makes these blondies taste like actually good lemon fruitcakes.

MAPLE-PECAN BLONDIES

This is a variation on a theme. Blondies are delicious as they are, but with pecans and maple syrup, we can begin to play with flavors, textures, and different sugars. This is a good example of how we can take one simple recipe and branch out into dozens of different paths. —Sara

Makes one 9-inch square pan

1 cup chopped pecans

Cooking spray

1⅓ cups all-purpose flour

1 teaspoon baking powder

½ teaspoon kosher salt

1 stick (½ cup) butter, softened

⅔ cup lightly packed light brown sugar

¼ cup pure maple syrup (not Aunt Jemima)

2 extra-large eggs

1 teaspoon pure vanilla extract

1. Preheat the oven to 350°F. Spread the pecans evenly on a baking sheet and bake for 8 to 10 minutes, or until lightly toasted. Set aside to cool.

2. Spray a 9-inch square baking pan with cooking spray or butter it generously. For ease, I recommend lining the pan with parchment paper and spraying that, too.

3. In a medium bowl, whisk the flour, baking powder, and salt.

4. In the bowl of a stand mixer fitted with the paddle attachment, beat the butter and sugar on medium-high speed for 2 minutes, until fluffy. Add the maple syrup, eggs, and vanilla, beating after each addition. Add the flour mixture to the butter mixture and beat until incorporated. Stir in the toasted pecans.

5. Spread the batter evenly in the prepared pan and bake for 25 to 30 minutes, depending on how gooey you want the middle to be. Just use a toothpick test to make sure the center is baked through.

6. Let the pan cool on a wire rack before cutting into bars.

↑ Brown-Butter Blondies, page 85

↓ Maple-Pecan Blondies

BUTTERSCOTCH-BOURBON BLONDIES

Enjoy these blondies with some Appalachian banjo pickin' playing in the background. —*Sara*

Makes one 9-inch square pan

Cooking spray

1½ cups all-purpose flour

¾ teaspoon baking powder

½ teaspoon kosher salt

1 stick (½ cup) butter, softened

¾ cup butterscotch chips

¾ cup lightly packed light brown sugar

1 extra-large egg

½ teaspoon pure vanilla extract

¼ cup bourbon

1. Preheat the oven to 350°F and spray a 9-inch square baking pan with cooking spray or butter it generously. For ease, I recommend lining the pan with parchment paper and spraying that too.

2. In a medium bowl, whisk the flour, baking powder, and salt.

3. In a small saucepan over medium heat, melt the butter and ¼ cup of the butterscotch chips until the mixture is smooth. Transfer it to the bowl of a stand mixer.

4. Beat the brown sugar into the butter mixture, then the egg. Add the vanilla and bourbon and beat until combined. Add the flour mixture and beat until incorporated. Stir in the remaining ½ cup butterscotch chips.

5. Spread the batter into the prepared pan and bake for 25 to 30 minutes, or until a toothpick inserted into the center comes out with not too much stuck to it. Let cool before cutting.

WHITE CHOCOLATE–MACADAMIA BLONDIES

We all know and appreciate the deliciousness that is a white chocolate–macadamia nut cookie, but why not take that concept and ramp it up to make awesome blondies? These blondies are moist and chewy, with all that white chocolate flavor and the crunch of the macadamia nuts really adding to their texture. White chocolate and macadamia is a cliché, I know, but it's also delicious. Don't hate. *—Sara*

Makes one 9-inch square pan

Cooking spray

2⅓ cups white chocolate chips

1 stick (½ cup) butter, softened

1 tablespoon pure vanilla extract

2 extra-large eggs

½ cup granulated sugar

2 tablespoons light brown sugar

¾ teaspoon kosher salt

1¼ cups all-purpose flour

⅓ cup chopped unsalted macadamia nuts

1. Preheat the oven to 350°F and grease a 9-inch square baking pan with butter or cooking spray.

2. Place 2 cups of the white chocolate chips and the butter in a medium saucepan over medium heat. Stir constantly until the mixture is melted and smooth. Stir in the vanilla.

3. In a big bowl, beat the eggs on medium speed until frothy. Add the sugars and salt and beat until combined. Slowly add the white chocolate–butter mixture, mixing until smooth. Stir in the flour and mix until just combined and smooth.

4. Stir in the remaining ⅓ cup white chocolate chips and the macadamia nuts.

5. Spread the batter into the prepared pan and bake for 20 to 25 minutes, or until a toothpick inserted into the center comes out clean. Let cool on a wire rack before cutting.

6. Wrap in plastic and store at room temperature or in the freezer.

MUFFINS & QUICK BREADS, SCONES & BISCUITS

I have a real soft spot for muffins and quick breads, because after I got my sea legs baking cornbread and biscuits at my first real restaurant job, the chef asked me to make some muffins and quick breads for the brunch service. I asked her for some recipes, and she gave me a baking book and told me to pick some. I had a few questions about some of the methods, like "creaming the butter and sugar," but on the whole I understood the concepts. I baked a few loaves of a butterscotch-walnut and a zucchini bread that Saturday night for service the next day. It was early in the evening, probably 7 p.m., and we usually worked till 2 a.m. I let the loaves cool and put them on my rack and went about my night, baking the cornbread and biscuits for that evening's meal and prepping for the guys on the line when they ran out of stuff. I kept seeing the cooks and the servers in and around my station. Also, I was good at frothing the milk for espresso drinks, and when they were busy, the servers would ask me to froth milk and pull shots for them, which I didn't mind because I was trying to hook up with one of the cuter servers anyway.

So the night went on, and we finished strong, had a beer, and cleaned up the kitchen. The chef asked me to show her my loaves—she wanted to try one. I was super proud, so I went into my corner to get the loaves off the rack, and there was nothing there! Well, that's not quite true. There were a few heels and some crumbs.

Now, I was playing ice hockey and lacrosse at the time, and somebody was going to die. I turned around, and the whole kitchen was laughing, *including the chef*! I knew I'd just got hazed. That's cool. So I laughed, too. Then something magic happened. The chef pulled me into her office and told me that our grill guy (big nasty Peruvian dude named Henry who made me eat a bunch of wasabi once by telling me it was guacamole) saw my loaves and cut off a piece and ate it. He then cut a few more pieces and gave them to the rest of the guys on the line. The line cooks told the servers there was a snack for them on the baker's rack. The chef even started snacking. She loved my breads, and I was so stoked that I wasn't mad. That was a great feeling. I knew I was good at something that I knew I wanted to do, and that validation was exactly what I needed. The chef smiled, gave me the keys to the restaurant, and told me to re-make the loaves for brunch the next day and lock up when I was done. That was cool; I knew where the beer was.

The great thing about muffins and quick breads is that they're awesome for learning the basics of baking. They employ a lot of fundamental techniques that you'll use over and over again. Quick breads are also very forgiving, which will give you more confidence to try baking new things. But the best thing about muffins and quick breads is that they're delicious!

Let's talk about biscuits for a sec. There's a special place in my heart for biscuits. If it weren't for biscuits, I wouldn't be a baker today. I don't even know if I'd be cooking. I landed my first fine-dining job only because I was willing to do anything to get into the best restaurant in Baltimore and work for the best chef in the city. At the time, I wanted to be a chef. I didn't even know what a pastry chef was. I just knew I wanted to be one of those bandana-wearin' cutthroats working the line of a badass kitchen working with fire and meat.

Well, I wasn't ready for the bigs yet, but Chef Cindy Wolf took a chance on me and taught me how to bake real Southern buttermilk biscuits with lard and real sweet cornbread muffins in cast-iron pans. Boy, did I take to baking! I loved it. I had so much pride in my biscuits and cornbread, and I was the low man on the totem pole, but I swear my zeal for perfection was infectious. Everybody in that kitchen loved my enthusiasm, and it spread from me to sauté to grill to garde manger. Cindy thought I was something of a freak (I had white-guy dreads and a spiral shaved into my head), but nothing could keep me from baking the best cornbread and biscuits in Maryland. And I believe that. I had two jobs. Biscuits and Cornbread. Dad always told me to do the best at whatever you're doing, whether it's running the show or mopping the floor—always do your best. And I did. I really was, for two years, baking the best cornbread and biscuits in the state.

One thing that I discovered by accident was that if I didn't mix the biscuit dough too much and left little clumps of cold lard in it, the biscuits would be flaky. If I dry-mixed the dough enough to incorporated the lard evenly, I'd get mealy biscuits. I liked the flaky ones, so that's how I made the biscuits—then and now.

The same rule goes for scones. Scones are basically slightly sweet, fruity biscuits, and they're usually made with butter, not lard. Lard is delicious, but the most important thing about both biscuits and scones is that they're vehicles. Scones and biscuits are the most efficient and delicious way of conveying butter, jam, cream, and gravy to your mouth. Scones are naturally a bit on the dry side, so serve them with milk or coffee. You can serve them with clotted cream, but we Americans don't really like the word "clotted," so don't think you're breaking with tradition by not doing so. Almost all baked goods are really just effective delivery systems for high-fat dairy products. When you take a good macro look at biscuits and scones, their utility is both obvious and beautiful.

BLUEBERRY MUFFINS

When you're looking for the ideal blueberry muffin, what do you look for? Bursting with blueberries? Light and fluffy, with just the right amount of sweetness? The awesome crisp of a streusel topping? These muffins will satisfy all these blueberry muffin must-haves and more! They're sure to make anyone's morning start off just right. —*Sara*

Makes 12 muffins

STREUSEL TOPPING

⅓ cup granulated sugar

⅓ lightly packed light brown sugar

¼ cup all-purpose flour

¼ teaspoon kosher salt

¾ stick (6 tablespoons) cold butter, cut into ½-inch cubes

¾ cup old-fashioned rolled oats (not instant)

MUFFINS

2⅓ cups all-purpose flour

1 cup plus 2 tablespoons granulated sugar

1 tablespoon baking powder

½ teaspoon baking soda

¾ teaspoon kosher salt

2 extra-large eggs

½ cup canola oil

½ cup buttermilk

½ teaspoon pure vanilla extract

2 cups fresh blueberries

1. Preheat the oven to 375°F and line a 12-cup muffin tin with paper liners or grease it generously with butter.

2. To make the streusel: In a medium bowl, mix the sugars, flour, and salt. Add the butter and start to blend it in using your hands or a pastry cutter. Add the oats after a minute or two and continue to break up the butter until it resembles a coarse meal. Set aside.

3. To make the muffins: Whisk the flour, sugar, baking powder, baking soda, and salt in a large bowl.

4. In a medium bowl, lightly whisk the eggs, oil, buttermilk, and vanilla. Add to the flour mixture and whisk just until smooth. Fold in the blueberries.

5. Divide the batter among the muffin cups, filling them to about ¼ inch from the top. (If you have extra batter, by all means make more muffins!)

6. Top each with a sprinkle of the streusel topping.

7. Bake for 25 to 30 minutes, or until a toothpick inserted into the middle of a muffin comes out clean.

8. Let the muffins cool for 5 minutes in the tin before moving them to a wire rack.

LEMON-POPPY SEED MUFFINS

Another staple in the muffin world, lemon–poppy seed muffins are a light, refreshing addition to brunch that can totally stand on their own. A little spread of butter or jam isn't necessary, but it would certainly kick up breakfast several notches. —*Sara*

Makes 12 muffins

1½ cups all-purpose flour

1½ teaspoons baking powder

½ teaspoon baking soda

½ teaspoon kosher salt

½ stick plus 1 tablespoon (5 tablespoons) butter, softened

¾ cup sour cream

3 large eggs

1 teaspoon pure vanilla extract

Zest of 2 lemons

Juice of 1 lemon

½ cup sugar

¼ cup poppy seeds

1. Preheat the oven to 375°F and line a 12-cup muffin tin with paper liners or grease it with cooking spray or shortening.

2. In a medium bowl, whisk the flour, baking powder, baking soda, and salt.

3. In a big bowl, whisk the butter, sour cream, eggs, vanilla, lemon zest, and lemon juice. Whisk in the sugar until smooth.

4. Add the flour mixture and whisk until just combined and smooth. Add the poppy seeds and stir to incorporate.

5. Scoop or spoon the batter evenly among the 12 muffin cups, filling them no more than three-quarters full.

6. Bake for 15 to 20 minutes, or until they're golden brown on top and a toothpick inserted into the middle comes out clean. Let them cool for a few minutes in the pan, then transfer to a wire rack to cool.

OLD-FASHIONED RAISIN BRAN MUFFINS

Bran muffins can get a bad rap for being boring or too healthy-tasting, but these are absolutely delicious, and with golden raisins and pecans, they're totally not boring. Get some bran in you—that's good fiber right there. You can find wheat bran online or at any decent health food store or specialty baking store. —*Sara*

Makes 12 muffins

1½ cups wheat bran

¾ cup all-purpose flour

¾ cup lightly packed light brown sugar

½ teaspoon baking powder

½ teaspoon baking soda

½ teaspoon ground cinnamon

¼ teaspoon kosher salt

1 extra-large egg

2 tablespoons honey

½ cup canola oil

1 cup buttermilk

1 cup golden raisins

1 cup chopped pecans (optional)

1. Preheat the oven to 350°F. Line a 12-cup muffin tin with paper liners or grease it with cooking spray or shortening.

2. In a big bowl, whisk together the bran, flour, brown sugar, baking powder, baking soda, cinnamon, and salt.

3. In a medium bowl, whisk together the egg, honey, oil, and buttermilk.

4. Whisk the wet mixture into the dry mixture just until combined.

5. Fold in the raisins and nuts, if using, and scoop or spoon the batter among the 12 muffin cups, filling them no more than three-quarters full.

6. Bake for 23 to 28 minutes, or until a toothpick inserted into the center comes out clean.

7. Let the muffins cool in the pan for a few minutes before transferring them to a wire rack.

APPLE STREUSEL MUFFINS

This muffin really is a star all on its own. It's like a dessert you're allowed to convince yourself is a break-fast food. The brown sugar–cinnamon streusel on top is the icing on the cake. (Sorry, bad pun.) —*Sara*

Makes 12 muffins

STREUSEL

2 tablespoons old-fashioned rolled oats (not instant)

1 tablespoon all-purpose flour

1 tablespoon light brown sugar

1 tablespoon granulated sugar

½ teaspoon ground cinnamon

1 tablespoon butter, melted

½ teaspoon pure vanilla extract

¾ cup buttermilk

1 large apple (Granny Smith is my favorite), cut into ½-inch dice

MUFFINS

1½ cups all-purpose flour

2 teaspoons ground cinnamon

1½ teaspoons baking powder

1 teaspoon baking soda

½ teaspoon kosher salt

3 tablespoons butter, melted

2 tablespoons granulated sugar

½ cup lightly packed light brown sugar

1 large egg plus 1 egg yolk

1. To make the streusel: Combine the dry ingredients in a small bowl. Drizzle the butter on top and stir lightly to combine. Set aside.

2. To make the muffins: Preheat the oven to 375°F and line a 12-cup muffin tin with paper liners or grease it with cooking spray or shortening.

3. In a medium bowl, whisk together the flour, cinnamon, baking powder, baking soda, and salt. Set aside.

4. In a big bowl, cream the butter and sugars until fluffy. Add the egg, egg yolk, vanilla, and buttermilk and whisk to combine.

5. Mix the flour mixture into the buttermilk mixture until just combined. Fold in the apple.

6. Scoop or spoon the batter among the 12 muffin cups, filling them no more than three-quarters full, and top each with a sprinkle of streusel.

7. Bake for 18 to 20 minutes, or until a toothpick inserted into the middle comes out clean. Let cool for a few minutes in the pan, then transfer them to a wire rack.

HOT PICKLED PEPPER–CORN MUFFINS

A lot of people have had jalapeño cornbread, but here's a fun trick: looking at a "surprise" ingredient that isn't a surprise anymore and trading it for a variation on a theme. I happen to be going through a pickling phase—why not?—and I've pickled everything in my fridge, so this just kinda popped into my head. Here's a spicy, sweet, salty, sour muffin that would also make an incredible polenta, but that's another book. —*Duff*

Makes about one 10-inch round pan, 18 standard muffins, or a whole bunch of mini muffins

Cooking spray

1½ cups all-purpose flour

1½ cups yellow cornmeal

2 teaspoons kosher salt

½ cup sugar

½ teaspoon baking soda

1 teaspoon baking powder

1 tablespoon honey

1 cup buttermilk, at room temperature

3 large eggs, at room temperature

1 cup chopped spicy pickled peppers, drained well, at room temperature (pepperoncini work awesome here, too)

2 sticks (1 cup) butter, softened

1. Preheat the oven to 375°F and grease 18 standard muffin cups (or a 10-inch pan or mini muffin tin) with cooking spray.

2. Get two big mixing bowls. In one, mix well the flour, cornmeal, salt, sugar, baking soda, and baking powder. In the other, whisk the honey, buttermilk, eggs, and peppers.

3. Make a well in the center of the flour mixture and stir in the liquid mixture. When the liquid is incorporated, mix in the butter.

4. Fill the muffin cups to within ½ inch of the top. Bake for 20 to 25 minutes, or until a toothpick inserted into the center of a muffin comes out clean. For a 10-inch pan, bake for 40 to 45 minutes. Mini muffins will bake faster, maybe 12 to 15 minutes. Also, if you wanted to sneak some shredded cheddar or mozz on top before baking these, I won't tell if you won't.

SARA'S CORNBREAD

My mom used to call this cornbread "corny cornbread" because the creamed corn not only makes this quick bread crazy moist, but it adds kernels of corn to really up the flavor! Serve warm with some butter or honey (or both!) and you'll be in cornbread heaven. Oh, and mine is better than Duff's. It's awesome warm because it melts the butter and sucks it up. Mmmmm . . . —*Sara*

Makes a 9-inch square pan or 12 muffins

2 extra-large eggs

1¼ cups yellow cornmeal

1 cup all-purpose flour

½ teaspoon baking powder

½ teaspoon baking soda

1 teaspoon kosher salt

2 teaspoons sugar

¼ cup vegetable oil

1 cup sour cream

1 (14.75-ounce) can cream-style corn

1. Preheat the oven to 375°F and butter a 9-inch square pan or 12-cup muffin tin.

2. In a big bowl, lightly whisk the eggs. Mix in the remaining ingredients.

3. Pour the batter into the prepared pan and bake for 35 minutes for a square pan (30 minutes for muffins), until a toothpick inserted into the center has only a few crumbs stuck to it.

4. Let it cool for 5 to 10 minutes, then dig in!

DUFF'S CORNBREAD

My first fine-dining job was working for Chef Cindy Wolf in Baltimore. She took a chance on me when I really didn't know how to cook, like, at all. She made me bake the cornbread for the restaurant, and it taught me that no matter what you're doing, do it the best you can. She'll tell you that I made the best damn cornbread in the state. This is my adaptation of Chef Cindy Wolf's recipe, but to be honest, every time I open the oven, I'm doing something that Cindy taught me how to do.

Bake these as soon as they're mixed, because the acid in the buttermilk will set off the baking soda and you want to get the most lift out of your leavening agent. And make your mouth happy and serve with homemade honey butter—roughly a 2:1 ratio of butter to honey, whipped until soft and awesome. —*Duff*

Makes one 9 x 13-inch pan or 12 muffins

1 cup yellow cornmeal
1 cup all-purpose flour
½ cup sugar
1 teaspoon baking powder
1 teaspoon baking soda
Big pinch of kosher salt
2 extra-large eggs plus
   1 egg yolk
1 cup buttermilk

1. Preheat the oven to 375°F and grease a 9 x 13-inch baking dish or cake pan, or a 12-cup muffin tin.

2. In a big bowl, whisk together all the dry ingredients.

3. In a medium bowl, whisk the eggs and buttermilk to a uniform color.

4. Quickly but gently fold the liquid mixture into the dry mixture. It should be a loose batter, not a dough. If not, add some more buttermilk or even some cream, but just a tad; these ratios are right.

5. Pour the batter into the pan or divide it among muffin cups and bake for about 22 minutes (15 to 18 minutes for muffins), or until the top is golden and a toothpick comes out somewhat clean. Let cool for 7 minutes, then turn them out upside-down so they develop a nice thin crust on the baked edge.

BANANA BREAD

My mom made this banana bread a lot. She could throw it together quickly and easily, using a couple bananas that were past their prime. Once the bread was done and the house smelled delicious, we would eat banana bread for breakfast, lunch, and dessert for days (I don't think my mom would let us eat banana bread for dinner). Feel free to play with it a little bit, mix up the nuts added to it, add chocolate chips, go bananas! Sorry, couldn't help myself with that one. —*Sara*

Makes one 9 x 5-inch loaf

1½ cups all-purpose flour

½ teaspoon baking soda

½ teaspoon kosher salt

1 teaspoon ground cinnamon

1 cup sugar

2 large very ripe bananas, mashed with a fork

2 extra-large eggs

½ cup plus 2 tablespoons vegetable oil

⅔ cup chopped walnuts (optional), lightly toasted (10 minutes at 350°F)

1. Preheat the oven to 350°F and grease and flour a 9 x 5-inch loaf pan.

2. In a big bowl, mix the flour, baking soda, salt, cinnamon, and sugar.

3. In a medium bowl, combine the rest of the ingredients.

4. Add the wet ingredients to the dry ingredients and stir until just combined.

5. Pour the batter into the prepared pan and bake for 1 hour, or until a toothpick inserted into the middle of the loaf comes out clean.

6. Let cool 10 for 15 minutes, then turn it out onto a wire rack.

Options: If you want, brush the top of the banana bread with a simple glaze (see page 297) about 10 minutes before you take it out of the oven. It makes a nice, sweet little crunch on top. Also, it's not traditional (but then, neither am I)—but you can bake it with a streusel topping (see page 45).

PUMPKIN BREAD

This autumnal quick bread is super-fast and easy to make, so it's the perfect treat to have around the kitchen during the season. Then you have breakfast, a snack, or dessert (or dinner, I'm not judging) all ready to go for a few days, and you can focus on pretty fall leaves, Turkey Day plans, and football games.

—*Sara*

Makes one 9 x 5-inch loaf

2 cups all-purpose flour

¾ teaspoon kosher salt

1 teaspoon baking soda

¾ teaspoon baking powder

1½ teaspoons ground cinnamon

½ teaspoon ground nutmeg

¼ teaspoon ground cloves

¾ stick (6 tablespoons) butter, softened

1½ cups sugar

¼ cup vegetable oil

2 extra-large eggs

2 tablespoons molasses

1 cup pumpkin puree (not pumpkin pie filling)

1. Preheat the oven to 350°F and grease and flour a 9 x 5-inch loaf pan.

2. In a medium bowl, mix the flour, salt, baking soda, baking powder, and spices.

3. In a big bowl, cream the butter and sugar until fluffy, scraping down the sides. Add the oil, eggs, molasses, and pumpkin and mix thoroughly, scraping down the sides at least once more.

4. Add the dry ingredients to the pumpkin mixture and mix until incorporated. Scrape down the sides.

5. Pour the batter into the prepared loaf pan and bake for 50 to 60 minutes, or until a toothpick inserted into the center comes out clean.

6. Let cool for 10 minutes, then turn the loaf onto a wire rack to finish cooling.

ZUCCHINI-PINEAPPLE BREAD

Looking for a quick bread that's easy to throw together but a little bit out of the box flavor-wise? Give this one a try. Zucchini gives the bread beautiful color, and the sweetness of the pineapple eliminates the need for added sugar! If you're feeling extra crazy, use both green and yellow zucchini for an even brighter look. And yes, there's no butter in this loaf. *—Sara*

Makes two 9 x 5-inch loaves

3 extra-large eggs

1¾ cups sugar

1 cup vegetable oil

2 teaspoons pure vanilla extract

2 cups unpeeled shredded zucchini, drained (about 3 large zukes)

1 tablespoon lemon zest

1 (8¼-ounce) can crushed pineapple, drained

3 cups all-purpose flour

2 teaspoons baking soda

1 teaspoon kosher salt

½ teaspoon baking powder

1½ teaspoons ground cinnamon

1 teaspoon ground nutmeg

1. Preheat the oven to 350°F and grease and flour two 9 x 5-inch loaf pans.

2. In the bowl of a stand mixer fitted with the whisk attachment, or in a large bowl with a wire whisk, beat the eggs and sugar until blended. Add the oil and vanilla and beat until thick and foamy.

3. Stir in the zucchini, zest, and pineapple.

4. Combine the rest of the ingredients in a medium bowl. Mix them into the wet mixture and stir until just combined.

5. Divide the batter between the loaf pans and bake for 1 hour, or until a toothpick inserted into the center comes out clean.

6. Let cool in the pan for 10 minutes, then turn out the loaves onto a wire rack.

GINGERBREAD

There's gingerbread that you make cute little houses out of (like the kind on page 84) and that talk sassy in the movie *Shrek,* and then there's the moist, tender loaf that punches your whole house in the face with the smell of Christmas. I learned this recipe when I was just going to culinary school and the mother of one of my friends slipped this little 3 x 5-inch card to me all inconspicuous-like and said, "If you're ever having trouble on a test, just bake this and you'll get an 'A.'" It totally worked—I got a 100 percent in quick breads. I've tinkered with it a bit, but not much. —*Duff*

Makes one 9 x 5-inch loaf

Cooking spray

1 cup all-purpose flour

1 cup cake flour

1½ teaspoons ground cinnamon

Pinch of ground cloves

1 teaspoon ground ginger

Pinch of kosher salt

2 teaspoons baking powder

1 cup half-and-half, at room temperature

1 extra-large egg, at room temperature

1 tablespoon cheap olive oil (this doesn't bake hot, so it won't smoke)

2 tablespoons molasses, at room temperature (or ¼ cup brown rice syrup for a more butterscotchy flavor)

¼ cup maple syrup, at room temperature

1. Preheat the oven to 325°F and spray a 9 x 5-inch loaf pan with cooking spray.

2. In a big bowl, whisk together the flours, spices, salt, and baking powder.

3. In a medium bowl, whisk together the half-and-half, egg, oil, molasses, and maple syrup.

4. Make a well in the center of the flour mixture, pour in the wet mixture, and mix well to combine. (Unlike most quick breads, this batter is hard to overmix.)

5. Pour the mixture into the prepared pan and bake for 45 to 50 minutes, or until a toothpick inserted into the center comes out mostly clean. Don't bake more than 1 hour, so the gingerbread stays moist.

6. Let the bread cool in the pan on a wire rack for 20 minutes before unmolding it to cool further. There isn't much gluten in this recipe, so the gingerbread will crumble if you unmold it too soon.

CINNAMON COFFEECAKE

When I first started baking, I thought coffeecake was supposed to taste like coffee. I asked the chef why coffee was missing from the recipe she gave me to bake, and needless to say, I was the kitchen joke for at least a week.

This is a good, solid recipe that can be modified as you like. It has orange flower water, which gives a very subtle flavor that adds an unexpected complexity to the bread while hiding well behind the cinnamon flavor. Add nuts, raisins, chocolate chips—you name it, it all works. —*Duff*

Makes two 9 x 5-inch loaves, four 5 x 3-inch loaves, or 12 muffins

Cooking spray

2 sticks (1 cup) butter, softened

1¼ cups granulated sugar

1 cup lightly packed light brown sugar

1 tablespoon pure vanilla extract

2 teaspoons orange flower water

1 teaspoon baking powder

Pinch of kosher salt

3 cups all-purpose flour

2 cups crème fraiche

4 extra-large eggs

¼ cup ground cinnamon

1 recipe Streusel (page 45)

1. Preheat the oven to 350°F. Lightly spray the loaf pans or a 12-cup muffin tin with cooking spray.

2. With a hand or stand mixer, cream the butter, 1 cup of the granulated sugar, and the brown sugar until light in color (it won't get super light because of the brown sugar). Add the vanilla and orange flower water and beat for 30 more seconds. Scrape the sides of the bowl.

3. In a medium bowl, whisk the baking powder, salt, and flour. Gradually add half the flour mixture to the butter mixture, then half the crème fraiche and 2 of the eggs, then the rest of the flour mixture, then the rest of the crème fraiche and remaining 2 eggs, mixing until just combined but homogeneous.

4. Pour half the batter into the prepared pan.

5. In a small bowl, mix together the remaining ¼ cup granulated sugar, the cinnamon, and ¼ cup water. With a bamboo skewer, quickly draw a zig-zag line all the way across the surface of the batter. Pour the cinnamon mixture on top of the batter and gently spread with the back of a spoon. Pour the remaining batter on top of the cinnamon layer.

6. Sprinkle the streusel on top and bake for 45 minutes (35 minutes for smaller loaves and 25 to 30 minutes for muffins), or until a toothpick inserted into the center comes out clean.

7. Let the coffee cake cool in the pan for 15 minutes, then unmold it onto a wire rack to cool.

JALAPEÑO, CHEDDAR & BACON BISCUITS

Do I really need to explain why this recipe is in here? These biscuits are so dang good, 'specially for breakfast, and 'specially to make breakfast sandwiches with, to which you can add even more cheese and pork products to them. Breakfast of champions. —*Duff*

Makes 10 to 12 biscuits

DOUGH

3 tablespoons cornmeal

¼ cup chopped crisp-cooked bacon

1 cup shredded Cheddar cheese

1 teaspoon cayenne

2 tablespoons finely diced jalapeño (seed the jalapeños first, if you're a wimp)

1 tablespoon kosher salt

1 tablespoon baking powder

½ teaspoon baking soda

2 tablespoons sugar

Drizzle of honey

1 stick (½ cup) butter, softened

½ cup buttermilk

1½ cups all-purpose flour, plus more as needed

EGG WASH

2 extra-large eggs

2 tablespoons sugar

1. Preheat the oven to 375°F and line a baking sheet with parchment paper.

2. To make the dough: In a big bowl, combine all the dough ingredients except for the flour and mix them up real good. Once all that goodness is mixed up, add the flour and gently stir until just combined. Turn the sticky mess out onto a floured table, flour the top of it, and push it together so you have one dough pile.

3. To make the egg wash: In a small bowl, whisk the eggs and sugar together. Set aside.

4. With a rolling pin, roll out the dough to about 1¼ inches thick. Using a 2¾-inch biscuit cutter, cut out the biscuits and place them a few inches apart on the prepared baking sheet. (Go ahead and reroll the scraps—just be gentle with the dough or the resulting biscuits will be tough.) Brush the top of each biscuit with egg wash.

5. Bake for 20 to 25 minutes, or until they look awesome. Let cool right on the pan on a wire rack.

Buttermilk Biscuits, page 116

Jalapeño, Cheddar & Bacon Biscuits

Mini Sesame-Cheddar Biscuits, page 117

BUTTERMILK BISCUITS

Yo, this recipe is the jam. Old-school buttermilk biscuits, blank-canvas style. Bake 'em just like this and you're stoked. Add all kinds of crazy flavors to them—then you got a party!

   This recipe calls for lard. Don't be shy. It's easy to find—if it's not at the grocery store, go to a Latin market and look for *manteca*. This dough is super wet, sloppy, and delicate. Don't overmix this dough, or you get crap biscuits. The dough should barely hold itself together. —*Duff*

Makes about 20 biscuits

DOUGH

5 cups all-purpose flour, plus more as needed

2 tablespoons kosher salt

2 tablespoons sugar

1 tablespoon baking powder

1 tablespoon baking soda

10 ounces (1¼ cups) cold lard*

1½ cups buttermilk

EGG WASH

2 extra-large eggs

2 tablespoons sugar

Buttermilk Biscuits are pictured on page 115.

1. Preheat the oven to 375°F. Line a baking sheet with parchment paper.

2. To make the dough: In a big bowl, mix together the flour, salt, sugar, baking powder, and baking soda. Mix it real good. Start tearing off chunks of lard and massage them into the flour— you want the flour to become sandy, but you also want to leave small chunks of lard. Pour in the buttermilk and gently massage the dough until it's just formed. Don't make it smooth—you want it lumpy and ragged-looking.

3. Flour a table and turn the dough out onto it. Flour the top of the dough and roll it out to 1½ inches thick. Cut out the biscuits with a 3½-inch cutter and place them on the prepared baking sheet so they're almost touching.

4. To make the egg wash: In a small bowl, whisk the eggs and sugar to make an egg wash. Brush all the biscuits with the egg wash.

5. Bake for 20 to 22 minutes, or until they look nice and golden brown. You may need to cut them apart when they cool, and that's totally okay. Let cool right on the pan on a wire rack.

* You can use butter here, but I promise that lard is the way to go.

MINI SESAME-CHEDDAR BISCUITS

This is a fun recipe that's quick and easy and uses a store-bought biscuit mix. I like goofing around with baking mixes—there's a lot you can do with them, and it's a great way to get familiar with baking and your oven. It's also a fantastic introduction to baking for the kids—they love eating what they make. —*Duff*

Makes like 40 tiny little biscuits

1 cup all-purpose flour, plus more as needed

2 cups Bisquick biscuit mix

1 teaspoon cayenne

¼ cup sesame seeds

1 teaspoon baking powder

¼ teaspoon baking soda

2 teaspoons kosher salt

Pinch of garlic powder

1 cup shredded Cheddar cheese

½ cup buttermilk

1 stick (½ cup) butter, softened

Milk or lightly beaten egg, for brushing

Mini Sesame-Cheddar Biscuits are pictured on page 115.

1. In a big bowl, whisk together the flour, biscuit mix, cayenne, sesame seeds, baking powder, baking soda, salt, garlic powder, and cheese.

2. Mix in the buttermilk and butter until well incorporated.

3. Turn the dough onto a floured surface and roll it into a snake about 1¼ inches wide. Place the snake on a piece of parchment paper. Lightly flour the snake, roll it up really tight in the paper, and refrigerate for 25 minutes, or freeze the dough for later.

4. Preheat the oven to 400°F and line a baking sheet with parchment paper.

5. Unroll the dough and cut it into ½-inch-thick slices with a sharp knife.* Place them on the baking sheet and brush them with a little milk or egg.

6. Bake for about 8 minutes, or until lightly browned. Let cool on the pan.

* These biscuits are also awesome made larger. Cut them into 2-inch pieces. Bake at 375°F for 15 to 20 minutes.

APPLE-CINNAMON SCONES

Scones aren't just for tea parties anymore. A good scone can be an easy breakfast or snack any time! These apple-cinnamon scones are moist, light, and delicate, but packed with flavor. The key to a good scone is handling it as little as possible so that it stays light in texture in the end. Feel free to switch out the apples for pears or peaches or maybe some reconstituted dried fruits. —*Sara*

Makes 8 scones

SCONES

2 cups all-purpose flour, plus more as needed

1/3 cup sugar

1 tablespoon baking powder

1/2 teaspoon kosher salt

1 teaspoon ground cinnamon

1 stick (1/2 cup) plus 2 tablespoons cold butter, cut into 1/2-inch cubes

2 apples (I like Mutsu and Fuji applies for this recipe), cored and cut into 1/2- to 3/4-inch cubes

1 cup buttermilk

GLAZE

2 tablespoons heavy cream

1/4 cup sugar

1 tablespoon ground cinnamon

1. Preheat the oven to 350°F and line a baking sheet with parchment paper.

2. To make the scones: In a big bowl, stir together the flour, sugar, baking powder, salt, and cinnamon.

3. Add the butter and use your hands to rub it into the flour mixture slightly, still leaving it in chunks. Think dime- to quarter-size pieces.

4. Gently mix in the apples. I do all of this just with my hands.

5. Gradually add the buttermilk while very lightly folding the dough with your hand. Mix until just combined, turn out the dough onto a floured surface, and pat it into a circle 1 to 1½ inches thick. Cut the dough into 8 wedges and place them a few inches apart on the prepared baking sheet.

6. To glaze the scones: Brush the tops of the scones with the cream. Mix together the sugar and cinnamon and sprinkle the scones with a bit of the cinnamon sugar.

7. Bake for 25 to 30 minutes, or until the scones are golden brown on top and a toothpick inserted into the center comes out clean. Let cool on a wire rack.

CRANBERRY-ORANGE SCONES

Don't spend money at the coffee shop on a scone to go with your latte in the morning. Make your own—they're super easy and you'll know they'll be good. These cranberry-orange scones have a holiday season lean to them, but they taste just as good in April—promise! —*Sara*

Makes 8 scones

SCONES

2 cups all-purpose flour

½ cup sugar

1 tablespoon baking powder

½ teaspoon kosher salt

½ cup (1 stick) plus 2 tablespoons cold butter, cut into ½-inch cubes

2 tablespoons orange zest

1 cup dried cranberries

1 cup heavy cream

EGG WASH

2 tablespoons milk

1 extra-large egg

Turbinado sugar (Sugar In The Raw), for sprinkling (optional)

1. Preheat the oven to 350°F and line a baking sheet with parchment paper.

2. To make the scones: In a big bowl, stir together the flour, sugar, baking powder, and salt.

3. Add the butter and use your hands to rub it into the flour mixture slightly, still leaving it in chunks. Think dime- to quarter-size pieces.

4. Gently mix in the orange zest and cranberries.

5. Gradually add the cream while just very lightly folding with your hand. Mix until just combined, turn out the dough onto a floured surface, and pat it into a circle 1 to 1½ inches thick. Cut the scones into 8 wedges and place them a few inches apart on the baking sheet.

6. Make a quick egg wash with the milk and egg and brush the tops of the scones. You can also sprinkle on some turbinado sugar to give the scones a nice, sweet crunch on top.

7. Bake for 25 to 30 minutes, or until the scones are golden brown on top and a toothpick inserted into the center comes out clean. Let cool on a wire rack.

CHORIZO-MANCHEGO-SCALLION SCONES

As a baker, sometimes you need a break from sweet stuff. Savory baking is so much fun because it gives us a chance to work with ingredients that we don't necessarily get to use all the time, like chorizo (I just can't seem to get it to work in the oatmeal cookie recipe). Combining something as heavenly and wonderful as chorizo with a flavorful and delicious Spanish cheese such as Manchego is a natural fit. Add some scallions to deepen the flavor and add some sweetness and bite and you have an awesome scone, indeed. —Sara

Makes 8 scones

SCONES

6 ounces fresh Mexican-style chorizo (not the dried kind)

2¼ cups all-purpose flour, plus more as needed

2 teaspoons baking powder

1 teaspoon kosher salt

¼ teaspoon freshly ground black pepper

1 stick (½ cup) cold butter, cut into ½-inch cubes

1 cup grated Manchego cheese

¼ cup minced scallions (about 2; don't use the tips of the dark green tops or the hairy root part, but everything else is okay)

½ to ⅔ cup heavy cream

EGG WASH

1 extra-large egg

2 tablespoons milk or cream

1. Preheat the oven to 350°F and line a baking sheet with parchment paper.

2. To make the scones: Cook the chorizo in a medium sauté pan over medium heat for 5 to 6 minutes, or until cooked through, breaking it up into little pieces as it cooks. Remove from the heat. Pat some of the grease off with a paper towel if you wish. Set aside to cool a bit.

3. In a big bowl, stir together the flour, baking powder, salt, and pepper.

4. Add the butter and either cut it in with two knives or use your palms to slightly rub it in, being sure to leave the butter in small chunks.

5. Gently mix in the Manchego, chorizo, and scallions.

continued on following pages

6. Gradually add in the heavy cream, mixing it in by hand as you add it. I like to do all of this by hand so that I can feel the consistency of the dough and nothing gets overmixed. This is important. Do not fully incorporate the butter or overmix this dough or the scones will turn out too dense and chewy.

7. When the dough is able to hold its shape (you might need another drop of heavy cream, but you don't want it sticky), place it on a floured surface and pat it into a circle about ½ to ¾ inch thick. Cut it into 8 wedges and place them a few inches apart on the baking sheet.

8. For a pretty finish to the scones, make a quick egg wash with the egg and milk or cream and lightly brush the tops of the scones with it. (If you have any Manchego left over, you can sprinkle it on top of the scones, too. But that's silly—if there was any leftover Manchego, you would have eaten it by now.)

9. Bake for 20 to 25 minutes, or until the scones are golden brown on top and a toothpick inserted into the center comes out clean. Let cool on a wire rack.

REAL BREAD

I f someone pointed a gun at my head and told me to pick one thing to do for the rest of my life, I would, without hesitation, choose to bake bread. It's the most elemental of baking disciplines, a dance with a living organism. It offers endless variety and fodder for constant thought, reflection, and speculation. As a bread baker, you pay attention to the weather. Is it going to be hot tomorrow? Humid? What season is it? Am I baking with summer or winter wheat? What elevation am I at? Much like the difference between a farm-raised fat, lazy trout and a wild trout that has had to fight streams and dart for food, trout is not just trout, and wheat is not just wheat.

Baking bread is a physical activity. You and your dough have a clearly delineated relationship between material and craftsman that only exists in a few workplaces. The smell of bread baking or rising or cooling is almost, if not in fact, the aroma of the Buddha of Samsara, or the cycle of birth, life, death, and rebirth. Bread starts with a few simple ingredients: flour, water, salt, and yeast. It's also the product of time and energy. The energy is heat and friction; the time is mixing, rising, baking, and cooling.

These are the things that make bread. There are some colorful and fun distractions, like oil and butter and herbs and grains and honey and eggs and countless other things that make different breads. There are a million shapes, from baguettes to boules to *pain épi* to rolls to crackers to pockets. But the root of bread is flour and water and salt and yeast, and the branches are higher, broader, and more various than those on any tree— even the banyan that our bread Buddha sat under—could ever be. Understanding why bread does what it does is enough to keep the most inquisitive mind busy for decades. I know it sounds like the semi-poetic musing of a person who's trying to capture the essence of something intangible, and it is, but it's no less true for that.

Now that I have thoroughly scared you from ever trying to actually bake a loaf of bread, let me bring this back down to earth. All living things have compassion, and that includes bread. Bread is surprisingly forgiving, and if you don't hold yourself too rigidly, your bread will become what it will become, and you'll accept that bread with all its faults and beauty, just as you would any other living creature. Bake some bread and you'll understand what I mean.

As I said at the beginning of the book, I want you to bake. Everybody in the world should bake one loaf of bread in their lives. It's easy. It's flour, water, salt, and yeast. Listen to the bread, and listen to me, and listen to yourself. You will succeed. I promise.

SOURDOUGH STARTER

Okay, sourdough is the easiest thing in the world to make. Well, one of them—but before we get into the making of sourdough, there's something we need to clear up. The only place you'll find San Francisco sourdough is in San Francisco. If you live anywhere outside the Bay Area, don't waste your money buying "authentic" San Francisco sourdough. It's a complete rip-off. Here's why: Yeast lives everywhere, and even if your great-grandma brought over her sourdough from the old country and you've been keeping it alive this whole time in Kalamazoo, you now have a Kalamazoo sourdough that has nothing to do with wherever your ancestors came from. Every sourdough takes on the characteristics of the environment in which it lives—ergo, your sourdough is alive and well with the native yeast from wherever it resides.

I know it sounds like I just told you that the Easter Bunny and Santa don't exist, but the fact that you have a starter that's been going for almost a hundred years is amazing, and you should cherish the fact that some tiny part of the sour in your fridge does indeed contain a little bit of great-grandma's starter, and you, dear baker, are carrying on the tradition of baking the bread for your family. That's awesome, and don't ever stop.

Now, let's say that you don't have a family starter that you're keeping alive. In that case, start one! That way, while your great-grandkids are huddling under the shelter of the nuclear bunker of their dystopian futuristic existence, they can say that their great-grand-whatever started this sourdough, and that's how we're keeping humanity alive. Isn't that a warming thought? —*Duff*

All-purpose flour*

10 or so organic
    blueberries**

SPECIAL EQUIPMENT

You need a big clean
    2-gallon plastic bucket
    that comes with a tight-
    fitting lid and fits in your
    fridge. Get one from
    a commercial kitchen
    supply place.

1. Mix 2 cups of the flour, 2 cups room-temperature water, and the blueberries in the bucket until it's a thick, goopy paste. Put the lid on firmly or wrap the top very tightly with plastic wrap and leave it on the counter.

* You can use any kind of flour you want—whole wheat, rye, spelt, whatever—but I've found that most of the time it's best to use a neutral all-purpose flour and then add the neutral all-purpose flour starter to whatever kind of bread you're going to make.

** Get your fruit from the farmers' market, not the grocery store, and you greatly reduce the risk of introducing chemicals into your starter that could otherwise kill all those poor, innocent yeasts. Also, you can use almost any organic fruit or vegetable you want—a peach, some strawberries, a scallion—as long as it contains some naturally occurring sugar, it will have yeast on it. The produce you initially start with doesn't affect the flavor of the starter or ultimately the bread—you're just harvesting the yeast.

2. The next day, open the bucket. Smell it. Does it smell yeasty and awesome, slightly vinegary and carbonated? Is it bubbly and flour-colored? Then proceed—it's perfect. Does it smell crazy, and is it rusty orange or red? Throw it away and go back to step 1.

3. Add 1 more cup of flour and 1 more cup of water. Put the lid back on and let it sleep on the counter until the next day.

4. Repeat steps 2 and 3.

5. Repeat steps 2 and 3 again.

6. One more time, repeat step 2, but this time put the sour in the fridge (don't add more flour and water). It should now be ready to use.

HOW TO USE YOUR SOURDOUGH STARTER

Sourdough starter is a living yeast, but it moves more slowly than store-bought yeast. You can add it to any bread recipe, but be patient—the bread will take longer to rise. But it will taste *so* much better.

Using your starter is very simple. For every tablespoon (or packet) of instant dry yeast, use 1 cup of sourdough starter instead. Don't just swap out half the yeast, though—it's all or nothing or your yeast could be too strong.

HOW TO TAKE CARE OF YOUR SOURDOUGH STARTER

Give it a name. If it has a name, you are more likely to take better care of it. The sour I have at home is named Gazpacho. I love that word. Now, when you use your sourdough, you can't use the whole thing—you have to leave some in the bucket and feed it. If you use three-quarters of the starter, fill it back up 1:1 flour to water and let it do its thing. The yeast is eating the starch (sugar) in the flour. Even if you don't use it, you have to treat it the same way—just throw some away (or put it in a Tupperware and make a friend use it) and fill it up with fresh water and flour. If you're going away for a while (like, a week), feed your starter 4 cups flour and no water and it will go real slow, but even so, have a friend stop by after day 3 and make sure there isn't a yeast monster exploding in your fridge.

SOURDOUGH BREAD

Okay, so you've made a sourdough starter, you've kept it alive for at least a week, and you've even given it a name. Fantastic! Using your sourdough starter will make you really feel like a wizard. You captured wild yeast from thin air, and now it's time to put those tamed wild animals to work.

This recipe is a basic white sourdough that's delicious on its own, or you can use it as a canvas and create your own bread formula. You can try combinations of different flours like rye and whole wheat, you can add grains, and you can even adapt other recipes and make sweet sourdough risen desserts and pastries like panettone.

Here's what you need to know. To use sourdough starter as the yeast in your formula, you need a ratio of starter to flour and water of somewhere between 1:3 and 1:2 *by weight*. What I'm about to say is debatable, and isn't a very accurate way of doing things, but it's a rough framework to work with. One cup of flour weighs about 4.25 ounces, so, if a recipe calls for 4 cups of flour and 1½ cups of water, that's about 1 pound, 13 ounces. 33 percent of 29 ounces is 9.5 ounces, which is about 1.5 ounces more than a cup of starter if we accept that starter weighs 8 ounces per cup.

All that being said, bread is done very much by sight. All the times in any bread baking formula are correct for that particular kitchen with that particular oven in that particular elevation. You'll have to play with any formula to make it right for your environment. Bread will teach you how to be present and observant in your kitchen. I can't effectively put into words what it's like harvesting your own yeast and then baking a loaf of bread with it; you just have to try it for yourself. Then you'll understand why people like me have dedicated their lives to it.

Note: I call for bread flour in this recipe. I mean it. You can use all-purpose, but the bread won't be as chewy or have big holes the way it should. Also, all bread is better when it's baked with spring or distilled water. Yeast is sensitive, and chlorine from tap water can inhibit yeast growth.

Makes 2 or 3 loaves

5 cups bread flour (unbleached and unbromated; I like Giusto's flour), plus more for dusting

1½ cups Sourdough Starter (page 128)

1½ tablespoons kosher salt

Olive oil

1. In the bowl of a stand mixer fitted with the dough hook attachment, combine the flour, 1¾ cups room-temperature water, and the starter. Mix on medium speed for about 12 minutes, or until the dough is smooth and you can stretch it so you can see daylight through it without it tearing. You may need to add a bit more water, a tablespoon at a time. Add the salt and mix for 1 full minute.

2. Grease a large bowl with some olive oil and transfer the dough to the bowl. Lightly flour the top of the dough and cover the

bowl with plastic wrap. Let the dough rise for about 1½ hours, or until it's almost doubled in size.

3. Punch down the dough, fold it a few times, return it to the bowl, cover it, and let it rise again for another hour. Pinch a corner of the dough: If you feel tiny little bubbles popping under your fingers, the dough is ready to be shaped.

4. Turn the dough out onto a floured surface and divide it into two or three equal parts. Shape each part into a round (you can find lots of videos on how to do this online).

5. Now you have some decisions to make. You can let the loaves rise right on your counter, or you can proof them in a *banneton*, which is a small round basket. You probably don't own a *banneton*, so for each loaf, line a small bowl with a clean kitchen towel, dust the towel liberally with flour, add the dough, cover the dough loosely with plastic wrap, and let it rise in there. (I suggest using a bowl so transferring the bread to the oven will be *much* easier.)

6. Let the dough proof for about 1½ hours, or until it springs back when you gently poke it, then proceed to the next step. *Or,* if you want to be a superstar, place your bread in the fridge overnight. This is called *retarding* the dough, and it lets the dough ferment for much longer, creating that signature sourdough flavor. Also, the crust on a loaf that has been allowed to rise overnight undergoes its own fermentation, and you get a thicker, flakier crust that makes an absolute mess when you eat it but is exactly why we love bread in the first place. Lightly flour the tops of the loaves and cover loosely with plastic wrap. You want the loaves to be airtight so they don't form a skin but you want them to have room to grow and not be restricted by the plastic wrap.

7. Set two baking sheets in the oven and preheat the oven to 450°F. When the oven and baking sheets are hot, pull out one baking sheet at a time and gently turn the dough out onto it. Remove the towel and brush off any excess flour. With a sharp

knife or razor blade (I use a straight razor), cut one, two, or three lines about 1½ inches deep across the top of the loaf. Place the baking sheet back in the oven and throw a handful of water at the back the oven to create steam. Close the door for 5 to 10 seconds. Pull out the next baking sheet and repeat with the second dough round (don't forget to throw some water into the oven before you close it). Two loaves can fit on one sheet, so you can bake two on the same sheet, one on each sheet, or two on one and one on the other.

8. Bake for about 25 minutes, or until the bread is a deep golden brown and sounds hollow when you tap on the bottom. Turn the oven temperature down to 325°F and bake for 15 minutes, then crack the oven door (stick the handle of a wooden spoon in there to hold it open) and bake for 7 minutes. If you chose to retard the dough, you should see thousands of little tiny bubbles of various shades of brown all over the crust.

9. Turn off the music or TV or the noises in your own head and pull the bread out to cool on a wire rack. Place your ear close to the bread and listen. The bread should talk to you and tell you that you did a good job. You'll hear it cracking and popping as it cools. Cooling bread is very important. If you cut open or eat the bread while it's still hot, you aren't giving the gelatinized proteins a chance to solidify and become the body of the bread, and thus you're depriving yourself of the full amount of pleasure the bread can provide. You can always heat it up in the oven (gasp!) if you want to enjoy it warm, but the cooling process is just as important to the bread's structure as the mixing and the baking.

FOCACCIA

Focaccia is a delicious Italian bread that, when done right, is amazing. But unfortunately it's rarely done right. Focaccia should be thick, with big holes in it. It should be chewy and salty, not mealy. I've made thousands of pounds of focaccia as a bread baker in Napa Valley and for Todd English and beyond, and this focaccia will be the best you ever tasted, promise. —Duff

Makes one 11 x 17-inch pan

DOUGH

2 (¼-ounce) envelopes active dry yeast

1 tablespoon sugar

2 tablespoons olive oil, plus more as needed

2 cups all-purpose flour, plus more as needed

2 cups bread flour

3 tablespoons kosher salt

Fine cornmeal for dusting

TOPPINGS

½ cup chopped fresh basil

¾ cup olive oil

½ cup sliced red onion

¼ cup grated Parmesan

1 tablespoon kosher salt

1. To make the dough: In a big bowl, mix the yeast, sugar, and 2 cups warm water and let it sit until it bubbles, about 7 minutes. Add the oil, flours, and salt and mix until sticky and wet. This is a wet dough.

2. Turn out the dough onto a floured surface (get all the dough out or you'll have to wash the bowl) and knead by hand for 10 minutes, until smooth and soft but still wet and sticky. Oil the bowl well and place the dough back in the bowl. Cover tightly and let it rise for about 1 hour in a warm spot, like on top of the fridge, or until doubled in size.

3. Pour a light coating of olive oil onto a half sheet pan or 11 x 17-inch cake pan—you want about 1/16 inch of oil on the bottom of the pan. Sprinkle on the cornmeal, as much or as little as you want.

4. Punch the dough down and turn it out into your pan. Push the dough around so it's roughly even across the whole pan. Oil the top and let the dough rise for another 30 minutes, or until doubled in size (or the size of my big grape head).

5. To make the toppings: In a blender, puree the basil with the olive oil.

6. Preheat the oven to 425°F.

7. Don't punch the dough down, but make a claw with your fingers and poke deep holes all over the dough, going all the way to the bottom. Arrange the onion slices on top, pour on

the basil oil, and let the oil settle into the finger holes. Sprinkle the Parmesan and salt all over the dough.

8. Bake for 25 to 30 minutes, or until the bread has a good, dark color to it (it could be up to 45 minutes, depending on the thickness and the mood of the bread). Focaccia should be pretty dark, not blond like you see at chain restaurants. Pull the bread out and let it cool. The oil on the bottom of the pan will have boiled and basically deep-fried the bottom, so it should be well browned and crispy when you take it out of the pan. Let cool completely and enjoy at room temp or warmed up in the oven.

Options: You can top the focaccia with anything you like—olives, sun-dried tomatoes, garlic, scallions, bacon bits, whatever. Focaccia is the granddaddy of pizza, remember that. Also, remember that different veggies cook for different times, so don't put garlic on at the beginning—let the bread bake most of the way through and then add it. Garlic is delicious, but burn it and it becomes disgusting. Same thing with anchovies.

SIMPLE WHITE FRENCH BREAD

This recipe is the basis for hundreds of different shapes and sizes of bread. If you want to shape this into baguettes or boules, go for it. Here, we'll make a ciabatta—a delicious country loaf that ferments a long time and grows big holes on the inside. Big holes means it can hold more butter, and what's bread if not a vehicle for butter? —*Duff*

Makes 1 large boule or 2 smaller loaves

1 tablespoon sugar

2 (1/4-ounce) envelopes active dry yeast

2 cups all-purpose flour, plus more as needed

1 1/2 cups bread flour

1 tablespoon kosher salt (more if you want it)

Olive oil

1. In a small bowl, stir up the sugar, yeast, and 1¾ cups warm water. It'll start bubbling and getting foamy after 7 minutes or so—that's good.

2. Combine the flours and salt in a big bowl. Keep that bag of flour out—you're gonna need it (get it? "knead?").

3. Make a well in the center of the flour mixture and pour the yeasty water in there. Stir the mixture until you can't anymore.

4. Turn the sticky mass onto a floured work surface. Scrape the bowl clean so that you use all the dough, then wash the bowl. Knead the dough for about 10 minutes—if you're gonna eat all this bread, you may as well get in a good tricep workout while you're at it.

5. Once the dough looks nice and smooth, use a paper towel to oil the inside of the bowl lightly. Put the dough in the bowl, oil the top of the dough, and cover the bowl tightly with plastic wrap.

6. Put the bowl in a warm spot, such as on top of the fridge, and let it rise until it's almost triple in size and poofy, about 45 minutes, give or take.

7. Turn the dough out on the work surface, punch it down, knead it for a minute, and repeat with another rise. It should go faster this time—about 25 minutes.

8. Heat the oven to 450°F and stack three matching baking sheets in there to get hot. If you have a baking stone, use that instead.

9. Turn the dough out again, punch it down, and roll it to about 2½ inches thick. Cut the dough into two VHS tape–sized rectangles with a sharp knife or a bench scraper, move them about 5 inches apart on the floured surface, flour the tops, and cover with more plastic. Let the dough rise for another 25 minutes.*

10. Open the oven door wide and use a baking peel or the floured back of a baking sheet to place the loaves onto the hot baking sheets or stone, working gently but quickly so as not to deflate them. Bake for about 10 minutes, then open the oven door and throw a few handfuls of water at the bottom of the oven to make steam. Close the door quickly. Bake for another 12 minutes and take a look. Do they look well browned? If not, bake until they do, up to 10 more minutes, then turn the oven down to 325°F and bake for 15 more minutes, or until they look like bread you want to eat. Bread gets darker than pie.

11. Pull the bread out of the oven and let it cool on a wire rack. Listen to it crackle as it cools—that's a good sound. Serve at room temp; only heathens eat warm bread.

Options: This bread is a blank canvas, so get creative with it. Add herbs, nuts, olives, or cheese and make a bread of your own—you really can't go wrong. You can also salt the top of the bread or brush with olive oil and freshly ground black pepper. The sky is the limit.

* Or you can let the loaves rise slowly overnight in the fridge. This gives the bread more flavor, as the fermentation process is longer; it gives the crust of the bread layers and bubbles, which really add to the crunch and texture of the bread; and it makes your bread look absolutely beautiful when it comes out of the oven. Just flour the loaves, cover them loosely with plastic, and bake them right out of the fridge in the morning.

PRETZELS

This recipe is one of my favorites. I love pretzels, and this really embodies the magic of baking for me. It shows that you can make something that you might have thought came from some mysterious place. These pretzels are buttery and delicious, and easy enough for the kids to make, too.

Now, real industrial pretzels are dipped in lye for that chewy outside, and it really does make a difference, but do you want to be messing around with lye? I didn't think so. Remember *Fight Club*? This recipe uses a much safer solution of baking soda. Let's just stick with safe, buttery, and awesome.
—*Duff*

Makes 12 to 16 big fat pretzels

DOUGH

1 (¼-ounce) envelope active dry yeast

2 tablespoons sugar

½ stick (¼ cup) butter, melted

1 tablespoon kosher salt

2 extra-large egg yolks

2 cups bread flour

2 cups all-purpose flour

Olive oil

FINISHING

½ cup baking soda

1 stick (½ cup) butter, melted

Cooking spray

Ramekin of pretzel salt

1. To make the dough: In a big bowl, mix the yeast, sugar, and 1⅓ cups warm water and let it sit until the yeast blooms, about 7 minutes. Add the butter, salt, egg yolks, and flours and knead the dough until smooth, 15 to 20 minutes.

2. Grease the bowl and the dough with a bit of olive oil, set the dough in the bowl, and cover it tightly with plastic wrap. Let it rise on top of the fridge or any warm, dry place for 30 to 40 minutes, or until doubled in size.

3. To finish the pretzels: In a saucepan, mix the baking soda and 4 cups warm water until it is milky and then bring to a simmer over low heat.

4. Preheat the oven to 425°F, cover four or five baking sheets with parchment paper, and spray them with cooking spray.

5. Punch down the dough and cut it into 12 to 16 pieces. Let the dough rest for 5 minutes. Roll out each piece to about 2 feet long and shape into a pretzel (figure it out, I'm not explaining this in words). Dip each pretzel into the simmering baking soda liquid for 30 seconds, flipping once. Remove from the liquid, shake off any excess, and place the pretzel on a prepared baking sheet* using a spider or two wooden spoons. Plan on getting three pretzels per sheet. Lightly flour the pretzels, cover them loosely in plastic wrap, and let them rise for 20 minutes. Gently brush them with melted butter, and use

cooking spray to grease any little corners you can't reach with butter. Sprinkle on the pretzel salt.**

6. Bake the pretzels until they're brown. About 8 minutes should do it. Let cool for a few minutes and serve with coarse German mustard.

* This is the same dough I use for pretzel rolls and buns, so if you want to make a roll instead of a pretzel, you're good. Just finish them as directed and bake at 400°F for 12 to 15 minutes.

** Salt is awesome on these, but top them with herbs, garlic, cheese, seeds, or anything else you want. Do I smell cinnamon-sugar?

LAVASH

Lavash is a Middle Eastern flatbread that's more like a cracker. It's an unleavened bread, but it's not the bread of affliction—we'll get to that on page 147. When I was first introduced to lavash, it had this wonderful dark purple spice on it that was piquant and acidic. I asked the baker what it was and he told me "sumac." Well, when I was growing up and running around outside, the word *sumac* had a definite stigma attached to it, because if you touched it, it was apparently ten times worse than poison ivy. So when I was eating my first lavash, I had a moment of thinking my throat was about to close, but then I learned that poison sumac is a very different plant from the sumac used for lavash and other Middle Eastern cooking. Look for sumac in any well-stocked spice shop. You might have to order it online, but it's worth it. It also makes a great infusion for olive oil.

This recipe is written for a stand mixer, as lavash requires a lot of mixing—or overmixing, I should say. You can do it by hand, of course—just get ready for a workout.

I made this bread famous in Vail, Colorado, when I was a pastry chef there. People still ask about it. I'm kind of a big deal. —*Duff*

Makes 3 baking sheets

DOUGH

3 cups all-purpose flour

2 teaspoons kosher salt

1 tablespoon sugar

1 extra-large egg

3 tablespoons olive oil,
   plus more as needed

TOPPINGS

Olive oil

Ground sumac

Sesame seeds

Kosher salt

Poppy seeds

Ground turmeric

Dried thyme

1. To make the dough: Put all the dough ingredients in the bowl of a stand mixer fitted with the dough hook. Mix on medium speed for 18 to 20 minutes, slowly adding 1 cup room-temperature water until the dough forms a ball and becomes soft and stretchy.

2. Preheat the oven to 400°F. With a paper towel, oil some baking sheets with sides (jelly roll pans). Cut three tennis ball–size pieces of dough, roll them thin, and hook one corner of the baking sheet with a corner of the dough.

3. Gently stretch the dough over the baking sheet until it is paper thin, let it rest for 5 minutes, and cut off the extra dough. The dough will naturally fall flat onto the baking sheet.

4. To top the dough: Let the dough rest for 10 minutes, brush it with olive oil, then sprinkle or drizzle with all your chosen toppings. Using a pizza cutter, cut the lavash into long triangles.*

5. Bake the lavash for 8 to 10 minutes, or until it starts to brown. It will go real fast; it is very thin, so don't walk away. Let cool on the pan for 10 minutes, then move to a wire rack.

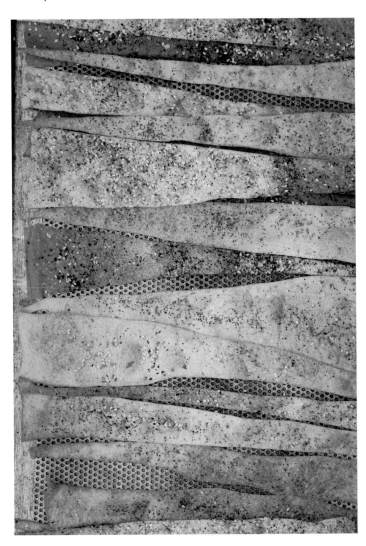

* The long triangles are traditional, as are rounds, but you can cut the dough into any shape you want. Go crazy!

PIZZA DOUGH

This is my go-to pizza dough recipe. Nothing fancy, and it works for the oven or the grill. It's a very versatile, soft, and sticky dough that makes a great crispy thin crust or a chewy thick crust. Make pizza from scratch with the kids and you're basically a Jedi. —*Duff*

Makes three 12-inch pizzas; maybe more, but you can make breadsticks with the leftovers

2 (¼-ounce) envelopes active dry yeast

1 tablespoon sugar

3 cups bread flour

2½ cups all-purpose flour, plus more for kneading

½ cup cornstarch

2 tablespoons kosher salt

¼ cup olive oil, plus more for oiling the dough

1. In a big bowl, mix the yeast, sugar, and 2 cups warm water. Let the yeast rest and bloom, about 7 minutes. When the yeast is bubbling, add the flours, cornstarch, salt, and oil. Mix well, then turn the dough out onto a floured surface (get all the dough out of the bowl or you'll have to wash it) and knead for about 15 minutes. Get your dough nice and smooth. Oil the bowl, oil the dough, put the dough in the bowl, and cover it with plastic wrap. Let it rise on top of the fridge for 30 to 40 minutes, or until bubbles show on top and the dough is straining against the plastic, like a big dough zit.

2. Punch the dough down, turn it out onto a floured surface, cut it into three equal pieces, and shape them into balls. Cover with a towel and let the dough rest for about 15 minutes (it won't roll out if you don't let it rest).

3. Preheat the oven to 425°F and place three baking sheets in there to get hot (or use a baking stone). Roll out each dough ball into a rough circle (don't worry if it doesn't look like Papa Domino's) and put on your toppings. Using an upside-down, floured, cool baking sheet (or a pizza peel), gently slide each pizza onto a hot baking sheet and bake until done. I don't know how long—could be 10 minutes, could be 20, depends on how thick your dough is. Don't pop the bubbles! If you get bubbles, they will be super crispy and awesome. Bake the pizzas one at a time if you have a regular house oven, or more if you can fit them. You want to bake as many as possible so they are all hot and fresh and everyone burns their tongues on hot cheese. Also, you can put the ingredients on the pizza after you place it on the hot baking sheet, but then it cools down. If you are confident, load up your pizza on the back of a cool, cornmeal- or flour-dusted baking sheet and then slide it onto the hot surface.

PITA BREAD

This is one of the most satisfying and self-affirming breads you can make at home. I was in the Arab quarter in Jerusalem, and I watched as a woman cooked pita bread on a smooth hubcap over an open fire. I ate, like, four of them, hot and fresh, and they cost about half a shekel. I'll never forget that pita, and every time I make it now, I'm always reminded that we're all just people who love to eat and cook stuff. —*Duff*

Makes 10 medium pitas

2 (¼-ounce) envelopes
   active dry yeast

1 tablespoon sugar

6 cups all-purpose flour

2 tablespoons kosher salt

1. In a big bowl, mix the yeast, sugar, and 1½ cups warm water until the yeast bubbles, about 7 minutes.

2. Add the flour and salt and mix until a ball forms. Turn the dough out onto a floured surface and knead for 12 minutes, or until the dough is smooth.

3. Oil the bowl and the ball of dough, place the dough in the bowl, cover it, and let it rise in a warm spot for 2 to 2½ hours, or until doubled in size.

4. Put a baking sheet on the bottom oven rack and remove the other racks so you have room to work. Preheat the oven to 500°F.

5. Punch the dough down and cut it into 10 pieces.

6. Form each into a little ball and roll the balls out into rough circles about ¼ inch thick.

7. Lay the pitas on the hot baking sheet (about three per sheet) and bake for 4 minutes on one side and 1 to 2 minutes on the other, until they have a warm, light brown spot or two in the middle. Flip them with a metal spatula or be a real baker and use your hands.* As you pull them out of the oven, stack them with a paper towel in between each one. Repeat to bake the rest.

* The pitas will balloon in the oven. Let them. Only when they've come out of the oven do you want to push them flat for storage. You can store them at room temperature, but honestly, eat them as soon as possible. You can also freeze them, but at that point you obviously don't care about bread and have hurt my feelings, so just go to the store and buy some packaged crap, you peasant.

MATZAH

I made matzah for my mom once for Passover, and every year she begs me to do it again. It's not that it's hard—it's super easy. It's just that around Passover, I like to chill and let Mom do the cooking.

Homemade matzah rules. The stuff that comes out of the box may be kosher for Passover, but it's also cardboard. I say make it from scratch and enjoy the feast. But that's just me—I also have tattoos and love bacon like a nice Jewish boy. —*Duff*

Makes 12 to 15 matzahs

5 cups all-purpose flour

2 teaspoons kosher salt, plus extra for topping

¼ cup olive oil

1. Mix all the ingredients in a big bowl with 1½ cups warm water, turn the dough out onto a floured surface, and knead until smooth, 10 to 12 minutes. Let the dough rest for 15 minutes, then cut it into 12 to 15 tennis ball–size pieces.

2. Place a baking sheet on the bottom oven rack and remove the other racks so you have room to work. Preheat the oven to 450°F.

3. Roll out the pieces of dough to about 1⁄16 inch thick and about a foot square. Prick the dough all over with a fork—make lots of holes, just like real matzah. (This *is* real matzah.) Sprinkle each piece with a bit of salt—just a smidge.

4. One at a time, transfer the matzah to the hot baking sheet and bake for 1½ to 2 minutes, then flip and bake for another 45 seconds. Don't overbake—you should have a good variety of color on there. Repeat with the remaining matzah.

5. As each matzah comes out of the oven, let it cool on a wire rack, and stack them only when they cool to room temperature. *Voilà!* The bread of affliction!

CHALLAH

A nice Jewish boy can't write a book about baking without including a recipe for challah. But my inclusion of it is less than godly. See, when I was in college, I used to bake challah in the communal kitchen in the dorms. Let's just say, it never failed to make me popular with the ladies.

You can bake this bread in a loaf pan, or you can braid it, which is a little tricky, but with practice you can do it! —*Duff*

Makes 2 big-ass loaves of challah. No, it's not too much. Either you'll eat it all right away or you'll make French toast with it in the morning.

DOUGH

2 (¼-ounce) envelopes
    active dry yeast

½ cup sugar

¼ cup honey

⅓ cup olive oil

2 extra-large eggs plus
    3 egg yolks

2 tablespoons kosher salt

3 cups bread flour

6½ cups all-purpose flour

EGG WASH

2 extra-large eggs

2 tablespoons sugar

1. To make the dough: In a big bowl, mix the yeast, sugar, honey, and 3 cups warm water, then let the yeast bloom for about 7 minutes.

2. Add the oil, eggs, yolks, and salt and mix well. Add the flours and mix until sticky. The dough should be a nice creamy yellow color.

3. Turn the dough out onto a floured surface (get all the dough out of the bowl or you'll have to wash it) and knead for 12 to 15 minutes, or until smooth. Oil the bowl, place the dough in the bowl, cover tight with plastic wrap, and let it rise on top of the fridge for about 1½ hours, or until doubled.

4. Punch the dough down, cover it, and let it rise for another 45 minutes. Punch it down again and cut it into six equal pieces. Let them rest for about 10 minutes, and then roll them into snakes about 14 inches long that taper at each end. On an oiled baking sheet, braid the three snakes loosely—you want to give them space to grow. Fold the ends under. Repeat to make the second loaf on a second baking sheet. Oil the loaves lightly, cover with plastic wrap, and let rise until they look good and poofy, about 25 minutes.

5. Preheat the oven to 375°F.

6. Whisk the egg wash ingredients lightly in a small bowl. Gently brush the loaves with the egg wash, taking care not to deflate them.

7. Bake for 45 minutes, or until the loaves are a beautiful golden color. Tap on the bottom of the loaf: if it sounds hollow, it's done. Let them cool completely before slicing. This is a very tender bread, and if you slice it too warm, it will grab the knife and mush.

Options: If you want to sprinkle on poppy seeds or sesame seeds, go to town, but remember that you'll be making French toast with the leftovers.

BRIOCHE

Brioche is like Christian challah. It's an enriched dough (a dough with fat in it), and what really makes it different from challah is that it has dairy as well and is very slightly glazed. It's super delicious and you really can't go wrong with it, 'specially for breakfast right before a day of snowboarding.

There are many ways to bake a brioche, but I like mine in a traditional loaf pan—I find that the inside of the bread stays more moist than if it is baked in smaller individual tins. —*Duff*

Makes two 9 x 5-inch loaves

DOUGH

2 (¼-ounce) envelopes
   active dry yeast

⅔ cup sugar

½ cup whole milk,
   warmed

2 extra-large eggs plus
   3 egg yolks

1 tablespoon kosher salt

4 cups all-purpose flour,
   plus more as needed

3½ sticks (1¾ cups)
   butter, softened

EGG WASH

2 extra-large eggs

¼ cup sugar

* Brioche is really good if you let the dough rise overnight in the fridge, before or after shaping. The flavor gets more complex and awesome. But it's your call.

1. Butter and flour two 9 x 5-inch standard loaf pans.

2. In a big bowl, combine the yeast, sugar, milk, and ½ cup warm water. Let the yeast bloom for about 7 minutes. When it's bubbly, whisk in the eggs, yolks, and salt. Add the flour and mix until sticky.

3. Turn the dough out onto a floured surface and begin to knead, slowly adding butter as you do. Keep extra flour around because your hands will get sticky. Knead until the dough is smooth and manageable. Return the dough to the bowl, cover with plastic wrap, and let it rise in a warm place for about 1½ hours, or until doubled in size.*

4. Punch the dough down, turn it out, and let it rest for about 15 minutes. Cut the dough in half and shape each piece into rectangles that will fit into the loaf pans. Place the dough in the pans, cover the pans with plastic wrap, and let them rise to just below the top of the pan.

5. Preheat the oven to 375°F.

6. Whisk the egg wash ingredients lightly in a small bowl. Gently brush the loaves with the egg wash,

7. Bake for 30 to 40 minutes, or until the brioche looks super shiny and sounds hollow when tapped on the top.

8. Turn the loaves out of the pans and let them cool on a wire rack. Serve with a generous amount of butter.

RUSTIC WHOLE-WHEAT BREAD

This is a good, classic whole-wheat loaf that I've been baking for years. It's a tad sweet, but earthy and delicious and shapes really well. It's very simple, and you'll feel like a real homesteader when you make it! Goes well with butter. Lots of butter. —*Duff*

Makes 3 boules or large, round loaves

DOUGH

3 (¼-ounce) envelopes active dry yeast

½ cup clover honey (or regular honey)

Pinch of sugar

1 cup whole milk, warmed

2 tablespoons kosher salt

½ stick (¼ cup) butter, melted

5 cups bread flour or high-protein flour, plus more as needed

4 cups whole-wheat or graham flour

BUTTER AND SUGAR WASH

1 stick (½ cup) butter, melted, plus more as needed

2 tablespoons sugar

1. In a big bowl, mix the yeast, honey, sugar, 2 cups warm water, and milk. Let the yeast bloom for about 7 minutes, or until bubbly.

2. Whisk in the salt and butter. Add the flours and mix until sticky. Turn the dough out onto a floured surface (get all the dough out of the bowl or you'll have to wash it) and knead the dough until somewhat smooth.

3. Oil the bowl. Return the dough to the bowl, cover it tightly with plastic wrap, and let it rise in a warm spot, like on top of the fridge, for about 1½ hours, or until doubled in size. Punch the dough down and let it rise for another 45 minutes, or until it doubles in size again.

4. Prep three baking sheets with a thin dusting of flour. Cut the dough into three pieces, shape each into a boule or round loaf, and place one on each sheet. Let them rise for about 30 minutes.

5. Preheat the oven to 350°F.

6. In a small bowl, make a wash with the butter and sugar. Brush the tops of the loaves generously but gently with the butter and sugar wash, leaving a little extra for after the loaves are baked. With a very sharp knife, cut the boules across the top about ¾ inch deep; you can even do an "X" cut.

7. Bake for 30 minutes, or until dark golden brown. When you pull the loaves out, brush them with a bit more butter wash and let them cool completely.

HEARTY SEVEN-GRAIN BREAD

I love this bread. It's a great vehicle for all those crunchy brown things that taste good and are really good for you. If you make it in a loaf pan, it makes a strong sandwich bread, or shape it into something cool and it's a beauty bread to have around, or an awesome housewarming gift for that cutie who just moved in a few doors down. (What?!? Why do you think I learned how to cook?)

If any of these ingredients are hard to find, go to the closest hippie health food store and they'll have everything, plus some advice on how to make variations of this bread. I didn't include it here, but you can add pepitas, nuts, or really anything else you want. I like this mix for its texture and flavor, but experiment and make it your own. —*Duff*

Makes two 9 x 5-inch loaves

DOUGH

1 cup wheat berries

1 cup bulgur

2 (¼-ounce) envelopes active dry yeast

1 cup whole milk, warmed

¼ cup honey

½ cup old-fashioned rolled oats (not instant)

½ cup flaxseed

½ cup shelled, unsalted sunflower seeds

¼ cup black sesame seeds

⅓ cup poppy seeds

3 cups bread flour, plus more as needed

2½ cups whole wheat or graham flour

2 tablespoons kosher salt

1 stick (½ cup) butter, melted

Cooking spray

EGG WASH

2 extra-large eggs

1 tablespoon sugar

1. To make the dough: Place the wheat berries in a saucepan and add water to cover by 2 inches. Bring to a boil over high heat, then turn the heat down to low and simmer for 1 hour. Meanwhile, put the bulgur in a large bowl and add warm water to cover. Set the bulgur aside to soak for 30 minutes, then drain through a sieve to remove any excess water.

2. In a large bowl, mix the yeast, 1½ cups warm water, the milk, and the honey. Let the yeast bloom for about 7 minutes.

3. Combine the oats, flaxseed, sunflower seeds, sesame seeds, and poppy seeds in a medium bowl. Scoop out one-third of the seed mixture and set it aside in a smaller bowl. Add the rest to the yeast mixture and stir. Add the flours, wheat berries, bulgur, salt, and half the melted butter. Mix well, then turn the dough out onto a floured surface and knead for about 12 minutes, or until you have a smooth, manageable ball.

4. Oil the bowl and return the dough to it. Cover the bowl tightly with plastic wrap and let the dough rise in a warm spot for about 1½ hours, or until it almost doubles.

5. Punch down the dough, then cover and let it rise for another 45 minutes, or until it rises again.

6. Preheat the oven to 400°F. Grease two 9 x 5-inch loaf pans with the rest of the melted butter.

7. Punch the dough down, cut it in half, and shape two rectangles that will fit into the loaf pans. Place the dough into the pans, spray them with cooking spray, and let the loaves rise for 30 to 40 minutes, or until they're just below the top of the pan.

8. In a small bowl, whisk together the eggs and sugar to make an egg wash. Brush the tops of the loaves gently with the egg wash, and then sprinkle the reserved seed mixture on top.

9. Bake for about 45 minutes, or until the loaves are nice and brown, bordering on dark. Turn the loaves out on a wire rack to cool. Kaboom, fiber!

COMMUNIST RYE BREAD

My people come from the lands where they kicked out anybody they didn't like—Russia, Germany, Poland, Serbia, and so on—so it's no wonder that I have a genetic affinity for this bread. Most Jews will call matzah the "bread of affliction," but if such a title exists, I could make a case that it should go to rye bread. On that cheerful note, I really do love this bread, especially with deli mustard and a heaping pile of pastrami and Dr. Brown's Black Cherry Soda. Bake this one freeform. You can bake it in a loaf pan, but my people didn't have nice things, so out of respect, I bake it round and delicious. —*Duff*

Makes 2 medium loaves

2 (¼-ounce) envelopes
   active dry yeast

2 cups whole milk,
   warmed

¼ cup molasses

3 tablespoons sugar

2 tablespoons kosher salt

¼ cup malt vinegar

3 cups dark rye flour

3½ cups bread flour, plus
   more as needed

¼ cup caraway seeds

* Quick note: Rye flour doesn't make gluten the way white flour does, so this bread will not rise as much as white bread. Don't freak out—it's meant to be a dense bread. Play with the ratio of rye to white flour until you like the texture. Take notes so that you know what you did each time—that's how you make my recipes your recipes.

1. In a big bowl, mix the yeast, ½ cup warm water, and the milk, molasses, and sugar. Let the yeast bloom for about 7 minutes. Add the salt, vinegar, flours, and caraway seeds and mix until sticky.

2. Turn the dough out onto a floured surface and knead it for about 10 minutes, or until you don't feel strands. Oil the bowl, put the dough back in, cover it tightly with plastic wrap, and let it rise in a warm place for an hour, or until doubled in size.*

3. Punch the dough down and knead it for another 10 minutes. Cover again and let it rise for another 45 minutes.

4. Punch it down again and turn it out onto a floured surface. Cut the dough in half and shape it into two rounds. Place the rounds on a well-floured baking sheet and cover with a bit of flour and a towel. Let them rise for another 30 minutes.

5. Preheat the oven to 425°F.

6. Score the tops of the loaves with a sharp knife. Bake the loaves for 15 minutes, throwing a handful of water on the floor of the oven to make some steam every 5 minutes.

7. Turn the heat to 350°F, stop throwing water in the oven, and bake for 40 minutes more, until the bread sounds hollow when you tap on it.

ROSEMARY-GARLIC POTATO BREAD

I learned the joys of putting potatoes in bread during my time in the Napa Valley, so the flavors here are resonant of that magical place, but don't be afraid to change up the herbs or play with nuts and olives. You can't mess it up. Well, you can—I certainly have more than once—but you know what I mean. You can do this by hand, but it's messy, so I wrote this recipe with directions for using a stand mixer. —*Duff*

Makes 2 round loaves

2 large russet potatoes, well baked and still warm (see page 158)

1 garlic head, roasted and still warm (see page 158)

2 (¼-ounce) envelopes active dry yeast

2 tablespoons sugar

3 tablespoons olive oil, plus extra for brushing

2 teaspoons kosher salt, plus more for sprinkling

4 cups all-purpose flour, plus more as needed

4 cups bread flour

1½ tablespoons chopped fresh rosemary

1. Peel and coarsely chop the potatoes. Squeeze the garlic from the garlic head into a medium bowl and add the potatoes.

2. In the bowl of a stand mixer fitted with the dough hook, combine the yeast, 2 cups warm water, and the sugar and let the yeast bloom for about 7 minutes, or until bubbly. Add the olive oil, potatoes, garlic, salt, and flours. Mix on medium speed for 15 minutes.

3. Turn the dough out into an oiled bowl, cover it with plastic wrap, and let it rise in a warm place for 1½ hours, or until doubled in size.

4. Punch it down and let it rise again for 1 hour. Punch it down again and cut the dough in half. Shape each loaf into a ball, place them on a baking sheet, and let them rise for 45 minutes, or until nice and poofy.

5. Preheat the oven to 400°F.

6. Brush the loaves with olive oil and sprinkle them with a wee bit of salt and some rosemary. Cut a big slash across the top of each and bake for about 45 minutes, or until the loaves are a nice rich brown and sound hollow when tapped. Let cool on a wire rack. Never refrigerate!

BAKED POTATOES
(PREFERABLY RUSSET POTATOES—THE BIG, BROWN, UBIQUITOUS ONES)

OVEN METHOD

Rub the potatoes with a bit of olive oil, kosher salt, and pepper. Stick 'em with a fork like 20 times all over the place to let the steam out. Place them on a baking sheet and roast at 425°F for 1 hour. The skin will get nice and crispy and you can scoop out the potato meat really easy, and also enjoy the skins as a snack while you bake. (As a poor culinary student, I always saved my potato skins as dinner. How did that bacon end up in my backpack? That's weird! ;)

MICROWAVE METHOD

Let's get this straight. I hate microwaves—I don't trust anything that cooks and I can't see the fire. That said, nuking potatoes is a very quick and effective way to cook them. Punch 'em with a fork like 20 times all over the place, place in a microwave-safe dish, uncovered, and cook them on full blast for 5 minutes. Turn them over and hit 'em again for another 5 minutes. That should do it. If not, cook in 2-minute increments until a fork will slide easily all the way to the center of the spud. Don't bother seasoning the potatoes—nuked potato skins are good for feeding the llama in the backyard. Or set up a skillet and make some corned beef hash with 'em. Or shallow pan-fry them.

WATER METHOD

This is best for potatoes with a thinner skin and less starch than a big ol' russet, such as Red Bliss, Yukon Gold, Rose Gold, Inca Gold, Adirondack, or Purple Peruvian. Skin the potatoes first, because harvesting the potato meat is difficult with a boiled potato. Fill a pot with cold water and whole peeled potatoes. Set the pot on a high flame and bring to a boil. Check them after 15 minutes and boil them longer if necessary—it's much better to overcook than undercook, as you're creating an ingredient, not a stand-alone dish.

ROASTED GARLIC

You should know how to roast garlic—it may save your life one day. Heat the oven to 425°F. Chop off the pointy end of the head of the garlic and expose the cloves. Drizzle olive oil right onto the exposed garlic, wrap it tightly with aluminum foil, place on a baking sheet, and roast for 35 to 40 minutes. Really, though, don't time it—just roast them until they smell amazing. You'll know it when you smell it. You'll also know very quickly if you over-roast it—it'll smell awful and burnt. Throw that crap away and start over.

PUMPERNICKEL

I've always been fascinated by pumpernickel. I especially love the tiny little loaves that are sliced for tea parties. You can make cold deli-meat sandwich sliders with them. This recipe is good and works well, but as you get more proficient with darker breads, don't be afraid to play with the darkness or the texture. This bread ain't black, but it's tasty. —*Duff*

Makes 2 large loaf pans or one 2-pound Pullman pan (pictured)

2 (¼-ounce) envelopes active dry yeast

1 cup whole milk, warmed

¼ cup dark molasses

2 tablespoons instant espresso granules or coffee granules

2 tablespoons light brown sugar

¼ cup unsweetened natural cocoa powder

¼ cup kosher salt

4 cups bread flour, plus more as needed

1½ cups rye flour

⅓ cup cornmeal

Cooking spray

* I like when this bread is real dark on top, but if it's looking too charred for you, cover it lightly with foil for the last 10 minutes or so of baking.

1. In a big bowl, mix the yeast, 1 cup warm water, the milk, molasses, instant coffee, and sugar. Let the yeast bloom until bubbly, about 7 minutes.

2. Add the cocoa powder, salt, flours, and cornmeal and mix well.

3. Turn the dough out onto a floured surface and knead for about 10 minutes. Oil the bowl, return the dough to the bowl, and cover it tightly with plastic wrap. Let the dough rise in a warm spot for 1½ hours, or until it's about two-thirds bigger.

4. Punch the dough down, knead it for 5 minutes, cover, and let it rise again for 1 hour.

5. Preheat the oven to 400°F. Coat two large loaf pans with cooking spray.

6. Punch the dough down, cut it into thirds, and push it into the loaf pans. Cover and let the loaves rise for 30 to 40 minutes, or until they look poofy.

7. Bake the loaves for 5 minutes, then turn the heat to 350°F and bake for 30 to 35 minutes more, or until very dark.* Turn the bread out onto a wire rack and cool completely before serving.

PIE

Pie has been around for a *long* time. In Ancient Egyptian and Medieval times, pie was mostly savory. India has long had samosas. If I had to hazard a guess, I would say that pie might even pre-date the sandwich. Joffrey choked on his pigeon pie in *Game of Thrones,* and who knows when that was? Bilbo liked pie. So did the trolls that tried to cook him into one. Every culture has some sort of pie, and pie was probably the first fast food.

Let's skip forward to today's America. We think of pie as a flaky crust (or a number of other creative crust options) with a filling that's creamy, fluffy, rich, or all of the above. It's hard to pick a favorite pie because they're just so damn versatile. You can have a favorite fruit pie, a favorite cream pie, a favorite savory pie. Pairing your crust with your filling is crucial . . . a ground spiced gingersnap crust pairs awesomely with an autumn pumpkin or sweet potato pie. A coconut crust is killer with a banana cream or coconut cream pie. No matter what, though, you want a light, buttery, salty, flaky crust! Texture is the life or death of your pie (and you want the thing to *live,* for goodness' sake!). Ancient recipes make it clear that anything can be used in a pie filling—I've seen everything from pigeon to persimmon. Get creative! Pie is the family go-to, the communal dessert that's meant to be shared, and the comfort food you love to love.

Having a strong pie game is huge when it comes to creating your own personal myth as the family baker. Pies can be a bit tricky and need to be handled gently. People who can bake a good pie get mad respect. Everybody loves pie. Love your pie and I promise, everyone will love you.

BOYSENBERRY PIE

Boysenberry pie served warm with ice cream. Nothing beats that. Boysenberries are a little difficult to find fresh when it's not summer, but blackberries, raspberries, blueberries, strawberries, or gooseberries will work as delicious substitutes. Or just combine them all, why not? —*Sara*

Makes one 9-inch pie

6 cups boysenberries (or whatever berries you want)

½ cup sugar

¼ cup boysenberry preserves (or whatever berry you're using)

2 teaspoons freshly squeezed lemon juice

3 tablespoons instant tapioca (find it in the baking aisle)

1 recipe Pie Dough (page 39)

EGG WASH

1 extra-large egg

1 teaspoon milk

Boysenberry Pie is pictured on page 180.

1. In a large bowl, gently combine the berries, sugar, preserves, lemon juice, and tapioca. Don't smash your berries! Set aside.

2. Preheat the oven to 400°F.

3. Divide the dough in half. Roll one piece out on a floured surface into a 14-inch round that's ¼ inch thick. Carefully drape the dough over the rolling pin and lay it gently into a 9-inch pie pan, making sure that the pan is completely lined with the dough. Trim the edges of the dough with a paring knife, leaving about ½ inch of dough beyond the edges of the pan.

4. Roll out the other piece of dough to make the top crust. The top crust needs to be ready to go on your pie as soon as you fill it.

5. Fill the bottom crust with the berry mixture and add your top crust. You can cover the whole top (just add slits before baking so that steam can escape) or get fancy and do a lattice design (see the Sour Cherry Pie on page 177 for directions). Seal the top crust to the edges of the bottom crust with a little water on your finger. Make the edges look nice.

6. Make an egg wash by whisking together the egg and milk. Brush the exposed crust with the egg wash.

7. Cover the pie very lightly with foil and set it on a foil-covered baking sheet in case it bubbles over.

8. Bake the pie for 25 minutes, then remove the foil from the top of the pie and bake for about 30 minutes more, or until the crust is a nice golden brown.

9. Let the pie cool completely before you cut it so that the filling sets up and the crust doesn't fall apart.

STRAWBERRY-RHUBARB PIE

Probably the most perfect summer pie there is, this is the ideal pie alongside a scoop of vanilla ice cream. Duff had the privilege of working under an amazing pastry chef when he first started working for Todd English in Boston. She had wise words that he remembers to this day: "Anyone who says they like rhubarb is a *liar!*" He thought it was hilarious at the time, and completely untrue, but if you're baking for a restaurant, don't make too many of the rhubarb desserts. They just don't sell as fast as chocolate things. —*Sara*

Makes one 9-inch pie

1 recipe Pie Dough
   (page 39)

2½ cups ½-inch slices
   rhubarb

2½ cups hulled and
   quartered ripe
   strawberries

1½ cups sugar

1 teaspoon orange zest

1 tablespoon plus
   2 teaspoons cornstarch

1 tablespoon instant
   tapioca

1 teaspoon freshly
   squeezed lemon juice

Pinch of ground cinnamon

1 teaspoon pure vanilla
   extract

2 tablespoons butter, cut
   into small chunks

1 extra-large egg

1. Roll out half the dough on a floured surface into a 14-inch round that's ¼ inch thick, reserving the rest of the dough. Carefully drape the dough over the rolling pin and lay it gently into a 9-inch pie pan, making sure that the pan is completely lined with the dough. Cut the crust to the edge of the pan with a paring knife. Chill the pan in the fridge for at least 20 minutes.

2. Preheat the oven to 425°F.

3. In a big bowl, combine all the remaining ingredients except the butter and egg and pour it into the chilled crust. Dot the top of the filling with the butter chunks and wet the edges of the bottom crust with water.

4. Roll out the top crust and gently drape it over the pie. Trim the edges to match the bottom crust and crimp the bottom and top crusts together with your fingers.

5. In a small bowl, beat together the egg and 1 tablespoon water to make an egg wash and lightly brush it over the exposed pie crust. Using a paring knife, make four 1½-inch slits in the top crust.

6. Cover the crimped edge with a bit of foil and set the pie on a baking sheet so it doesn't make a mess in your oven. Bake for 20 minutes, then reduce the temperature to 375°F and bake for 35 minutes more.

7. Remove the foil and bake for 10 to 15 minutes more, or until the filling is bubbling.

8. Let the pie cool completely before serving. Serve with vanilla ice cream with a touch of cinnamon.

BANANA CREAM PIE
WITH A PRETZEL CRUST

Okay, the title actually doesn't do the pie justice. It's a banana cream pie with a crust of ground pretzels and peanut butter–filled pretzels, a layer of dark chocolate coating, a smooth pastry cream with fresh bananas layered throughout, and a whipped cream topping, drizzled with dark chocolate. Sounds pretty awesome, right? It's better than that. —*Sara*

Makes one 9-inch pie

CRUST

2¾ cups finely ground pretzel crumbs (use the long, thick rod pretzels)

¾ cup finely ground peanut butter–filled pretzel crumbs

1½ tablespoons sugar

1 stick (½ cup) butter, melted

4 ounces unsweetened baking chocolate (semisweet will work fine, too)

FILLING

4 extra-large egg yolks

¾ cup sugar

¼ teaspoon kosher salt

⅓ cup cornstarch

3 cups whole milk

2 tablespoons butter

1 teaspoon pure vanilla extract

3 to 4 ripe bananas

continued

1. Preheat the oven to 325°F.

2. To make the crust: In a big bowl, combine the pretzel crumbs and sugar. Gradually add the butter, using your hand to distribute it throughout the crumbs. The mixture should hold together when squeezed in your hand.

3. Press the crumb mixture into the bottom and sides of a 9-inch pie pan.

4. Bake the crust for 10 minutes, or until firm. Set aside to cool completely.

5. Melt the chocolate over a double boiler or (gasp) in the microwave in 30-second intervals until completely melted and smooth. Pour it into the cooled shell and very gently smooth it over the bottom and lower ½ inch of the sides of the shell. Set the crust aside to set up completely.

6. To make the filling: Fill a large bowl with ice and water. In a big bowl, lightly whisk the egg yolks, sugar, salt, and cornstarch. In a medium saucepan over medium heat, bring the milk to a boil; as soon as it starts to boil, remove from the heat. Working ¼ cup at a time and whisking constantly, pour the hot milk into the egg mixture. When three-quarters of the milk has been whisked in, transfer the mixture back to the saucepan and cook for 6 to 8 minutes, still over medium-low heat, until quite thick, still whisking constantly.

1½ cups heavy cream

1 tablespoon powdered
sugar

½ teaspoon pure vanilla
extract

2 ounces dark chocolate
(optional, for drizzling)

7. Remove the pan from the heat and stir in the butter and vanilla. Pour the pastry cream into a cool mixing bowl. Set the bowl in the ice bath, whisking every 5 minutes or so, until it's lukewarm, then cover the pastry cream surface with a piece of plastic wrap and refrigerate until cooled completely.

8. When both the crust and filling are cooled, cut the bananas into ¼-inch slices and line the bottom of the pie crust with just a single layer. Scoop half the pastry cream over the bananas and smooth it to cover them evenly. Add another layer of bananas and the rest of the pastry cream. Cover and refrigerate.

9. To make the topping: In a big bowl or stand mixer, whip the cream until it starts to thicken. Add the sugar and vanilla and beat until peaks form. Do not overwhip. Smooth the whipped cream over the entire pie and use the back of a spoon to create pretty soft peaks.

10. If desired, melt the dark chocolate, make sure it isn't piping hot, and drizzle it over the pie.

11. Let the pie set completely for at least 1 hour in the fridge and serve it cold, refrigerating any leftovers.

COCONUT CUSTARD PIE

My family almost always ate this pie during Christmastime. An old staple in Southern baking, custard pie has long been a favorite in my mom's family. This pie is extra awesome because it's so easy to make! Simple ingredients, simple instructions, lots of flavor—especially when accompanied by a giant dollop of homemade whipped cream. —*Sara*

Makes one 9-inch pie

½ recipe Pie Dough
 (page 39)

4 extra-large eggs, slightly
 beaten

¼ teaspoon kosher salt

½ cup sugar

2 cups milk

1 cup half-and-half

1 teaspoon pure vanilla
 extract

1½ cups sweetened
 shredded coconut

Pinch of ground nutmeg

1. Preheat the oven to 425°F.

2. Roll out the dough on a floured surface into a 14-inch round that's ¼ inch thick. Carefully drape the dough over the rolling pin and lay it gently into a 9-inch pie pan, making sure that the pan is completely lined with the dough. Trim and crimp the edges.

3. In a large bowl, beat the eggs, salt, and sugar until smooth. Slowly stir in the milk, half-and-half, and vanilla. Fold in the coconut.

4. Pour the filling into the pie crust and sparingly sprinkle the top with nutmeg.

5. Bake for 10 minutes, then lower the oven temperature to 325°F and bake for 35 to 45 minutes more, or until a knife inserted into the middle comes out clean.

6. Let the pie cool completely. Serve at room temperature but store in the fridge, covered.

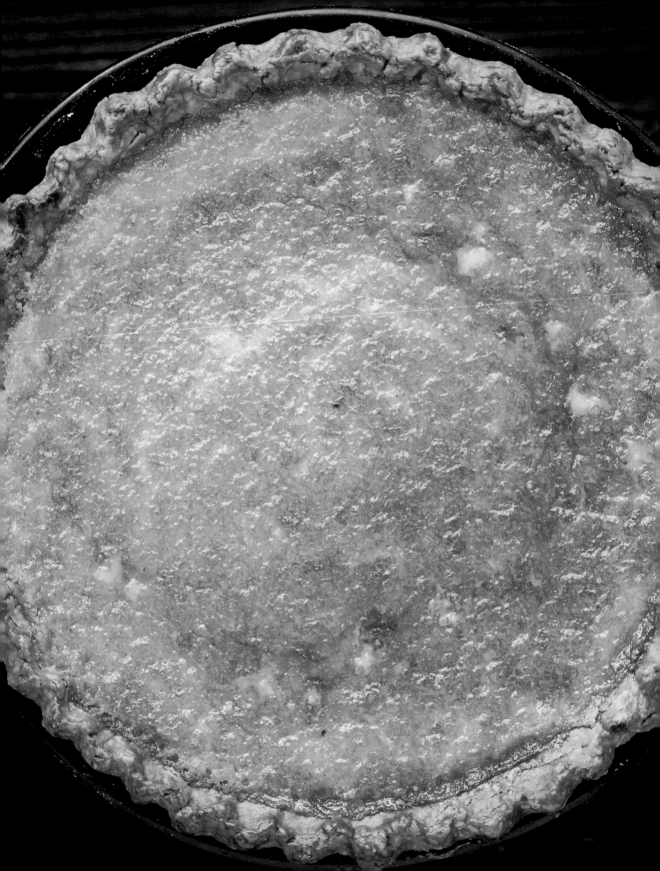

LEMON CHESS PIE

A true Southern and Colonial staple pie, chess pie is traditionally a somewhat gelatinous filling made unique by the addition of cornmeal. This lemony version is nice and tart and decidedly refreshing. Serve at room temperature with a cup of coffee or a cold glass of milk. My friend Rodney Henry from Dangerously Delicious Pies introduced me to chess pie. That man is the pie master. —*Duff*

Makes one 9-inch pie

½ recipe Pie Dough
   (page 39)

1 stick (½ cup) butter

2 extra-large eggs plus
   6 egg yolks

¼ teaspoon kosher salt

1½ cups granulated sugar

½ cup lightly packed light
   brown sugar

1 teaspoon pure vanilla
   extract

2 tablespoons yellow
   cornmeal

1½ tablespoons all-
   purpose flour

½ cup buttermilk

1 tablespoon lemon zest

2 tablespoons freshly
   squeezed lemon juice

1. Preheat the oven to 375°F.

2. Roll out the pie dough on a floured surface into a 14-inch round that's ¼ inch thick. Carefully drape the dough over the rolling pin and lay it gently into a 9-inch pie pan, making sure that the pan is completely lined with the dough. Trim and crimp the edge.

3. Lay a circle of parchment paper and some pie weights or dry beans on the bottom of the crust. Blind bake the crust for 5 minutes, remove the weights, and bake for 4 more minutes, until the crust is a matte blond color. Set aside.

4. To brown the butter, slowly simmer it in a small saucepan over medium-low heat until the solids have separated and lightly browned, taking care not to burn it. Remove it from the heat but make sure it stays melted.

5. In a large bowl, lightly whisk the eggs and salt, then whisk in (one at a time) the sugars, vanilla, cornmeal, flour, buttermilk, browned butter, lemon zest, and lemon juice.

6. Pour the mixture into the crust and cover the edges of the crust with foil.

7. Bake for 50 to 60 minutes. Remove the foil and bake for 10 to 15 minutes more, until the pie looks mostly set, just slightly jiggly in the very center.

8. Let it cool completely, then chill it in the fridge for at least 1 hour. Let the pie return to room temperature before slicing and serving.

CHOCOLATE CREAM PIE WITH OREO CRUST & MARSHMALLOW MERINGUE

For the sweet tooth of the sweet-toothed, this knockout pie is sure to be a hit. Combining the classic taste of Oreos and chocolate pudding is enough, but adding fluffy marshmallows too?! Pro tip: Easily make this a tasty S'mores pie by using a graham cracker crust (page 186) instead of the Oreo one! —*Sara*

Makes one 9-inch pie

CRUST

24 Oreo cookies

½ stick (¼ cup) butter, melted

FILLING

2½ cups whole milk

3 ounces unsweetened baking chocolate

2 tablespoons all-purpose flour

3 tablespoons cornstarch

1 cup sugar

¾ teaspoon kosher salt

4 extra-large egg yolks, lightly beaten

2 tablespoons butter

2 teaspoons pure vanilla extract

MARSHMALLOW MERINGUE

4 cups mini marshmallows

1 tablespoon milk

2 extra-large egg whites

3 tablespoons sugar

½ teaspoon pure vanilla extract

¼ teaspoon kosher salt

1. To make the crust: In a food processor, finely grind the cookies. Mix in the melted butter and press the crumbs evenly onto the bottom and sides of a 9-inch pie pan.

2. To make the filling: In the top of a double boiler (see page 25), heat 2 cups of the milk until it is scalded (almost but not quite boiling). Add the chocolate and stir until it's completely melted. Set aside.

3. In a big bowl, whisk together the flour, cornstarch, sugar, and salt. Whisk in the remaining ½ cup milk.

4. Stir the flour mixture into the hot chocolate mixture and return it to the double boiler. Return the double boiler to the heat and cook, whisking constantly, until the mixture is very thick,

8 to 10 minutes. Whisk in the egg yolks and cook for another 2 minutes, whisking constantly.

5. Remove the pan from the heat and whisk in the butter and vanilla. Set aside to cool, stirring occasionally.

6. Unless you plan to use a blowtorch to color the meringue, preheat the oven to 425°F.

7. For the meringue: In a medium saucepan over medium heat, warm the marshmallows and milk until the marshmallows are almost completely melted. Remove from the heat and fold until the mixture is smooth and fluffy.

8. With a hand or stand mixer, beat the egg whites until foamy. Gradually add the sugar and beat until the mixture is stiff, then beat in the vanilla and salt.

9. Gently fold the marshmallow mixture into the egg white mixture.

10. Pour the cooled pie filling into the crust and smooth the top evenly. Spread the meringue topping over the filling and bake for just 2 to 3 minutes to brown the meringue, or use a blowtorch (see page 19).

11. Let the pie cool completely, then chill it for 30 minutes before serving.

↓ Sour Cherry Pie

Apple Crumb Pie,
page 182 ↓

SOUR CHERRY PIE

As much as it may tempt you to make this pie—if only to do one of those cartoon pie-in-the-face gags so you can see your buddy with the classic red goop sliding down his face—I advise you strongly to have a slice to yourself first, or make two pies, because this one is killer. The perfect combo of tart and sweet with a light flaky crust, the only "pie-in-the-face" that's going to happen here is me eating the entire thing. —*Sara*

Makes one 9-inch pie

1 recipe Pie Dough
   (page 39)

2 pounds sour cherries,*
   pitted

1 cup sugar

⅓ cup all-purpose flour

¼ teaspoon almond
   extract

1 extra-large egg white,
   lightly beaten

1 extra-large egg

* Sour cherries are not Bing or Rainier cherries. You can find them frozen or at a good farmers' market in the summertime.

1. Preheat the oven to 375°F.

2. Roll out half the dough on a lightly floured surface into a 14-inch round that's ¼ inch thick. Carefully drape the dough over the rolling pin and lay it gently into a 9-inch pie pan, making sure that the pan is completely lined with the dough. Leave ½ inch of dough over the edge to crimp later. Set the pan in the fridge to chill for 15 minutes.

3. In a large saucepan over medium-high heat, combine the cherries, sugar, and flour. Bring to a boil and let boil for 1 minute, stirring constantly. Remove from the heat and let cool to room temperature. Stir in the almond extract.

4. Brush the bottom crust lightly with the egg white. Fill it with the cooled cherry filling.

5. Roll out the top crust. You can do a solid crust by just draping the top crust over the pie, crimping the edges, and cutting a few slits on top for ventilation, or if you have the time, do a lattice-topped pie. For the lattice top, roll the top crust to a 14-inch diameter and use a knife (or, ideally, a pastry wheel) to cut straight lines ½ to 1 inch apart through the dough. Taking care not to rip the strips of crust, carefully weave the strips of dough together on top of the pie, then crimp the edges so they're pretty. Weaving is done more easily by laying all the horizontal strips first, then going back and weaving in the vertical ones. I bet there are about a thousand videos online showing you how to do this!

6. Make a quick egg wash by whisking the egg and 1 tablespoon water in a small bowl. Brush the egg wash on any exposed crust. Put the pie on a baking sheet so you don't drip cherry goo all over the oven.

7. Bake the pie for 40 to 45 minutes, or until the crust is golden brown. Let it cool completely on the windowsill overlooking the tire swing and serve at room temperature.

PUMPKIN PIE

This is an absolute staple in a baker's repertoire. Pumpkin pie is great all year round, but if I don't get any between November 1 and New Year's Day, I get grumpy. They sell billions of pre-made pumpkin pies in stores, especially around the holidays, but I seriously recommend you make your own. They're not difficult, and the result is night and day versus a store-bought pie. Another fun thing to do is pour a thin layer of maple syrup on this pie when it cools off, then torch the syrup. —Duff

Makes one 9-inch pie

½ recipe Pie Dough
   (page 39)

2 cups pumpkin puree (not
   pumpkin pie filling!!!)

2 tablespoons cream
   cheese, softened

2 tablespoons molasses

½ cup granulated sugar

¼ cup lightly packed light
   brown sugar

1½ teaspoons ground
   cinnamon

1 teaspoon ground nutmeg

1 teaspoon ground ginger

½ teaspoon ground cloves

3 extra-large eggs, lightly
   beaten

1½ cups half-and-half

Whipped cream, for
   serving

Pumpkin Pie is pictured
on page 180.

1. Preheat the oven to 425°F.

2. Roll out the dough on a lightly floured surface into a 14-inch round that's ¼ inch thick. Carefully drape the dough over the rolling pin and lay it gently into a 9-inch pie pan, making sure that the pan is completely lined with the dough. Crimp the edges to make them pretty.

3. In a big bowl, whisk the pumpkin, cream cheese, and molasses until smooth. Whisk in the sugars and spices.

4. Whisk in the eggs and half-and-half until well blended.

5. Pour the filling into the pie shell and bake for 10 minutes. Lower the oven temperature to 350°F and bake for 40 to 50 minutes more, or until a knife inserted into the center comes out clean. If the edges of the crust start looking dark after 30 minutes of baking, cover the edges with foil to keep them from burning.

6. Set the pie on a wire rack and let cool to room temperature. Serve at room temperature with whipped cream—seriously. Pumpkin pie with whipped cream is the business.

Pecan Pie ↓

↓ Boysenberry Pie,
page 164

↓ Key Lime P
page 186

Lemon Chess Pie, ↑
page 171

↑ Pumpkin Pi
page 179

↑ Lemon Meringue Pie,
page 184

PECAN PIE

If I had to pick one pie to eat for the rest of my life, it would be pecan pie. It's iconic, delicious, and good really any time of year, but when it starts getting cold out and you see a pecan pie, you know you're in for some turkey, some football, and a renewal on your gym membership. *—Duff*

Makes one 9-inch pie

½ recipe Pie Dough (page 39)

3 extra-large eggs

¼ cup lightly packed light brown sugar

1¼ cups dark corn syrup

¼ teaspoon kosher salt

1 teaspoon pure vanilla extract

1 cup chopped pecans plus about 1 cup pecan halves

1. Preheat the oven to 450°F.

2. Roll out the dough on a lightly floured surface into a 14-inch round that's ¼ inch thick. Carefully drape the dough over the rolling pin and lay it gently into a 9-inch pie pan, making sure that the pan is completely lined with the dough. Crimp the edges with your fingers and make it look nice. Refrigerate the crust while you prepare the filling.

3. In a large bowl, lightly beat the eggs. Add the brown sugar, corn syrup, salt, vanilla, and chopped pecans and whisk well to blend.

4. Pour the filling into the pie shell (don't overfill it!) and lay the pecan halves on top. Make it look nice—this is probably for a holiday, people!

5. Bake for 10 minutes, lower the oven temperature to 325°F, and bake for 30 minutes more, or until a knife inserted into the center comes out clean. Let cool on a wire rack for 2 hours. Serve at room temperature, or, if you're weird, eat it cold.

Options: One cool thing you can do to jazz up a pecan pie is to paint the inside of the crust with melted chocolate. Pecan pie is pretty sweet, so I would suggest using a darker chocolate. The chocolate kinda melds with the filling so it turns into a pecan pie filling/ganache-like thing.

APPLE CRUMB PIE

There are three kinds of apple pies in this world. There are apple pies with no top crust, apple pies with a top crust, and apple pies topped with streusel. Apple pies that are open for all the world to see (no top crust) are but a poor Communist imitation of a classic apple pie, and should be shunned accordingly. The apple pie that would have passed the test with Senator Joseph McCarthy is the traditional American apple pie with a pie crust on top. That's all well and good, but why the redundancy, senator? Do we not get enough pie crust from the bottom of the pie? I say we do, and I think many of my fellow Americans are with me.

Apple pie topped with streusel is a delicious thing; it screams patriotically, "Cover me with caramel or cover me with shame!" Streusel gives an excellent new texture to a standard apple pie, and it's always a good place to hide a few extra spices like ginger, mace, or cinnamon. Sometimes too much pie crust can happen—not often, but it does. Sometimes we get our hot little hands on some really delicious apples and we want to spotlight those flavors. Streusel is a great way to show off the color, texture, and flavor of those apples, uninterrupted by a crust that you have plenty of underneath said pie. My fellow Americans, ask not what your apples can do for your pie crust, ask what your pie crust can do for your apples.

I'm Duff Goldman, and I approved this message. *—Duff*

Makes 4 mini pies or one 9-inch pie

CRUST AND FILLING

½ recipe Pie Dough (page 39)

5 large apples, peeled, cored, and sliced (I like to go with Gala, Granny Smith, or Honeycrisp)

1 cup granulated sugar (if you're not using green apples, use ¾ cup)

Pinch of ground cinnamon

Pinch of kosher salt

1 tablespoon all-purpose flour

2 teaspoons freshly squeezed lemon juice

1. Preheat the oven to 425°F.

2. Roll out the dough on a lightly floured surface into a 14-inch round that's ¼ inch thick. Carefully drape the dough over the rolling pin and lay it gently into a 9-inch pie pan, making sure that the pan is completely lined with the dough. Refrigerate the crust while you make the filling.

3. In a big bowl, combine the apples, sugar, cinnamon, salt, flour, and lemon juice. Pour the filling into the pie shell.

TOPPING

½ stick (¼ cup) butter,
softened

2 tablespoons granulated
sugar

2 tablespoons light brown
sugar

½ cup all-purpose flour

Pinch of kosher salt

Pinch of ground cinnamon

A baked Apple Crumb Pie
is pictured on page 176.

4. To make the topping: Using the same bowl you used for the apples, hand-mix the ingredients until crumbly. Spread the topping evenly over the apple mixture.

5. Bake for 10 minutes, then lower the oven temperature to 350°F and bake for 25 to 30 minutes more, or until the apples are tender and the crumble is browned.

6. Let the pie cool before serving, but serve it at room temperature. Cold apple pie is stupid and un-American.

LEMON MERINGUE PIE

This pie definitely makes my top-five favorite pies list. Tart, creamy, and with the fluffy meringue, it's just delightful. When I was a kid, it was my favorite pie to watch my mom make because I liked seeing the tips of meringue turn nice and brown while it baked. Plus, it tasted awesome! —*Sara*

Makes one 9-inch pie

CRUST AND FILLING

½ recipe Pie Dough (page 39)

3 extra-large egg yolks (the whites are used in the meringue)

7 tablespoons cornstarch

1⅓ cups sugar

¼ teaspoon kosher salt

½ cup freshly squeezed lemon juice

1 teaspoon lemon zest

2 tablespoons butter

MERINGUE

3 extra-large egg whites

1 tablespoon freshly squeezed lemon juice

6 tablespoons sugar

Lemon Meringue Pie is pictured on page 180.

1. Preheat the oven to 350°F.

2. Roll out the dough on a lightly floured surface into a 14-inch round that's ¼ inch thick. Carefully drape the dough over the rolling pin and lay it gently into a 9-inch pie pan, making sure that the pan is completely lined with the dough. Crimp the edges as desired. Bake the crust for 13 to 15 minutes, or until lightly browned. You're not baking the crust all the way yet!

3. To make the filling: Lightly beat the egg yolks in a small bowl.

4. In a saucepan, whisk the cornstarch, sugar, and salt. Slowly stir in 1½ cups hot water. Bring to a boil over high heat, stirring constantly and cooking until the mixture is thick and clear. Remove from the heat.

5. Stir about ⅓ cup of the cornstarch mixture into the beaten egg yolks and mix well. Pour the yolk mixture into the saucepan and bring the mixture back to a boil over high heat. Turn the heat to low and cook, stirring constantly, for 4 to 5 minutes, or until it thickens.

6. Remove the pan from the heat and slowly stir in the lemon juice, lemon zest, and butter. Let the filling cool thoroughly at room temperature, then pour it into the baked pie shell.

7. To make the meringue: Using a hand or stand mixer with a very clean bowl, combine the egg whites and lemon juice. Beat on high speed until the whites are able to stand in soft peaks. Add the sugar 2 tablespoons at a time, beating well after each addition. Beat until the meringue stands in firm glossy peaks.

8. Spread the meringue over the cooled filling, taking care to spread it all the way to the crust. If you like, use the back of a spoon to create peaks across the top (or you can even pipe the meringue into a design if you're feeling fancy).

9. Bake (still at 350°F) for 15 to 20 minutes, or until the meringue has started to brown.*

10. Let the pie cool completely before serving. Store it chilled.

* You can use a blowtorch to brown the meringue, but if you expect the pie to live after one day, bake it. The meringue won't get all weepy that way.

KEY LIME PIE

Key lime pie makes me want to lie on a white beach in Miami. Maybe because it's the state pie of Florida? Or it got its origins in the Florida Keys? Or because its tart, cool, refreshing taste reminds me of one of those umbrella drinks? Whatever it is, Key lime pie is fantastic. Key limes are more aromatic and tart than the regular limes you see at the market, so if you can find them, use them. It really isn't "Key lime pie" if you use regular limes, but sometimes Key limes are tough to find. I won't judge. —*Sara*

Makes one 9-inch pie

GRAHAM CRACKER CRUST

24 graham crackers

¾ stick (6 tablespoons) butter, melted

FILLING

2 extra-large egg yolks

Pinch of kosher salt

3 (14-ounce) cans sweetened condensed milk

½ cup sour cream

¾ cup freshly squeezed Key lime juice (or regular lime juice if you can't find Key limes)

2 tablespoons grated lime zest (Key limes if you can!)

Whipped cream, for serving (optional)

Key Lime Pie is pictured on page 180.

1. Preheat the oven to 350°F.

2. To make the crust: Grind the crackers into fine crumbs in a food processor. In a big bowl, combine the crumbs and melted butter by hand until well mixed.

3. Carefully press the crumbs into a 9-inch pie pan, evenly covering the bottom and sides. Make sure the crumbs are pressed in tightly. Bake the crust for about 15 minutes, or until a slightly darker brown color.

4. To make the filling: In a big bowl, whisk the egg yolks and salt until well combined. Whisk in the condensed milk and sour cream. Add the lime juice and zest and whisk until well incorporated.

5. Pour the filling into the cracker crust. It should fill it almost to the top.

6. Bake for 8 to 10 minutes, or until tiny bubbles start to burst on top of the pie.

7. Let the pie cool slightly, then refrigerate it for 1 hour before serving. Top with whipped cream if desired!

APPLE-PEAR GALETTE

A galette may sound like a super fancy-pants French pastry, and it is, but it's actually incredibly easy to make, and you'll be super impressive to your guests! It's very versatile, too, so if you're more of a pear fan, use pears. Like some crunch? Add a handful of pecans.

This particular version combines tart apples and sweet pears with a hint of ginger that adds more depth to the flavor. —*Sara*

Makes one 10-inch galette

CRUST

2 cups all-purpose flour

½ teaspoon kosher salt

1¾ sticks (½ cup plus 6 tablespoons) cold butter, cut into small cubes

2 to 4 tablespoons cold milk

Cooking spray

FILLING

1 pound Granny Smith apples, peeled, cored, and cut into ⅛-inch-thick slices

½ pound Bartlett or Anjou pears, peeled, cored, and cut into ⅛-inch-thick slices

1 tablespoon freshly squeezed lemon juice

2 tablespoons granulated sugar

2 tablespoons light brown sugar

1 tablespoon all-purpose flour

1 teaspoon ground ginger

¼ teaspoon ground cinnamon

EGG WASH

1 extra-large egg

1. To make the crust: Sift the flour and salt into a big bowl. Use a pastry cutter or two knives to cut the butter into the flour until the mixture resembles small peas. Add 2 tablespoons of the cold milk and use your hands to mix until the dough starts to clump together (you may need to add 1 or 2 more tablespoons of milk). Form the dough into a ball, wrap it in plastic wrap, and refrigerate it for at least 30 minutes.

2. Preheat the oven to 400°F and line a baking sheet with parchment or foil and spray with cooking spray.

3. To make the filling: In a large bowl, combine the apples, pears, lemon juice, sugars, flour, ginger, and cinnamon and toss lightly to coat.

4. You want about a 14-inch crust that's ⅛ inch thick, and the easiest way to do this is to roll out the dough between two sheets of parchment so that you can handle it more easily. Roll out the dough, remove one side of the parchment paper, and then flip the crust onto the prepared baking sheet. Remove the top parchment.

5. Arrange the apple-pear filling in pretty concentric circles on the crust, leaving a 2-inch border. Fold 2 inches of crust in toward the center in a rustic fashion, partially covering the filling, and press lightly to seal.

6. Make a quick egg wash by whisking together the egg and 2 tablespoons water and lightly brush the edges of the crust.

7. Bake for 15 minutes, then lower the oven temperature to 350°F and bake for 30 to 35 minutes more, or until the crust is golden brown. Let cool for at least 10 minutes, then cut into wedges and serve at room temperature.

SAVORY BEEF HAND PIES

Hand pies rule. You can make them sweet or savory, and you can bake them, pan-fry them, or deep-fry them. This is a great snack to keep in your backpack when you're off to school or to protest whatever regime is oppressing you. —*Duff*

Makes 4 or 5 hand pies

2 tablespoons butter

1 pound ground beef

1 small unpeeled Red Bliss potato, diced small

1 cup green peas (frozen is totally cool)

1 shallot, minced

1 tablespoon curry powder

1 teaspoon cayenne pepper

2 tablespoons kosher salt

3 tablespoons all-purpose flour

½ recipe Pie Dough (page 39)

2 extra-large eggs

1. In a large skillet, melt the butter over medium-high heat. Add the ground beef, potato, peas, shallot, spices, and 1 tablespoon of the salt. Cook, stirring occasionally, until the potato is tender, about 25 minutes, then slowly add the flour and stir until the filling thickens up. Transfer the filling to a bowl and wash the skillet.

2. Roll out the pie dough on a floured surface to ¼ inch thick and cut it into four or five 8-inch circles. Use a plate as a template. Divide the filling among the circles, mounding it in the middle and leaving plenty of room around the edges. You can reroll the scraps once, but after that they will start to get tough. Toss them in hot oil and make some fry-bread with them.

3. Preheat the oven to 375°F.

4. Lightly whisk the eggs and remaining 1 tablespoon salt with a fork in a small bowl. Brush the egg wash all the way around the circles, then fold the circles in half. Press down the edges of the semicircles with a fork to lock in the filling. Transfer the pies to a baking sheet and chill them in the fridge for 15 to 20 minutes.

5. Brush the pies with egg wash. Bake for 15 to 20 minutes. Let cool a bit on the baking sheet, then serve warm.

CHICKEN POT PIE

When you work in restaurants, everybody takes turns making "family meal." That's the dinner that one cook makes for all the staff who are working that night. This chicken pot pie of mine is famous in restaurants across America, not because it was on the menu, but because the cooks in those restaurants used to get me to make family meal more often than it was really my turn. But that's okay—when the chefs all want your food, that's a compliment.

One of the things that makes this pie so good isn't the baking, but the caramelizing of the vegetables. Color, friends, is flavor. *—Duff*

Makes one 9-inch pie

1 stick (½ cup) butter

1 shallot, chopped

2 scallions, chopped

¼ cup chopped Vidalia or Maui onion

½ cup chopped cauliflower

2 celery ribs, sliced

2 carrots, washed and trimmed but not peeled, diced

2 chicken breasts, diced

1 tablespoon kosher salt

Freshly ground pepper

Pinch of cayenne

½ cup milk

¼ cup all-purpose flour

¼ cup cornstarch

2 cups chicken stock

1 cup frozen peas

1 recipe Pie Dough (page 39)

1. Preheat the oven to 400°F and butter a 9-inch pie pan well.

2. In a big saucepan over medium-high heat, melt 2 tablespoons of the butter. Add the shallot, scallions, onion, cauliflower, celery, and carrots and cook until caramelized, about 10 minutes. Add the chicken, salt, pepper, and cayenne, stir well, and cook until the chicken is cooked through and everything is nice and browned. Stir in the remaining 6 tablespoons butter and the milk and turn the heat to low.

3. In a small bowl, whisk together the flour, cornstarch, and chicken stock. Using a wooden spoon, stir the veggies and chicken quickly but gently while slowly pouring in the stock mixture.

4. Taste it. Is it good? Does it need more salt or pepper or heat? Season it until you like it. Now, add the peas and turn off the heat.

5. Roll out half the dough on a floured surface into a 14-inch round that's ¼ inch thick. Carefully drape the dough over the rolling pin and lay it gently into a 9-inch pie pan, making sure that the pan is completely lined with the dough. Leave about ½ inch of dough over the edge of the pan.

6. Fill the pie with the chicken mixture.

7. Roll out the remaining dough to make the top of the pie. Wet the edges of the bottom crust and lay the top crust on top.

Trim the crust with a sharp knife or scissors and crimp the edges as desired. With a paring knife, make 5 vent holes in the middle of the pie to let out the steam.

8. Bake the pie for 30 to 40 minutes, or until it looks done. Place a baking sheet under the pie just in case it drips, so you won't have to clean a mess out of your oven. The crimped edge might get really dark, but it acts like a savory cookie to scoop up extra pie filling.

9. Let the pie cool for about 10 minutes before serving or the filling will goo out all over the place.

RANDOM YUMMY STUFF

I like that title. It speaks volumes with its sort-of-poetical purity; it makes me want to eat everything in this chapter. Basically, these recipes are the magical things that most people don't make at home because you can get them for $0.99 at the state fair or the convenience store. I wanted to include these kinds of items in the book because there's a certain sense of accomplishment one gets from making things that are usually made in factories and on carts. One of my most fantastic days at culinary school was when we learned how to make Butterfingers, just like the candy bar, from scratch. It was like being five years old and getting to see how the machine that resets the bowling pins works. I was blown away that I now had the knowledge to create a candy that was, just hours before, a complete mystery to me. I felt that if I willed lightning to shoot from my fingertips, it would be as easy as writing my own name. I truly believe that making some of these hitherto mysterious treats will have the same empowering effect on you.

Consider the doughnut. Pretty standard fare—you see them everywhere. But how many people do you know who actually know how to make a delicious doughnut? I'm going to assume not many. And imagine the look on a child's face when you produce a hot, sweet funnel cake from your own kitchen, when that child had thought you could get them only after being very brave and riding the biggest roller coaster in the park. You'll rise to the status of wizard in that child's eyes.

Making a loaf of bread is one of the most rewarding things any of us can do. But making something that has a name or a logo or that's tied to a specific geographical location is another matter entirely. You've peeked beyond the curtain and bitten the apple of forbidden knowledge.

BLUEBERRY CAKE DOUGHNUTS

These are my favorite doughnuts ever. I've had an emotional attachment to them since I was living and working in Washington, D.C. I was super poor and there was a bakery stall in Eastern Market right on my way to work that would sell me two-day-olds for 50 cents, and I'd eat them while riding my bike to work. Oh, the salad days. I'll even eat the 7-Eleven ones in a pinch. I just love a blueberry cake doughnut. I've tried to sneak this doughnut onto the menu of every restaurant I've ever worked at. —*Duff*

Makes about 2 dozen regular doughnuts or 48 mini doughnuts

Cooking spray

1/3 stick butter, softened

1 cup sugar

Pinch of kosher salt

1 teaspoon pure vanilla
   extract

1 cup cake flour

2 cups all-purpose flour

1 teaspoon baking soda

2 teaspoons baking
   powder

2 extra-large eggs plus
   1 egg yolk

1 pint (2 cups) frozen
   blueberries, thawed

1 cup buttermilk

Basic Sugar Glaze
   (page 297)

SPECIAL EQUIPMENT

Doughnut pans (regular
   or mini)

Piping bag

1. Preheat the oven to 350°F and spray the doughnut pans liberally with cooking spray.

2. In the bowl of a stand mixer fitted with the paddle attachment, cream the butter, sugar, salt, and vanilla until light and fluffy.

3. In a separate bowl, whisk together the flours, baking soda, and baking powder.

4. Add the eggs and yolk to the mixer and cream until blended.

5. In 4 to 6 stages, alternately add the flour mixture and the buttermilk, mixing on medium-low the whole time and constantly scraping down the sides. Once the additions are done, turn the mixer to its lowest setting and gently add the blueberries, mixing just until evenly incorporated and the batter is a nice shade of blue.

6. Fill a large piping bag with the batter and fill each well in the pans about two-thirds full.

7. Bake for 18 to 20 minutes or until the dough springs back when poked for regular doughnuts, or 8 to 10 minutes for mini doughnuts.

8. When cool, dip the doughnuts into the glaze and shake off the excess. Place them on a wire rack so the glaze soaks in and gets a little crunchy on the outside.

CINNAMON ROLLS

Oh, cinnamon roll! You delicious, chubby goddess of warm, buttery, fluffy, cinnamon-ness! This recipe is one of the more technical ones in this book, and you'll have to allow a lot of time for the dough to rise, but it's truly a labor of love and, oh man, it is *so* worth it! —Sara

Makes 12 cinnamon rolls

DOUGH

1¾ cups plus
   2 tablespoons
   all-purpose flour

½ teaspoon kosher salt

1 tablespoon plus
   ¼ teaspoon
   granulated sugar

¾ cup whole milk

1½ teaspoons active
   dry yeast

½ stick (¼ cup) butter,
   cut into small cubes,
   plus more for the pan

1 extra-large egg, lightly
   whisked

* If you *don't* smell any yeast-like aroma, or the yeast doesn't look like it activated, do not proceed! If you pour that into the flour mixture, it's very likely you'll be wasting all those ingredients because the dough won't rise. Just toss it out, heat up some new milk, check to see that the yeast isn't past the expiration date, make sure your milk is at the correct temperature, throw a little sugar in, and try again.

FILLING

⅓ cup lightly packed light
   brown sugar

⅓ cup granulated sugar

1 to 2 teaspoons ground
   cinnamon

Pinch of kosher salt

Raisins (optional)

ICING

1 tablespoon butter, melted

2 teaspoons milk

1 cup powdered sugar

Pinch of kosher salt

½ teaspoon pure vanilla
   extract

1. To make the dough: In a big bowl, combine the flour, salt, and 1 tablespoon of the sugar.

2. In a small saucepan, heat the milk over low heat until it's just mildly warm. Immediately turn off the heat and very lightly whisk in the yeast. Sprinkle the surface of the milk with the remaining ¼ teaspoon sugar to give the yeast some food. Let it sit for 10 or so minutes while the yeast wakes up.

3. Meanwhile, add the cubed butter to the flour mixture and very lightly rub it between your hands. Don't rub it in too much! You want some chunks of butter left in the dough.

4. When the surface of the milk/yeast mixture looks like it's foaming a bit and smells yeasty, you're in the money.* Quickly add the egg, give it a little 3-second stir, then pour it into the flour mixture. With your hand, gently incorporate the liquid into the flour, just until combined—don't overmix.

5. Cover the bowl well with plastic wrap and let the dough rise about 6 hours or overnight in the fridge. It will have almost doubled in size.

6. Place the dough on a well-floured surface and use a floured rolling pin to roll it into a long rectangle, about 8 x 20 inches. Dust off the excess flour and fold the rectangle in thirds, like a business letter. You now have a smaller rectangle—roll it right back out to 8 x 20 inches again. Fold in thirds again, roll it out again, and fold it one last time.

7. Let this rectangle guy rest for a minute while you mix the filling ingredients together in a small bowl.

8. Generously butter a 9 x 13-inch baking pan and set it aside.

9. Making sure your surface is well-floured, roll out the dough to an 18 x 20-inch rectangle. This may take some time and muscle power, as the dough will be a bit elastic.

10. To make the filling: In a small bowl, combine the sugars, cinnamon, and salt. Sprinkle the filling mixture over the whole surface, to all the edges but one of the shorter ones. Leave 1 bare inch on that edge—this will be the

outermost edge of the bun, which will be sealed. Sprinkle on raisins, if using.

11. Starting with the edge opposite the bare one, roll up the dough, working firmly but not so tightly that you rip the dough. You'll now have an 18-inch cylinder.

12. Use your hands to make sure everything is looking even and cylindrical, then cut straight through the cylinder every 1½ inches, to give you 12 cinnamon rolls.

13. Place the rolls cut-side-up in the buttered baking pan. Don't fit them too snugly— they're going to rise like crazy! Cover the pan loosely in plastic wrap.

14. Preheat the oven to 325°F.

15. To make the icing: In a medium bowl, whisk all the icing ingredients together until smooth!

16. Remove the plastic from the pan and bake the rolls for about 25 minutes, or until the tops are golden and the rolls at the center don't look too doughy.

17. Place the pan on a wire rack and place a dollop of the icing on top of each roll while they're still very hot. Let cool just enough for safety, then dig in!

JAM-FILLED TOASTER PASTRY-LIKE ITEMS

There's just something magical and cool about making a pastry that exists in the store. I remember coming home from school as a kid and making Pop-Tarts in the toaster oven as a snack. I was like eight, and I could do this myself. There's certainly an element of nostalgia in this recipe, but more than that, they're delicious. —*Sara*

Makes about 8

CRUST AND FILLING

1½ sticks (¾ cup) butter, softened

⅔ cup granulated sugar

2 extra-large egg yolks

¼ teaspoon kosher salt

½ teaspoon pure vanilla extract

2 cups all-purpose flour

1 tablespoon heavy cream

Cooking spray

Any flavor preserves you'd like for filling: strawberry, blueberry, grape. *Or,* try a mixture of brown sugar and cinnamon to make my personal childhood favorite flavor.

1 extra-large egg whisked with a pinch of sugar

TOPPING

2 cups powdered sugar

½ cup milk

½ teaspoon ground cinnamon for the brown sugar–cinnamon flavor (optional)

Colored sprinkles or sanding sugar to make it cute

1. To make the crust and filling: With a hand or stand mixer, cream the butter and sugar until smooth. Add the yolks, salt, and vanilla and mix well. Gradually mix in the flour. While the mixer is going, add the cream and mix until the dough is smooth.

2. Wrap the dough in plastic wrap and refrigerate it for at least 1 hour.

3. Preheat the oven to 350°F, line a baking sheet with parchment paper, and spray it with cooking spray.

4. Roll out the dough on a lightly floured surface to about ¼ inch thick. Use a ruler to make uniform rectangles, or to be totally exact, trace a 3 x 5-inch card (that's how big a real

Pop-Tart is). Reroll the scraps, getting as many rectangles as you can until you're out of dough. Place half the rectangles on the prepared baking sheet.

5. Spoon about 2 tablespoons of filling into the center of half the rectangles, leaving a ½-inch edge uncovered. Don't overfill them! Try to make these look legit.

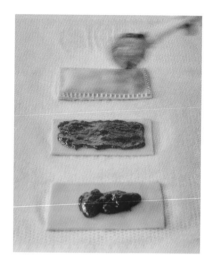

6. Using a finger or pastry brush, spread water around the ½-inch border of the filled rectangles.

7. Fit a top rectangle on each filled rectangle, pressing with the tines of a fork around the border to seal the top and bottom crusts together.

8. Brush each tart with a bit of egg wash and poke a few tiny holes in each so the steam can escape. Bake for 10 to 12 minutes, or until the edges start to turn golden. Let the tarts cool completely on a wire rack.

9. To make the topping: In a medium bowl, whisk together the powdered sugar and milk (and cinnamon, if using) to make the icing.

10. When the tarts are *completely* cool, ice them if desired, and add some sprinkles if you like. But seriously, add those sprinkles.

11. Let the icing set up for about 10 minutes and enjoy!

WHOOPIE PIES

Originally hailing from the Northern Midwest, these delightfully bad-for-you treats are essentially two cake-like chocolate cookies on either side of a marshmallow frosting. Why do they call it a pie? It's a giant cookie made out of cake. What about that says pie? I've always wondered. —*Sara*

Makes 12 whoopie pies

CAKES

Cooking spray

2⅓ cups all-purpose flour

1 teaspoon baking powder

½ teaspoon baking soda

¾ teaspoon kosher salt

1 stick (½ cup) butter, softened

1 cup lightly packed light brown sugar

1 teaspoon pure vanilla extract

1 extra-large egg

½ cup unsweetened natural cocoa powder

1 cup milk

2 cups semisweet chocolate chips

FILLING

1 cup shortening, softened

1 cup powdered sugar

1⅓ cups marshmallow cream (a little more than half a jar)

¼ teaspoon kosher salt dissolved in 1 tablespoon warm water

1½ teaspoons pure vanilla extract

1. Preheat the oven to 350°F. Line two baking sheets with parchment paper and lightly spray with cooking spray.

2. To make the cakes: In a medium bowl, whisk together the flour, baking powder, baking soda, and salt and set aside.

3. With a hand or stand mixer, beat the butter, brown sugar, and vanilla until creamy. Add the egg and beat until smooth. Beat in the cocoa powder. Add the flour mixture and milk alternately, mixing until the batter is smooth.

4. Stir in the chocolate chips.

5. Using a blue-handled 2-ounce scoop, portion the batter and drop it onto the baking sheets, leaving a few inches between the cakes. Grease your hand and pat each one on the head a couple times for doing such a good job.

6. Bake for 16 to 18 minutes, or until a toothpick inserted into the middle of a cake has only a couple crumbs stuck to it.

7. Let the cakes cool completely while you make the filling!

8. To make the filling: With a hand or stand mixer, beat the shortening, powdered sugar, and marshmallow cream until combined. Add the salt water and vanilla and beat until smooth.

9. Place the desired amount of filling between the flat sides of two cookies and press together. You can then either serve them right away or freeze them for later, but they don't keep too well in the fridge. If you want to make them ahead, freeze the cakes and make the filling fresh when you want to serve them.

PERPETUALLY FRESH YELLOW SUBMARINE-LOOKING PASTRY/ DOUGHNUT/CAKE THINGS

Yup. You can make your own version of Twinkies from scratch. —*Sara*

Makes 18

CAKE

Cooking spray

3 tablespoons butter, softened

¾ cup granulated sugar

2 extra-large eggs

1 teaspoon pure vanilla extract

1½ cups cake flour

2 teaspoons baking powder

½ teaspoon kosher salt

½ cup milk

FILLING

1 cup shortening, softened

1 cup powdered sugar

1⅓ cups marshmallow cream (a little more than half a jar)

¼ teaspoon kosher salt dissolved in 1 tablespoon warm water

1½ teaspoons pure vanilla extract

SPECIAL EQUIPMENT

Twinkie baking pans

1. Preheat the oven to 350°F and spray two Twinkie pans heavily with cooking spray. (You can use a doughnut pan or even muffin tins—they just won't be Twinkie shaped. Also, you'll have to experiment with baking times to get them perfect.)

2. With a hand or stand mixer, cream the butter and sugar for about 2 minutes, or until light and fluffy. Add the eggs one at a time, beating after each addition. Add the vanilla and beat on medium-high speed for about 1 minute.

3. In a medium bowl, whisk the flour, baking powder, and salt.

4. Mix half the flour mixture into the butter mixture, then the milk, then the rest of the flour mixture, making sure to scrape the sides of the bowl as you go and making sure each addition is well incorporated.

5. Divide the batter among the cake wells, filling each one no more than two-thirds full. (A piping bag makes this easier.)

6. Bake for 18 to 23 minutes, or until a toothpick inserted into the centers comes out clean. Set the pan on a wire rack to cool thoroughly.

7. To make the filling: In a large bowl using a hand mixer or in the bowl of a stand mixer fitted with the paddle attachment, beat the shortening, powdered sugar, and marshmallow cream until combined. Add the salt water and vanilla and beat until smooth.

8. Fill a piping bag with a medium-size plain tip with the filling and gently squeeze about 2 tablespoons of the filling into each cake through three spots on the flat side of the cake.

BEIGNETS

A long time ago when I was a culinary student, I found what someone told me was the original Café du Monde recipe for beignets. It wasn't, because the recipe didn't work, but I messed with it for a few years and made a recipe that works really well. It's pretty easy, it's delicious, and it makes awesome beignets. There's a great scene in the movie *Chef* where Jon Favreau's character takes his son to New Orleans and gets him beignets for the first time. In the scene, the son's face is covered in powdered sugar; you can tell Jon loves passing along the knowledge of a chef as he says, "You can only have your first beignet once." I love that line, and the scene, and it makes me so happy that the path I chose in life has led me here. —*Duff*

Makes about 15

1 (¼-ounce) envelope active dry yeast

¼ cup milk or cream, warmed

3 tablespoons granulated sugar

3 cups all-purpose flour

1½ cups bread flour

¼ stick (2 tablespoons) butter, softened

1 extra-large egg plus 1 egg yolk

1 teaspoon kosher salt

1 quart vegetable oil

2 cups powdered sugar

1. In a big bowl, combine the yeast, 1 cup warm water, and the milk and sugar and let the yeast bloom for about 7 minutes. When it's bubbly, add the flours, butter, egg, egg yolk, and salt. Mix the dough until it's sticky, then turn it out onto a floured surface and knead for about 15 minutes.

2. Oil the bowl. Put the dough back in the bowl, cover the bowl tightly, and let it rise overnight in the fridge.

3. The next day, in a deep pot over pretty high heat, bring the oil to 350°F on a deep-fry thermometer. Add the powdered sugar to a large bowl and set it aside along with a wire rack to drain the beignets.

4. Punch the dough down and roll it out onto a floured surface to 1 inch thick. With a pizza cutter, cut 2-inch squares out of the dough. Fry them immediately, about 90 seconds per side and flip them only once, until they're golden brown.

5. Drain the beignets on the wire rack, and while they're still hot and somewhat oily, toss them in the bowl of sugar. If you want to be a rock star, make little envelopes with parchment paper to hold the beignets. Serve them immediately with Café du Monde chicory coffee for a legit experience.

FUNNEL CAKES

I remember eating my first funnel cake at Disneyland when I was super young. Later, when I made my own funnel cakes, I remember eating my first one, and I tried hard to make them extra awesome because I was probably making someone else's first funnel cake and I remembered how awesome mine was.

Make life easy for yourself and prep four or five disposable plastic piping bags with batter. Funnel cakes can be very messy to make, and this will totally help. —*Duff*

Makes 8

1 quart vegetable oil

3 cups all-purpose flour

2 teaspoons baking powder

1 teaspoon kosher salt

1 teaspoon ground cinnamon

½ cup granulated sugar

3 extra-large eggs

2 cups milk or cream

2 cups powdered sugar

1. Add the oil to a deep pot and heat it over medium-high heat until it registers 375°F on a deep-fry thermometer. Set up a work surface with 4 or 5 plastic piping bags, scissors, tongs, parchment paper, and a wire rack with parchment paper underneath.

2. In a big bowl, whisk the flour, baking powder, salt, cinnamon, and granulated sugar. Add the eggs and milk and whisk well. Get all the lumps out!

3. Fill all the piping bags with batter. Cut the tip off one bag and drizzle the batter straight into the hot oil in a swirly, crazy pattern. Toss the piping bag. When one side is golden brown, about 75 seconds, carefully flip the funnel cake with tongs and fry the other side, another 75 seconds. Fry the rest of the batter.

4. Drain the funnel cakes on the wire rack. While they're still warm and shiny, dust them with powdered sugar using a wire-mesh strainer. Serve immediately!

CHURROS

Last winter, I was at a park in Tulum, Mexico, a few hours north of Belize, and there was a fiesta going on, with all these street vendors selling corn and sweets and tacos and stuff on sticks. I thought it would be clichéd if I got a churro, but I did, and I'm glad, because I realized I'd never had a real churro before in my life. I hope you find these authentic, because the real churros are crunchy, sweet, and incredible. Or just go to Mexico. It's a good excuse. —*Duff*

Makes about 15 churros

2 cups plus 2 tablespoons sugar

½ cup ground cinnamon

1 stick (½ cup) butter

¼ teaspoon kosher salt

1 cup all-purpose flour

3 extra-large eggs

2 to 3 quarts vegetable oil

SPECIAL EQUIPMENT

Large Dutch oven, or a pan at least 12 inches wide and 4 inches deep

Hella (lots of) paper towels

Sifter (or sieve)

Stand mixer with a paddle attachment

Kitchen thermometer that reaches at least 400°F

Large, sturdy piping bag (double up when using disposable plastic bags)

Large closed-star metal decorating tip*

Metal tongs

1. Combine 2 cups of the sugar and the cinnamon in a large, shallow dish or pan that's big enough to roll the churros in (at least 8 inches wide). Set aside.

2. Set up a baking sheet lined with a bunch of paper towels for the finished churros.

3. In a medium saucepan over medium-high heat, bring the butter, the remaining 2 tablespoons sugar, the salt, and 1 cup water to a boil. Reduce the heat to low.

4. Sift the flour into the saucepan and stir for about 1 minute. The mixture will immediately form into a sticky ball.

5. Transfer the dough to a stand mixer fitted with the paddle attachment. With the mixer on low, add the eggs, one at a time. Mix until the eggs are well incorporated.

6. Fill the Dutch oven or pan with 2 to 2½ inches of oil and place it over high heat. You want the oil to be at 345°F to 365°F during the frying process; use the thermometer to monitor the temperature closely. When the oil hits 340°F, turn the heat down to medium and try to maintain the temperature range.

* Or something that looks comparable. A regular star tip will work, but the ridges of your churros won't be very defined. A way to combat this is to take a pair of needle-nose pliers and bend the points of the tips in slightly.

7. Fit the pastry bag with the metal tip and fill it three-quarters full of churro dough.

8. Squeeze the dough directly into the oil in 6- to 8-inch lengths, using a scissors or a paring knife to separate the dough from the bag. You can fry about 3 churros at a time, using the metal tongs to keep them separated. Fry about 2 minutes on each side, until the churros are a deep golden color all over.

9. Gently remove the finished churros with tongs and place them directly into the cinnamon-sugar mixture, rolling to coat them evenly. Place them on the paper towel–lined tray.

10. Repeat until you've used all the dough! Serve warm.

WHITE CHOCOLATE BREAD PUDDING

This classic bread pudding is presented here in a very simple form. It's a blank canvas that can be spiced and played with any way you want. It's a great vehicle for dried fruits, different kinds of chocolates, spices, and even roasted or candied nuts. Whatever you have on hand, most likely it will work in a bread pudding. But I tend to stay away from high-liquid items like fresh fruit. It's not that they don't work—I just don't like the way they stain the bread pudding around each piece, and they tend to disrupt the smoothness of the custard. It's a textural and visual thing for me, but this is *your* bread pudding. Do your worst.

Think of bread pudding as the stew of the bakeshop. There are usually eggs in the fridge, sugar in the pantry, and bread going stale in almost every kitchen. Using older bread that has started to dry out will allow it to soak up more of the custard and be delicious. If I know I'm going to be making a bread pudding, I always cube the bread and leave it out overnight to air-dry. —*Duff*

Makes one 9 x 13-inch pan

4 extra-large eggs plus
   7 egg yolks

1 tablespoon pure vanilla
   extract (or if you want
   to be a badass, 2 vanilla
   beans, scraped and
   scalded in the cream. You
   will absolutely notice the
   difference.)

2 cups milk

1 quart heavy cream

Pinch of kosher salt

1 cup sugar

6 to 8 ounces good white
   chocolate (no waxy
   stuff), chopped

4 cups 1-inch cubes day-old
   challah (page 148) or
   brioche (page 150)

SPECIAL EQUIPMENT

One of those big disposable
   aluminum roasting pans
   from the grocery store—
   something big enough to
   hold the baking pan

1. In a medium bowl, whisk together the eggs, yolks, and vanilla until smooth.

2. In a medium saucepan over medium-high heat, heat the milk, cream, salt, and sugar until just before they boil. Remove from the heat, add the white chocolate, and stir until the chocolate is melted. In a slow, steady stream, pour the cream/chocolate mixture into the egg mixture, whisking constantly. Set aside.

3. Preheat the oven to 350°F.

4. Place the bread cubes in a 9 x 13-inch baking pan and pour three-quarters of the egg/cream mixture evenly over the top. Let it sit for 10 minutes. Poke five large holes with your finger

in spots around the bread pudding and pour in the remaining custard. You want the bread to kinda float on top of a thin layer of custard.

5. Cover the pan with aluminum foil and place the entire pan inside a large disposable aluminum or other roasting pan. Fill a pitcher with hot water. Place the bread pudding in the oven and then fill the roasting pan with the water until it is just below the level of the baking pan (you've made a bain marie! See page 24).

6. Bake for 30 minutes, then check the water level. Replenish if needed. Bake for another 30 minutes, then remove the foil and check the water again. Bake for 15 minutes more, or until the bread on top begins to brown.

7. Remove the baking pan from within the larger pan and cool it on a wire rack for 20 minutes, then place it in the fridge so the custard will set up.

8. Slice it cold, place each slice in a preheated 350°F oven for 6 minutes, and serve warm with a berry coulis (page 294) or a loose chocolate ganache (page 290) or some ice cream. Or just lean over the sink and eat it with a spoon like a hunchback—that's what I do.

SAVORY BREAD PUDDING WITH BACON, LEEKS & MUSHROOMS

Bread pudding has to be one of the most decadent, rich, delicious baked desserts there is. There are endless possible variations, as you can really throw in whatever complements the other ingredients. So why not make a savory version? A savory bread pudding is the ideal addition to brunch, or the perfect lunch entrée alongside a salad. Still based on bread, cream, and eggs, this savory version adds bacon, leeks, mushrooms, and a tasty blend of cheeses and herbs. —Sara

Makes one 9 x 13-inch pan

7 cups 1- to 1½-inch cubes of day-old brioche or challah

6 bacon strips, diced

¼ cup olive oil

6 leeks, washed well, white and light green parts sliced

2 garlic cloves, minced

½ pound cremini mushrooms, sliced

½ pound shiitake mushrooms, sliced

Leaves from 2 thyme sprigs, chopped

Leaves from 2 rosemary sprigs, chopped

1 teaspoon kosher salt

2 teaspoons freshly cracked black pepper

¼ cup chopped fresh parsley

6 extra-large eggs

1½ cups heavy cream

1½ cups chicken stock

8 ounces Gruyère cheese, grated (1½ cups)

2 ounces Parmesan cheese, grated (⅓ cup)

1. Dry out the bread by spreading it on one or two rimmed baking sheets and putting them in a 350°F oven for 12 minutes. Set aside.

2. In a large sauté pan over medium heat, cook the bacon in the olive oil for 6 minutes, or until crispy. Add the leeks and garlic and sauté about 10 minutes, or until the leeks are tender. Add the mushrooms, thyme, rosemary, salt, and pepper and cook until the mushrooms start to soften and the liquid starts to evaporate, 8 to 10 minutes. Remove from the heat and stir in the parsley.

3. In a big bowl, whisk the eggs, cream, chicken stock, and two-thirds of the cheeses.

4. Add the bread cubes and the mushroom mixture to the bowl and gently fold to coat the bread evenly. Let the mixture sit for 15 minutes, stir again, and let it sit for another 20 minutes so that the bread has a chance to soak up plenty of liquid.

5. Preheat the oven to 350°F.

6. Spread the bread pudding into the baking dish and sprinkle with the remaining cheeses. Bake for 40 to 50 minutes, or until the top is golden brown.

7. Let cool for 5 to 10 minutes, then serve warm!

CHOCOLATE MOUSSE

This is real, old-school French chocolate mousse taught to me by a real, old-school French pastry chef who was grumpy and would smack me with a wooden spoon if I ever screwed up, which was often. No joke, professional cooking is not for the faint of heart—I've been physically assaulted by at least four different chefs I worked for. It's part of the job. Don't worry, though, I tagged a few of them back. One of them I hip-checked into a hot pizza oven. Although once I got punched in the face, and this dude was big so I didn't do anything . . . I kind of deserved it.

Anyway, you really need a stand mixer for this recipe, and you need everything ready—once you start this process, you can't run around the kitchen looking for stuff. Get it all organized and you'll make amazing mousse. And when you make this mousse, put it into the container you want to serve it in—don't mess with it once it chills and sets up. Serve with whipped cream and a garnish of shaved chocolate. *—Duff*

Makes 6 to 8 servings

8 ounces chopped dark chocolate

½ stick (¼ cup) butter

Pinch of kosher salt

1 teaspoon pure vanilla extract

1 cup heavy cream

3 tablespoons sugar

7 extra-large eggs, separated

5 drops lemon juice

Whipped cream and chocolate shavings, for garnish

NOTE: READ THIS WHOLE THING CAREFULLY AND DO IT IN THIS ORDER OR YOU'LL MESS IT UP AND I'LL SMACK YOU WITH A WOODEN SPOON!

1. Gather the equipment you'll need and measure out all the ingredients. Fill a saucepan with a few inches of water and bring it to a simmer over medium-low heat.

2. Put the chocolate, butter, salt, and vanilla in the top of a double boiler (or in a heatproof bowl over simmering water).

3. In the bowl of a stand mixer fitted with the whisk attachment, whip the cream with 1 tablespoon of the sugar until thick but still smooth. Scrape it into a bowl, put it in the fridge, then clean the stand mixer bowl and the whisk really well.

4. In the clean stand mixer bowl using the clean whisk attachment, whip the egg whites, lemon juice, and 1 tablespoon of the sugar until you have a fluffy meringue, 7 to 10 minutes. Set aside at room temperature.

5. Without cleaning the bowl, whip the egg yolks and remaining 1 tablespoon sugar until light and fluffy. This will take a few

minutes, so go stir your chocolate. If it's melted, pull it off the heat and set it aside.*

6. When the yolks are light, creamy yellow, and fluffy, and the chocolate is slightly warmer than room temperature, fold them together. Next, fold in the meringue, and finally, fold in the whipped cream.

7. Immediately fill a piping bag with the mousse and pipe the mousse into 6 to 8 rocks glasses or ramekins. Put them in the fridge right away. After 5 minutes, cover them with plastic wrap. Let them chill for at least 1 hour.

8. Serve with whipped cream and a bit of shaved chocolate. This will be the best mousse you've ever tasted.

* At this point, stick your finger in the chocolate mixture and taste it. That is the taste of chocolate and butter and there is no finer thing in this world. Except maybe corgi puppies. Maybe.

DUFF'S GOOD-ASS FUDGE

The name might be a bit off-putting, but that's what this recipe is called. The first time I tried making it fifteen years ago, I was so surprised at how good it was, and the chef I made it for said, "Wow, that's good-ass fudge," so I wrote "Good-Ass Fudge" in my notebook. Now everybody I give the recipe to calls it "Duff's good-ass fudge." I think it might be because it really is good-ass fudge. Like, "Dang, that's a good-ass burger!"

I added walnuts to this one, so for anyone who has the original recipe, don't freak out—it's just good-ass fudge with nuts.

This fudge is the bane of my existence, though. I used to make it as a treat for customers when they got their bill, but the stupid waiters would eat all the fudge and make me make more. Nobody likes waiters. —*Duff*

Makes one 9-inch square pan

3¼ cups sugar

1 cup evaporated milk

¼ cup light corn syrup

½ cup unsweetened natural cocoa powder

1 stick (½ cup) butter

1 tablespoon pure vanilla extract

Pinch of kosher salt

1¼ cups walnuts, toasted (15 minutes at 350°F) and chopped

1. Line a 9-inch square pan with parchment paper and butter the paper very lightly. Set up a big bowl of cold water.

2. In a large saucepan over medium-high heat with the thermometer inserted, combine the sugar, evaporated milk, and corn syrup. Stir and cook just until the mixture is combined, then stop stirring. Don't mess with it! When it hits 236°F to 237°F (soft ball stage), pull the pan off the heat and place the bottom of the pan in the cold water to stop the cooling process. Add the cocoa, butter, vanilla, and salt. Stir for 60 seconds to incorporate and then add the walnuts, stir *once,* and pour the fudge into the prepared pan. Let it sit there for an hour, then cover it and let it sit for half a day before slicing and serving.

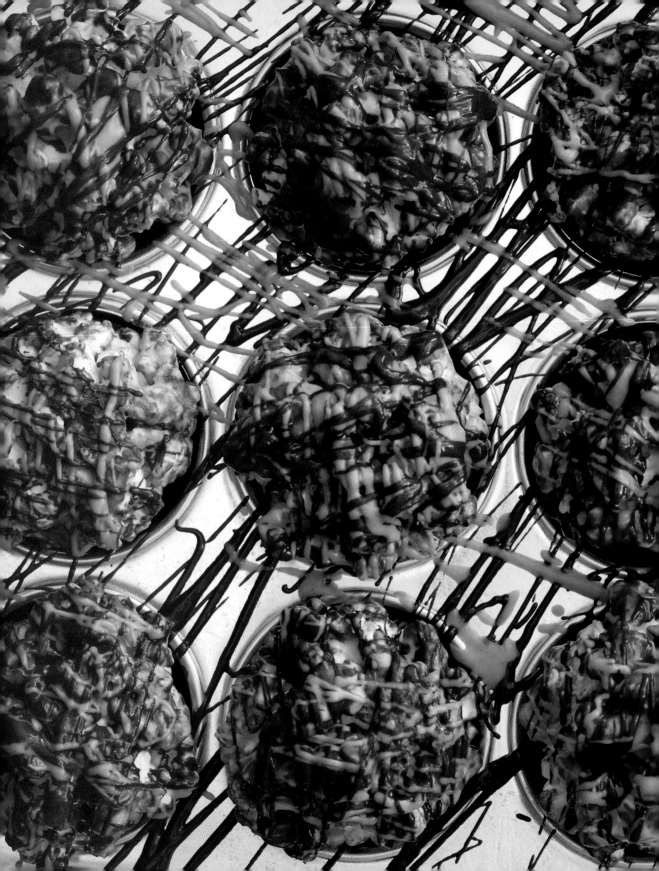

POPCORN BALLS

Popcorn balls are a great variation on Rice Krispies treats. They're super easy, fun to make with the kids, and you can customize them with anything you like. Mine have peanut butter and chocolate chips, but that's because I'm really just a five-year-old. —*Duff*

Makes 18 to 24 baseball-size balls

1 gallon plus 1 quart (that's 20 cups) plain popped popcorn (page 228)

1¾ cups peanut butter chips

1¾ cups milk chocolate chips

1 stick (½ cup) butter

2½ cups confectioners' sugar

¾ cup light corn syrup

1 cup mini marshmallows

Cooking spray

1. In a big bowl, combine the popcorn, 1¼ cups of the peanut butter chips, and 1¼ cups of the chocolate chips and toss to distribute evenly.

2. In a medium saucepan over low heat, melt the butter, sugar, corn syrup, and marshmallows, stirring constantly to keep the mixture from burning.

3. When the sugar mixture boils, pour it over the popcorn mixture and quickly but gently form balls. This isn't rocket surgery—make the balls the size you like. Place them in small bowls or the wells of a muffin tin that have been lightly coated with cooking spray so they hold their shape as they cool. Pretend you're making snowballs but don't pack them too hard.

4. In separate small saucepans over low heat, melt the remaining peanut butter chips and milk chocolate chips and drizzle the two over the cooled popcorn balls.

5. Wrap them in plastic when they're cool. *Do not* put them in the fridge—they'll get all melty and stale.

Options: One of the cool things about these balls is that they go great with savory flavors as well. Try them with chopped scallions and curry powder, or spicy Thai seasoning, or even Old Bay crab seasoning. Don't omit the sweet stuff if you want to make these savory, though—all the spicy, salty things you could add to these will only be that much more awesome when layered on top of sweetness.

POPCORN

In this day and age, everyone has a microwave and a mysterious white bag full of chemicals that when nuked, turns into popcorn. Don't be ridiculous. You're going to call yourself a baker and still pop popcorn in some weird machine that uses black magic to create heat? You're killing me, Smalls.

Makes 8 cups popped popcorn

3 tablespoons canola oil

¼ cup unpopped popping corn

1. In a large pot with a loose-fitting lid, heat the oil to 425°F (to measure the temp, carefully tilt the pot to one side and stick a deep-fry thermometer in the deepest part of the oil). When the oil is hot, turn the heat down to keep it at an even temperature. Toss in a few kernels and wait for them to pop.

2. Add the rest of the corn kernels. Place the lid slightly ajar to let steam escape but not the popcorn. Keep the popcorn on the heat until the popping begins to slow down. Shake the pot a few times to let the heavier unpopped kernels fall to the bottom and pop and to keep the popped popcorn from burning.

3. Remove the pan from the heat and let the popcorn continue to pop for a few minutes, until the popping sound stops.

4. Pour the popcorn into a bowl and either let it cool so you can work with it or butter and salt it so you can eat it.*

* Do not salt the kernels before they pop; it makes the popcorn tough and chewy. If you just want popcorn to snack on, butter and salt it after it's popped. Evidently you can also add Milk Duds or M&M's to it, but that's for weirdos. You can do fun things like adding curry powder or BBQ rubs or any other fun dried spice you have in your pantry. You can even go to 7-Eleven and get some of the nacho cheese goop they put on Big Bites.

SEA SALT–DARK CHOCOLATE TURTLES

These little candies are surprisingly easy to make, and crazy good. The addition of some butterscotch in the caramel gives it a unique twist and adding sea salt to contrast the sweetness just sends these turtles out of this world. Space turtles! —*Sara*

Makes 18 turtles

3 cups pecan halves

Cooking spray

1 stick (½ cup) butter

1 cup lightly packed light brown sugar

½ cup light corn syrup

⅛ teaspoon coarse sea salt, plus more for topping

1 cup sweetened condensed milk

¼ cup butterscotch chips

1 pound semisweet coating chocolate

1. Spread the pecans on a rimmed baking sheet and toast them at 350°F for about 10 minutes. Let cool.

2. Line three or four baking sheets with parchment paper and spray them with cooking spray. Arrange the cooled pecans in star-shaped clusters of five (the pecans should touch). One is the turtle's head and the other four are his feet!

3. To make the caramel, in a heavy saucepan over high heat with a candy thermometer attached, combine the butter, brown sugar, corn syrup, and salt. Stirring constantly, bring the mixture to a low boil. Stir in the condensed milk and keep stirring constantly as you bring the mixture to a full boil. Cook for about 20 minutes, or until the thermometer reaches 240°F.

4. Turn off the heat and add the butterscotch chips. Stir gently until they're completely melted and the mixture is smooth. Let the caramel cool until it's the consistency of thick honey.

5. Drop about 1 tablespoon of caramel onto the middle of each pecan cluster, making sure each pecan half is partly coated. If the caramel starts to get too thick to use, reheat over low heat, stirring constantly. Set the clusters aside to firm up.

6. Melt the chocolate until smooth, either in the large bowl of a double boiler or in the microwave in intervals of 30 seconds at low power. Spoon 1 tablespoon of the chocolate over each hardened turtle.

7. Sprinkle the tops of the turtles with sea salt and set aside to harden completely.

MARSHMALLOWS

I'm not sure I need to explain the majesty of making your own marshmallows, but the thing is, it's like a peek behind the curtain. If you could build a time machine and tell your ten-year-old self that you'll know how to make marshmallows from scratch, you'd think you were going to grow up to be like a wizard, but a really cool wizard that knows how to make candy. That's a win, yeah? —*Duff*

Makes 80 to 100 marshmallows

4(ish) cups powdered sugar

¼ cup powdered gelatin

2 cups granulated sugar

3 tablespoons light corn syrup

2 extra-large egg whites

Few drops of lemon juice

2 teaspoons pure vanilla extract

NOTE: Do this in exactly this order, okay? If you don't, you'll screw it up and I don't want to see your annoying tweets because you didn't listen to me.

1. Line a shallow 9 x 13-inch inch baking dish with plastic wrap and dust it very generously with powdered sugar.

2. Make sure the bowl for the stand mixer and the whip are super, super clean.

3. In a small bowl, bloom the gelatin in ¾ cup cold water and set it aside.

4. Fill a large bowl with cold water.

5. Put the granulated sugar, corn syrup, and ¼ cup water in a medium saucepan and turn the heat to high. Attach a candy thermometer to the pan.

6. Put the egg whites in the stand mixer and begin whipping them slowly with a few drops of lemon juice.

7. Cook the sugar mixture to the hard ball stage, or 260°F. At exactly 260°F, pull the pan off the heat and cool the bottom of the pan in the cold water.

8. Once the hot sugar has cooled a bit, stir in the bloomed gelatin.

9. Increase the speed of the mixer and add the vanilla to the egg whites, then slowly add the hot sugar mixture in a continuous stream, aiming it away from the whisk. Whip the hell out of it until it is bright white, shiny, and stiff.

10. Pull the marshmallow mixture off the mixer and quickly scrape the bowl clean into the plastic wrap–lined dish. Dust the top of the marshmallow mixture with powdered sugar from a sieve and place another piece of plastic on top. Push out all the air and let the marshmallow mixture sit at room temperature for at least 6 hours—overnight is best—to relax, cool, and set up.

11. Cut the marshmallows to your preferred size and lightly dust the cut edges with more powdered sugar to keep them from drying out. Keep your cutter or knife oiled to keep the marshmallows from sticking and tearing when you cut them.

Options: This recipe makes plain marshmallows, but you can add all kinds of awesome stuff to them in the mixer before they set up, like spices, nuts, chocolate chunks, food coloring, anything you can think of. Go nuts!

tapioca

lemons

potato
starch

garbanzo
flour

arrowroot

blueberries

coconut

white
rice
flour

VEGAN & GLUTEN-FREE BAKING

blackberries

almonds

almond
milk

xantham
gum

avocado

You might be thinking, cakes without eggs? Cookies without butter? Frosting without dairy? I do assure you that it's possible, and the most important thing is keeping an open and creative mind when it comes to substitutions. When dietary restrictions exclude dairy or gluten, there are almost always substitutions you can use to get around those ingredients. Earth Balance is a great butter substitute. Almond milk is a good thing. Rice flour, chickpea flour, and corn or potato starch can often work in place of flour. There are options out there!! This chapter will explore some of our tried and true (and *delicious*!) vegan and gluten-free recipes.

Vegan and gluten-free baking has gotten a bad rap because, when this first started being a thing, we bakers had to learn new ways of doing things and we made a lot of mistakes. You would be amazed at what bakers and pastry chefs have been able to come up with. Whether you're trying a diet for nutrition reasons or you have a dietary restriction, you don't have to suffer through gummy, nasty cakes anymore. Things have become so amazing that sometimes we serve our vegan chocolate cake to people without telling them. Not because we want to trick anybody, but because it is so delicious!

VEGAN CHOCOLATE CAKE

Possibly better than some more traditional chocolate cakes, this cake is moist, rich, and surprisingly light in texture. The coffee enhances the chocolate and lends a very decadent flavor. Vinegar is used in some vegan baking because its reaction with baking soda creates the leavening agent for the cake—and no, you can't taste the vinegar in the final product. —*Sara*

Makes one 2-layer, 9-inch round cake

2¼ cups all-purpose flour

1 cup plus 2 tablespoons granulated sugar

½ cup lightly packed light brown sugar

1½ teaspoons baking soda

¾ teaspoon kosher salt

⅓ cup unsweetened natural cocoa powder

1 cup plus 2 tablespoons soy milk

¾ cup brewed coffee, at room temperature

¾ cup vegetable oil

1½ teaspoons pure vanilla extract

1 tablespoon apple cider vinegar

Frosting of your choice (see page 254)

1. Preheat the oven to 350°F and grease and flour two 9-inch round cake pans.

2. In a big bowl, mix together all the dry ingredients.

3. In another medium bowl, mix together all the wet ingredients, adding the vinegar last.

4. Add the wet mixture to the dry and mix well.

5. Divide the batter evenly between the two cake pans and bake for 30 to 40 minutes, or until a toothpick inserted into the center comes out clean.

6. Let the cakes cool in the pans for 10 minutes, then turn them out upside down on a wire rack to cool completely. Frost with your favorite vegan and gluten-free frosting (see more on frosting cakes starting on page 302). Store in the fridge. This cake is best served within 1 or 2 days—you're not supposed to, but you're going to eat it before it goes stale.

VEGAN VANILLA CAKE

Here's a super-easy vanilla cake recipe for your favorite vegan, and it's also handy to have if you realize there are no eggs in the fridge. The cake is very moist and packs an awesome punch of vanilla flavor. Don't be shy; play around with the spices with this cake—it's a great vehicle for flavor. —*Sara*

Makes one 2-layer, 9-inch round cake

2⅔ cups all-purpose flour

1½ cups sugar

1½ teaspoons baking powder

1½ teaspoons baking soda

¾ teaspoon kosher salt

1½ cups soy milk

¾ cup vegetable oil

3 tablespoons pure vanilla extract

1½ tablespoons apple cider vinegar

Frosting of your choice (see page 254)

1. Preheat the oven to 350°F and grease and flour two 9-inch round cake pans.

2. In a big bowl, mix together all the dry ingredients.

3. In a medium bowl, whisk together all the wet ingredients, adding the vinegar last.

4. Add the wet mixture to the dry mixture and mix well.

5. Divide the batter evenly between the cake pans and bake for 30 to 40 minutes, or until a toothpick inserted into the center comes out clean.

6. Let the cakes cool completely in the pans on a wire rack. Turn them out of the pans and frost with your favorite vegan and gluten-free frosting (see more on frosting cakes starting on page 302).

VEGAN WHITE CAKE

Everybody loves white cake, and vegans have birthdays, too! —*Sara*

*Makes one 2-layer,
8- or 9-inch round cake*

1 cup all-purpose flour

1½ cups cake flour

¼ cup tapioca flour

1 tablespoon baking
powder

1 teaspoon baking soda

Big pinch of kosher salt

¾ cup sugar

¼ cup vegetable oil (or
olive or coconut oil)

1 tablespoon pure vanilla
extract

1½ cups almond or soy
milk

1 tablespoon freshly
squeezed lemon juice

Frosting of your choice
(see page 254)

1. Preheat the oven to 365°F and grease and flour two
   8- or 9-inch round cake pans.

2. In a medium bowl, whisk together the flours, baking powder,
   baking soda, and salt.

3. In another big bowl, whisk together the sugar, oil, and vanilla.

4. In a small bowl, whisk together the almond or soy milk and
   lemon juice. It'll look weird; don't worry. Let the mixture set for
   7 to 10 minutes, or until thickened, then whisk it into the sugar-
   oil mixture.

5. Very gently stir the dry mixture into the wet mixture until there
   are no lumps.

6. Divide the batter between the two pans and bake for
   20 minutes, or until it feels firm against your fingers.

7. Turn the cakes out upside down onto a wire rack to cool. Let
   the cakes cool completely and frost with your favorite vegan
   and gluten-free frosting (see more on frosting cakes starting
   on page 302).

VEGAN LEMON CAKE

Sometimes you just have to get a little fancier than vanilla or chocolate cake, and what to do if you avoid dairy? You go for a lemon cake. Even fancier? Add a little bit of ground lavender for a deep flavor boost! Believe me, people will be impressed, unless of course you refuse to share, which is entirely possible. —*Sara*

Makes one 2-layer, 9-inch round cake

2⅔ cups all-purpose flour

1½ cups sugar

1½ teaspoons baking powder

1½ teaspoons baking soda

¾ teaspoon kosher salt

2 teaspoons ground culinary lavender (optional)

1¼ cups soy milk

¾ cup vegetable oil

1 tablespoon pure vanilla extract

¼ cup freshly squeezed lemon juice

2 tablespoons lemon zest

1½ tablespoons apple cider vinegar

Frosting of your choice (see page 254)

1. Preheat the oven to 350°F and grease and flour two 9-inch round cake pans.

2. In a big bowl, mix together all the dry ingredients, including the ground lavender. (If you can't find ground lavender, a quick and easy way to grind it is in a large bowl with the end of a dowel-style rolling pin.)

3. In a medium bowl, whisk together the rest of the ingredients, adding vinegar last.

4. Add the wet mixture to the dry mixture and mix well, making sure there are no lumps. If so, just break them up with your fingers.

5. Divide the mixture between the cake pans and bake for 30 to 40 minutes, or until a toothpick inserted into the center comes out clean.

6. Let the cakes cool completely in the pans on a wire rack. Turn them out of the pans and frost with your favorite vegan and gluten-free frosting (see more on frosting cakes starting on page 302).

VEGAN CHOCOLATE-AVOCADO CAKE

I know—*avocado in a cake?! But why?!* Because avocado is amazing! It's butter that grows on trees! It has an awesome creamy texture, and it's high in all the healthy fats that aren't found in butter, so you can absolutely use it as a fat alternative in a cake. And the chocolate masks the flavor and color of the fruit, so your friends will really have no notion of the green intruder unless you tell them. —*Sara*

Makes one 2-layer, 9-inch round cake

Cooking spray

3 cups all-purpose flour

1/3 cup unsweetened natural cocoa powder

Pinch of kosher salt

2 teaspoons baking powder

2 teaspoons baking soda

1 ripe medium avocado, pitted, peeled, and pureed

1/4 cup coconut oil

1 cup brewed coffee, at room temperature

2 tablespoons apple cider vinegar

1 tablespoon pure vanilla extract

2 cups sugar

Frosting of your choice (see page 254)

1. Preheat the oven to 350°F and spray two 9-inch round cake pans with cooking spray. (Lining the pans with parchment circles is also helpful.)

2. In a big bowl, sift together the flour, cocoa powder, salt, baking powder, and baking soda. Set aside.

3. In a medium bowl, whisk the avocado and coconut oil.* Add the coffee, vinegar, vanilla, and 1 cup water and whisk until combined and smooth.

4. Whisk the sugar into the avocado mixture.

5. Stir the wet mixture into the dry mixture until just combined and smooth.

6. Divide the batter evenly between the pans and bake for 35 to 45 minutes, or until a toothpick inserted into the center of the cakes comes out clean.

7. Let cool at least 10 minutes in the pans, then invert the cakes onto wire racks. Let cool completely before frosting with your favorite vegan and gluten-free frosting (see more on frosting cakes starting on page 302).

* It's a whole lot easier to work with the coconut oil if you zap it in the microwave until it's soft and almost liquid. Coconut oil has a very low melting point; if it goes liquid and clear, that's totally cool.

VEGAN, GLUTEN-FREE & RAW CHOCOLATE MACAROONS

Okay, this one is *super*-easy, and if you have that one friend with a bunch of dietary limits and they want something sweet, make these. Everybody will love them. This is also a great recipe to experiment with. Use it as a base and try new flavors, such as orange zest, toasted almond, or freshly grated cinnamon. —*Sara*

Makes as many as you get

2 cups unsweetened shredded coconut, plus more to roll them in

½ cup coconut oil

½ cup plus 2 tablespoons unsweetened natural cocoa powder

¼ cup honey

1 teaspoon pure vanilla extract

Pinch of kosher salt

1. Blend all the ingredients in a food processor, mixing them in one at a time, in order.

2. Roll the mixture into 1- to 2-inch balls, roll the balls around in some more shredded coconut, and refrigerate or freeze them until firm to the touch. Serve cold but not frozen.

VEGAN & GLUTEN-FREE GRANOLA BARS

What can be said against granola bars? They're tasty, they're good for you, you can take them on the go, and they're an all-around great snack! Why pay money for them at the grocery store when you can make your own right in your kitchen?! This is a healthy, easy recipe that will make you leave those store-bought granola bars far, far behind. —*Sara*

Makes 18 bars

Cooking spray

4 cups old-fashioned rolled oats (not instant)

½ cup roughly chopped almonds

½ cup roughly chopped pecans

¼ cup sesame seeds

½ cup dried cranberries

3 tablespoons flaxseed meal

1 cup all-natural smooth peanut butter

½ cup honey

1 ripe banana, well mashed

½ teaspoon pure vanilla extract

1. Preheat the oven to 350°F. Spray a 9-inch square baking pan with cooking spray and line it with parchment paper long enough to extend over the edges of the pan. This will make it really easy to lift the bars out of the pan when they are ready.

2. In a big bowl, mix the oats, nuts, seeds, cranberries, and flaxseed meal until it's pretty evenly distributed.

3. In a medium saucepan over medium heat, combine the peanut butter, honey, banana, and vanilla. Stir until the peanut butter has melted and the mixture is combined and smooth, 3 to 4 minutes.

4. Pour the hot peanut butter mixture into the dry mixture and stir until evenly mixed.

5. Press the mixture into the baking pan, taking care to really press it firmly and evenly so that you end up with evenly sized bars.

6. Bake for 20 minutes, or until the edges are turning golden. Let cool completely, then refrigerate in the pan for at least 1 hour before cutting them.

7. To cut, turn the pan upside down over a cutting board and pull the parchment paper to release the 9-inch square onto the cutting board. Discard the parchment paper. For nice, uniform bars, use a ruler to cut them 1½ x 3 inches. This makes 18 perfect bars! Or cut them however you like.

VEGAN & GLUTEN-FREE TOASTED GRANOLA

This granola recipe is super-quick and easy to make, and it's a great snack for all day long. The coconut, spices, and vanilla make the house smell like Christmas while they're baking. Christmas. All year. —*Sara*

Makes 5 to 6 cups

Cooking spray

2 cups old-fashioned rolled oats (not instant)

1 cup unsalted sunflower seeds

1 cup sweetened shredded coconut

½ cup whole almonds

¾ cup pecan pieces

¼ cup coconut oil

¼ cup clover honey

1 tablespoon dark brown sugar

1 teaspoon pure vanilla extract

1 teaspoon ground cinnamon

½ teaspoon ground nutmeg

¼ teaspoon ground ginger

1 cup dried cranberries

1. Preheat the oven to 350°F. Line a baking sheet with parchment paper and lightly spray the paper with cooking spray.

2. In a big bowl, combine the oats, sunflower seeds, coconut, almonds, and pecans.

3. In a small saucepan over medium heat, whisk the remaining ingredients (except the cranberries) over medium heat until the coconut oil is melted and the brown sugar is dissolved.

4. Pour the coconut oil mixture over the oat mixture and use a spatula to fold until all the ingredients are evenly coated.

5. Pour the mixture onto the baking sheet and spread it in an even layer with the spatula. Bake for 15 minutes, stir, and bake 15 minutes more.

6. Stir in the dried cranberries, taking care to spread out the granola again. Bake for 5 minutes, then set aside to cool completely. Store at room temperature in an airtight container. This keeps for a while, like a month.

VEGAN & GLUTEN-FREE OATMEAL RAISIN COOKIES

No one wants to miss out on a delicious oatmeal raisin cookie just because they have dietary restrictions, right?! Of course not! Whip these up for the whole group and everyone will love them. —*Sara*

Makes 12 cookies

1 cup plus 2 tablespoons vegan butter substitute (I use Earth Balance sticks)

1 cup granulated sugar

1 cup lightly packed light brown sugar

2 tablespoons canola oil

½ ripe banana, well mashed

2 teaspoons pure vanilla extract

2 cups rice flour

¼ cup garbanzo bean or chickpea flour

1 teaspoon kosher salt

1 teaspoon baking soda

2 teaspoons ground cinnamon

2 cups raisins

1. Preheat the oven to 350°F and line a baking sheet with parchment paper.

2. With a hand or stand mixer, cream the butter substitute and the sugars for a few minutes, until light and fluffy.

3. Add the oil, banana, and vanilla and mix well.

4. In a medium bowl, mix the flours, salt, baking soda, and cinnamon. Add to the "butter" mixture and stir until combined. Stir in the raisins.

5. Form the dough into 1½-inch balls and place them on the prepared baking sheet at least 4 inches apart. I find it 100 percent easier to just use a 2-inch ice cream scoop, scraped flat to make uniform cookies. Slightly flatten each cookie with your hand to about 1 inch thickness.

6. Bake for 12 to 15 minutes, or until the cookies start to look golden around the edges.

7. Let the cookies cool on the baking sheet before you move them!

VEGAN & GLUTEN-FREE BLUEBERRY MUFFINS

In addition to being both gluten- and dairy-free, these muffins are soy-free, and they taste *amazing*. Seriously, like better than regular muffins. They're moist, fluffy, and absolutely brimming with blueberries. —Sara

Makes 12 muffins

MUFFINS

2½ cups white rice flour

½ cup garbanzo bean or chickpea flour

1½ cups granulated sugar

1½ teaspoons baking powder

1½ teaspoons baking soda

¾ teaspoon kosher salt

1½ cups almond milk

¾ cup canola oil

3 tablespoons pure vanilla extract

2 tablespoons apple cider vinegar

3 cups frozen blueberries

STREUSEL

2 tablespoons old-fashioned rolled oats (not instant)

2 tablespoons white rice flour

2 tablespoons brown sugar

2 tablespoons soy-free vegan butter (we like Earth Balance), melted

1. Preheat the oven to 350°F and line a 12-cup muffin pan with paper muffin cups.

2. In a large mixing bowl, whisk together the flours, granulated sugar, baking powder, baking soda, and salt.

3. In a large measuring cup, combine the almond milk, oil, vanilla, and vinegar. Add to the dry mixture and whisk to combine.

4. Fold in the blueberries. The batter will be somewhat thin, so I like to pipe the batter into the muffin cups (it's also much less messy). Fill each cup up three-quarters of the way with the batter.

5. Bake for 15 minutes.

6. Meanwhile, combine all the streusel ingredients and stir lightly until just combined.

7. Sprinkle the muffins evenly with streusel topping. Quickly return them to the oven and bake for 15 to 20 minutes more, or until a toothpick inserted into the center of a muffin comes out clean.

8. Let the muffins cool in the pan for a few minutes, then remove them from the pan and let them cool completely on a wire rack.

VEGAN & GLUTEN-FREE LEMON-GLAZED DOUGHNUTS

These little doughnuts are super fun to make and are incredibly delicious. Vegan and gluten-free baking really shines with these little guys. Make 'em small because they're nice bite-sized, and the baking time is reduced, which makes a much more moist doughnut. Serve them the same day—nobody likes day-old doughnuts! —*Sara*

Makes about 3 dozen little doughnuts

DOUGHNUTS

1 cup granulated sugar

¾ cup white rice flour

⅓ cup garbanzo bean or chickpea flour

½ cup potato starch

¼ cup arrowroot

1½ tablespoons baking powder

½ teaspoon xanthan gum

½ teaspoon kosher salt

¼ teaspoon baking soda

6 tablespoons unsweetened applesauce

¼ cup pure vanilla extract

1 teaspoon lemon extract

¾ cup hot water (not warm, *hot!*)

⅔ cup canola oil

1 tablespoon lemon zest

LEMON GLAZE

1 cup powdered sugar

1 tablespoon freshly squeezed lemon juice

2 teaspoons lemon zest

1 tablespoon almond milk

SPECIAL EQUIPMENT

Mini-doughnut pan

1. Preheat the oven to 350°F and liberally spray a mini-doughnut pan with cooking spray.

2. To make the doughnuts: In a big bowl, whisk the dry ingredients.

3. In a medium bowl, whisk the wet ingredients and lemon zest.

4. Pour the wet mixture into the dry mixture and whisk until well combined.

5. Pour the batter into a piping bag or a gallon-size plastic sealable bag (you'll have to cut off a corner of the bag). Pipe the batter into the wells of the pan, filling each mold about three-quarters full.

6. Bake for 8 to 10 minutes, or until the doughnuts spring back lightly when touched. Remove the doughnuts from the pan and set them on a wire rack to cool completely. Repeat with any remaining batter.

7. To make the lemon glaze: Whisk all the ingredients in a medium bowl.

8. Dip the tops of the doughnuts in the glaze and lay them on a wire rack to set up.

VEGAN & GLUTEN-FREE BANANA-WALNUT MUFFINS

It may be hard to believe that you can transform such a down-home comfort food into something you can find at a health food market, but these muffins will make you a believer. With their delightful combination of banana, spices, and toasted walnuts on top, these muffins are absolutely going to rule. —*Sara*

Makes 12 muffins

2½ cups white rice flour

½ cup garbanzo bean or chickpea flour

1½ cups sugar

1 tablespoon ground cinnamon

1 teaspoon ground nutmeg

1½ teaspoons baking powder

1½ teaspoons baking soda

¾ teaspoon kosher salt

1½ cups almond milk

¾ cup canola oil

3 tablespoons pure vanilla extract

2 tablespoons apple cider vinegar

2 VERY RIPE bananas, mashed

2 cups walnuts, roughly chopped

1. Preheat the oven to 350°F and line a 12-cup muffin pan with paper muffin cups.

2. In a big bowl, whisk the flours, sugar, cinnamon, nutmeg, baking powder, baking soda, and salt.

3. In a big measuring cup, combine the almond milk, oil, vanilla, and vinegar.

4. Combine the bananas, wet mixture, and dry mixture and whisk to combine.

5. The batter will be somewhat thin, so I like to pipe the batter into the muffin cups (it's also much less messy). Fill each cup up three-quarters full and top with a sprinkle of walnuts.

6. Bake for 25 minutes, or until the muffins are browned on the top and a toothpick inserted into the center comes out clean.

7. Let the muffins cool in the pan for a few minutes, then pull the muffins out to cool completely on a wire rack.

VEGAN & GLUTEN-FREE FRUIT & ALMOND SHORTBREAD BARS

These are an absolute favorite of everyone in the bakery (I have to yell at them to stop eating them); they can't believe these light, buttery-tasting shortbread bars are actually vegan and gluten-free. They're so good. I like to use blackberry or boysenberry preserves for these bars, but I've also used homemade cranberry and even store-bought apricot preserves and they all come out awesome! —*Sara*

Makes 16 bars

2 sticks (1 cup) vegan
    butter or margarine
    (we like Earth Balance)

½ cup sugar

½ teaspoon pure vanilla
    extract

½ teaspoon almond
    extract

1 cup almond flour

½ cup white rice flour

½ cup potato starch

¼ teaspoon kosher salt

1 cup fruit preserves

Sliced almonds, for topping

1. Preheat the oven to 350°F and grease an 8-inch or 9-inch square pan.

2. With a hand or stand mixer, beat the vegan butter and sugar until light and fluffy. Add the vanilla and almond extracts.

3. In a medium bowl, mix the flours, starch, and salt.

4. Add the dry ingredients to the "butter" mixture and mix until just incorporated.

5. Press two-thirds of the dough into the pan and bake for about 10 minutes, or until the crust is pale light brown. Remove it from the oven.

6. When the pan has cooled enough to handle, spread the preserves evenly over the crust.

7. Break the remaining dough into little tiny pieces and drop them evenly over the jam. Top with the almonds.

8. Bake for another 25 to 30 minutes, or until the top is a nice golden brown.

9. Cut into bars and serve immediately, while still warm, or store them in the refrigerator.

Options: To make in a non-GF/vegan version, use regular butter and substitute equal amounts all-purpose flour for the rice flour and potato starch.

VEGAN & GLUTEN-FREE "BUTTERCREAMS"

Cake needs frosting. Vegan cake needs vegan frosting. Here are two basic recipes that will get you started, but please—experiment! See where you can take these frostings. Add flavor, change texture, get wild with them. I always say that just because it's vegan doesn't mean it can't be awesome. —*Sara*

Makes enough to cover a
2-layer, 9-inch cake

VANILLA

½ cup vegan butter substitute (Earth Balance sticks work great), at room temperature

4 cups powdered sugar

2 teaspoons pure vanilla extract

¼ teaspoon kosher salt

4 to 6 tablespoons soymilk

CHOCOLATE

½ cup vegan butter substitute (Earth Balance sticks work great), at room temperature

3½ cups powdered sugar

½ cup unsweetened natural cocoa powder

2 teaspoons pure vanilla extract

¼ teaspoon kosher salt

5 to 7 tablespoons soymilk

"CREAM CHEESE"

¼ cup vegan butter substitute (Earth Balance sticks work great), at room temperature

¼ cup vegan cream cheese substitute, at room temperature (Tofutti is a good one)

3¾ cups powdered sugar

1 teaspoon pure vanilla extract

¼ teaspoon kosher salt

4 to 5 tablespoons soymilk

In the bowl of a stand mixer fitted with the paddle attachment, beat the "butter" (and "cream cheese," if using) until creamy. Add the sugar 1 cup at a time, mixing after each addition. Mix in the vanilla, salt, and/or any other flavorings or extracts. Add the soymilk or juice a bit at a time and mix to the desired consistency. Beat until smooth.

LEMON

½ cup vegan butter substitute (Earth Balance sticks work great), at room temperature

4 cups powdered sugar

Pinch of kosher salt

4 to 6 tablespoons freshly squeezed lemon juice

1 tablespoon lemon zest

ORANGE

½ cup vegan butter substitute (Earth Balance sticks work great), at room temperature

4 cups powdered sugar

Pinch of kosher salt

4 to 6 tablespoons freshly squeezed orange juice

1 tablespoon orange zest

ALMOND

½ cup vegan butter substitute (Earth Balance sticks work great), at room temperature

4 cups powdered sugar

1½ teaspoons almond extract

¼ teaspoon kosher salt

4 to 6 tablespoons soymilk

CAKES

I think about cakes all the time. I say the word hundreds of times a day. They consume my life, they haunt my dreams, and they bring me endless joy. But cakes are a bit tricky. Much like cookies, you have to pull them out of the oven at the right time. Beyond that, you have to treat your cakes right. Freeze them or keep them at room temperature, but don't put them in the fridge. Would you put Wonder bread in the fridge? Of course not. You know it would go stale in a day or two. Well, Wonder bread is really just cake without quite as much sugar. I'd explain the science of starch molecules, but it would probably bore you to death, so just respect your cakes enough to keep them out of the fridge. Once a cake is iced, keep it in the fridge but serve at room temperature, and obviously, keep cheesecakes in the fridge. And crabcakes, too.

Charm City Cakes probably has more than sixty cake flavors on the menu. I could write a whole book on just those, but let's let these nine suffice for now. These fantastic cake recipes can be tailored to your every whim. Once you have the basics of these cakes down, feel free to experiment and try new flavors. I really mean it when I say that baking is more spontaneous than most people realize, and cakes are a great example of this. Once you understand a particular cake base recipe, it's easy to doctor it and evolve the cake into anything you want.

That said, I'm the guy who makes cakes, and these recipes are awesome. So tinker at your own peril! I'm kidding; enjoy my cakes.

CHOCOLATE CAKE

Who doesn't love a good chocolate cake? A crazy person, that's who. —*Sara*

Makes one 2-layer, 9-inch round cake

2 cups all-purpose flour

2 cups sugar

1 teaspoon baking soda

1 teaspoon kosher salt

2 sticks (1 cup) butter

½ cup brewed coffee

⅓ cup unsweetened natural cocoa powder

3 extra-large eggs

½ cup buttermilk

2 teaspoons pure vanilla extract

Frosting of your choice (see page 282)

1. Preheat the oven to 350°F and grease and flour two 9-inch round cake pans.

2. In a big bowl, mix the flour, sugar, baking soda, and salt.

3. In a medium saucepan over medium heat, melt the butter. Whisk in the coffee, cocoa powder, and ½ cup water and heat it for a minute, stirring constantly. Pour the melted butter mixture into the flour mixture and whisk until well combined.

4. In a medium bowl, whisk the eggs, buttermilk, and vanilla. Add it to the batter and mix until smooth.

5. Divide the batter between the two cake pans, scraping all the batter from the bowl with a rubber spatula. Bake for about 40 minutes, or until a toothpick inserted into the center comes out clean. Let cool for 15 minutes in the pans and then turn out onto a wire rack to cool completely.

6. Frost with the frosting of your choice (see more on frosting cakes starting on page 302).

Variation: The water/coffee combo in this recipe can be switched up, but remember, coffee is to chocolate like salt is to beef. Coffee brings out the flavor of chocolate without making it taste like coffee, just as salt brings out the flavor of meat without making it taste salty. The liquid you use can be all water, or it can be a full cup of coffee for more of a mocha-flavored cake. And if you're feeling really bold, go ahead and use a cup of a dark stout beer instead. Top it with an Irish Cream buttercream (see the recipe on page 286 but use butter, powdered sugar, and Baileys). Get creative and experiment a little—after all, it is a science project.

You'll know a cake is done if the cake springs back when pressed lightly in the center or a toothpick inserted into the center comes out clean. The cake will slightly shrink away from the sides of the pans. To get your cake out of the pan, allow it to cool in the pan for 10 to 15 minutes, then run a small offset spatula around the outside of a layer to loosen it from the pan. Carefully flip the cake out of the pan onto a wire rack. Place the cake right-side up on the rack and let it cool completely before icing.

SOUTHERN WHITE CAKE

White cake is not angel food cake. They're similar in that they don't use the egg yolks, so the cake stays white, but white cake is denser, richer, and firmer than angel food. Serve this cake frosted with butter-cream and maybe some sweetened flaked coconut. This cake is a staple in any traditionally Southern home or bakeshop. —*Duff*

Makes one 3-layer, 9-inch round cake

8 extra-large egg whites

2½ cups sugar

3 sticks (1½ cups) butter, softened

Pinch of kosher salt

2 cups cake flour

2 cups all-purpose flour

1½ tablespoons baking powder

2 teaspoons pure vanilla extract

1 tablespoon vegetable oil

Frosting of your choice (see page 282)

1. Preheat the oven to 350°F and butter and flour three 9-inch round cake pans.

2. In the clean bowl of a stand mixer fitted with the whisk attachment, beat the egg whites and 1¼ cups of the sugar until you have a stiff, shiny meringue. Very gently transfer to a separate bowl and set aside.

3. Switch to the paddle attachment (no need to wash the mixer bowl) and cream the butter, remaining 1¼ cups sugar, and the salt until creamy.

4. In a medium bowl, whisk together the flours and baking powder.

5. Slowly add the flour mixture, vanilla, and oil to the butter mixture while the mixer is on low speed. Stop the mixer and gently fold in the meringue by hand until combined.

6. Divide the batter evenly among the three pans, scraping all the batter from the bowl with a rubber spatula. Bake for 20 to 25 minutes, or until a toothpick inserted into the center comes out clean.

7. Let the cakes set up in the pan for 15 to 20 minutes, then remove them a wire rack to finish cooling.

8. Frost with the frosting of your choice (see more on frosting cakes starting on page 302).

VANILLA BIRTHDAY CAKE

No one can pass up a slice of birthday cake! Buttery, fluffy, and moist, this vanilla birthday cake can be frosted with pretty much any buttercream of your choosing. Throw a candle on top and a scoop of ice cream on the side and you'll be struggling to get the Happy Birthday song out of your head for weeks—and don't forget to pick up pin-the-tail-on-the-donkey! —*Sara*

Makes one 2-layer, 9-inch round cake

Cooking spray

1½ sticks (¾ cup) butter, softened

1½ cups sugar

2 extra-large eggs plus 3 egg whites, at room temperature

2¼ teaspoons pure vanilla extract

3 cups cake flour

1 tablespoon plus 1 teaspoon baking powder

¾ teaspoon kosher salt

1 cup milk

½ cup sprinkles, jimmies, whatever you wanna call 'em

Frosting of your choice (see page 282)

1. Preheat the oven to 350°F. Grease two 9-inch round cake pans with cooking spray and line them with parchment paper rounds.

2. In the bowl of a stand mixer fitted with the paddle attachment, cream the butter and sugar for about 2 minutes, until light and fluffy.

3. Add the eggs one at a time, beating after each addition. Beat in the egg whites, scraping the sides of the bowl as you go. Add the vanilla and beat on medium-high speed for about 1 minute.

4. In a medium bowl, whisk the flour, baking powder, and salt.

5. Mix the flour mixture and milk into the egg mixture in three parts—flour-milk-flour—taking care to scrape the sides as you go and incorporating each addition well. Mix until smooth. Gently fold in the sprinkles by hand.

6. Divide the batter evenly between the cake pans, scraping all the batter from the bowl with a rubber spatula. Bake for 25 to 30 minutes, or until a toothpick inserted into the center of the cake comes out clean.

7. Let the cakes cool in the pans on a wire rack for 10 to 15 minutes, then turn them out onto the rack to finish cooling.

8. Frost with the frosting of your choice (see more on frosting cakes starting on page 302).

ANGEL FOOD CAKE

Top this deliciously light and fluffy cake with homemade whipped cream and sliced strawberries macerated (see page 24) in a tablespoon of sugar for a delightful strawberry shortcake dessert. Or, plate slices with the coulis on page 292. Add some ice cream in there, too! If you don't have superfine sugar, it's okay—just throw your regular sugar in the food processor for a couple minutes and it will be as fine as it needs to be. —*Sara*

Makes one 10-inch tube cake

1 cup cake flour

1½ cups superfine sugar

12 extra-large egg whites

1½ teaspoons cream of tartar

¼ teaspoon kosher salt

1 cup granulated sugar

1½ teaspoons pure vanilla extract

½ teaspoon lemon extract (optional)

1. Preheat the oven to 375°F. Make sure you have a nonstick 10 x 4-inch angel food pan. If you aren't sure if the pan is nonstick, you can lightly spray it with a cooking spray—*lightly*! The way an angel food cake works is that it climbs up the side of the pan as it bakes. You don't want the pan too slippery.

2. Sift the flour and superfine sugar into a medium bowl.

3. In the bowl of a stand mixer fitted with the whisk attachment, beat the egg whites, cream of tartar, and salt until foamy. Add the granulated sugar gradually—about 2 tablespoons at a time—beating constantly, until the meringue is stiff.

4. Lightly fold in the extracts, then fold in the flour mixture ¼ cup at a time—very, *very* gently.

5. Carefully spoon the batter into the pan and bake 30 to 35 minutes, or until the top of the cake springs back when tapped.

6. Let it cool in the pan for 5 minutes tops, then flip the pan over onto a wire rack and let the cake cool upside down, still in the pan. This keeps the cake from sinking in on itself. Remove the pan after 15 minutes and let it cool completely.

7. Frost with the frosting of your choice (see more on frosting cakes starting on page 302).

COCONUT MERINGUE CAKE

My grandmother lived in Wichita, Kansas, and she could no doubt cook, but she couldn't bake to save her life. Which is weird, because she was a silversmith and a photographer and had limitless patience. My great-grandmother could bake, my mom can bake, and I'm no slouch, but Nana's specialty was smokies (small, smoked breakfast sausages popular in the Midwest), and she'd make them in a cast-iron skillet every time we visited her.

But one thing she could bake—and did almost every time we'd visit—was this coconut meringue cake.

—Duff

Makes one 2-layer, 9-inch round cake

CAKE

2 cups cake flour

2 teaspoons baking powder

Pinch of kosher salt

1 stick (½ cup) plus 2⅔ tablespoons butter, softened

1¼ cups sugar

½ teaspoon coconut extract (optional but recommended)

1 teaspoon pure vanilla extract

3 extra-large eggs, separated

1 cup whole milk

ICING AND GARNISH

1½ cups sugar

2 extra-large egg whites

Pinch of cream of tartar

Pinch of salt

8 ounces mini marshmallows

1 teaspoon orange zest

1¼ cups sweetened shredded coconut

1. To make the cake: Preheat the oven to 350°F and grease and flour two 9-inch round cake pans.

2. Sift the flour, baking powder, and salt into a medium bowl.

3. With a hand mixer in a large bowl or in the bowl of a stand mixer fitted with the paddle attachment, cream the butter, sugar, coconut extract, and vanilla extract until light and fluffy, about 3 minutes. Add the egg yolks and beat thoroughly.

4. Add half the dry mixture, then the milk, then the rest of the dry mixture to the butter mixture, beating well and scraping the sides of the bowl after each addition.

5. In a separate large bowl, beat the egg whites with a whisk until stiff. Gently fold them into the cake batter.

6. Divide the batter between the pans, scraping all the batter from the bowl with a rubber spatula. Bake for 30 to 35 minutes, or until a toothpick inserted into the center comes out clean. Let the cakes cool completely in the pans. Lower the oven temperature to 325°F.

7. To make the icing and garnish: Combine the sugar, egg whites, cream of tartar, salt, marshmallows, remaining ½ cup coconut, and ⅓ cup water in the top of a double boiler. Over simmering water, whisk constantly for 8 to 10 minutes, or until the icing will hold a peak. Remove from the heat, add the orange zest, and whisk until the icing is cooled and thick enough to spread.

8. Frost with the icing and press the coconut all over the cake.

CARROT CAKE

Easily the entire bakery's favorite cake. Something about the spices and moistness and the cream cheese frosting and the . . . I don't know, it's just perfection. This recipe is a basic carrot cake, but— feeling crazy? Add some golden raisins, add pecans, add 'em both! I like all kinds of junk in my carrot cake. —*Sara*

Makes one 2-layer, 9-inch round cake

6 extra-large eggs

2¼ cups vegetable or olive oil

1¾ cups plus 1 tablespoon granulated sugar

¾ cup lightly packed light brown sugar

2¼ cups all-purpose flour

2 teaspoons baking powder

1½ teaspoons baking soda

2½ teaspoons ground cinnamon

¾ teaspoon ground nutmeg

Pinch of ground cloves

¾ teaspoon kosher salt

1½ pounds carrots, peeled and finely grated

¾ cup golden raisins (optional)

¾ cup chopped pecans (optional)

Cream Cheese Frosting (page 287)

1. Preheat the oven to 350°F and grease and flour two 9-inch round cake pans.

2. With a hand or stand mixer, mix the eggs and oil. Add the sugars and mix well.

3. In a medium bowl, mix the rest of the ingredients except the carrots (and raisins and nuts, if using).

4. Add the flour mixture to the sugar mixture and mix well.

5. Add the carrots (and raisins and nuts, if desired) and mix until incorporated.

6. Divide the batter evenly between the pans, scraping all the batter from the bowl with a rubber spatula. Bake for 35 to 40 minutes, or until a toothpick inserted into the center comes out clean.

7. Let cool in the pans for 15 minutes, then turn out onto a wire rack to cool completely. Frost with the Cream Cheese Frosting (see more on frosting cakes starting on page 302).

HUMMINGBIRD CAKE

I was in the Adirondack Mountains in upstate New York when I first heard of hummingbird cake. I was making a wedding cake for this awesome chef I used to work for, Steve Mannino, and his mom was this cool old Italian lady who decided that since I was a pastry chef and she was old, I would make all the cannoli. I worked in her kitchen and she sat in the corner and yelled at me for about four hours while I made all the shells and filling from scratch and set up the dipping station. Various members of the family would stop by and laugh as this four-foot-tall woman was ordering me around her kitchen like an intern. But it was awesome—she was a cool lady, and that cannoli lesson has stuck with me ever since.

What does this have to do with hummingbird cake? Steve's sister came by to laugh at my indentured servitude and asked me if I'd ever heard of hummingbird cake. I said no and she handed me a piece of paper with a recipe on it. It was like some kind of initiation or something.

Anyway, I made the cake when I got back to Baltimore, and it was delicious, so I added it to the Charm City Cakes menu. Here's the recipe, a bit doctored from the original, and whenever you make it, picture me getting hollered at by an old Italian lady while making cannoli in a tiny kitchen—and laughing the whole time. —Duff

Makes one 3-layer,
9- or 10-inch round cake

2½ cups all-purpose flour

2 cups cake flour

3 cups sugar

1½ teaspoons kosher salt

1 tablespoon ground cinnamon

Pinch of ground nutmeg

Tiny pinch of ground cloves

Tiny pinch of ground cardamom

1½ teaspoons baking soda

2 cups vegetable oil (olive oil works awesome; that's how I do it)

4 extra-large eggs plus 2 egg yolks

2 teaspoons pure vanilla extract

1 (12-ounce) can crushed pineapple, drained

2½ cups mashed-up over-ripe bananas

1½ cups toasted chopped pecans

Cream Cheese Frosting (page 287)

Sliced maraschino cherries (optional)

Pineapple rings (optional)

1. Preheat the oven to 350°F and prep three 9- or 10-inch round cake pans with butter and flour.

2. In a medium bowl, whisk the flours, sugar, salt, spices, and baking soda.

3. In a big bowl, whisk the oil, eggs, egg yolks, vanilla, pineapple, and bananas really well.

4. Add the flour mixture into the wet mixture and whisk gently until there are no lumps. Fold in ¾ cup of the pecans.

5. Divide the batter among the pans, scraping all the batter from the bowl with a rubber spatula. Bake for 35 to 50 minutes, depending on your oven. Be advised: This is a dense, moist cake and you'll be tempted to overbake it. Try not to. Once you start seeing color on top, keep pressing the top of the cake. When it's firm, it's done.

6. Turn out the cake layers onto a wire rack and let them cool completely. Frost with the cream cheese frosting (see more on frosting cakes starting on page 302) and garnish with the remaining ¾ cup pecans and—if you're feeling very Southern— sliced maraschino cherries. You can even brûlée some pineapple slices for the top of the cake.

RED VELVET CAKE

A Southern classic, but with many interpretations. "How much cocoa powder should *really* go in there?" "How much red food coloring?" "*My* grandmother didn't use vinegar." And so on, and so on. Everyone has their special recipe, and here's a relatively traditional version we use at Charm City Cakes. —*Sara*

Makes one 2-layer, 9-inch round cake

2 extra-large eggs

1½ cups sugar

1½ cups vegetable oil

1½ teaspoons white vinegar

2½ cups cake flour

1 teaspoon baking soda

½ teaspoon baking powder

2 tablespoons unsweetened natural cocoa powder

1 cup buttermilk, at room temperature

1 teaspoon pure vanilla extract

2 tablespoons red food coloring (you can find larger bottles of food coloring at any cake and candy supply store or online)

Cream Cheese Frosting (page 287)

1. Preheat the oven to 350°F. Generously grease two 9-inch round cake pans and line them with parchment circles if available.

2. With a hand or stand mixer and the paddle attachment, cream the eggs, sugar, oil, and vinegar until creamy.

3. In a medium bowl, whisk the flour, baking soda, baking powder, and cocoa powder.

4. While beating, add the flour mixture to the creamed mixture, then slowly add the warm buttermilk, vanilla, and food coloring.

5. Divide the batter between the pans, scraping all the batter from the bowl with a rubber spatula. Bake for 30 to 35 minutes, or until a toothpick inserted into the center comes out clean.

6. Let cool in the pans for 10 minutes, then invert the cakes onto wire racks and let them cool completely.

7. Frost with the Cream Cheese Frosting (see more on frosting cakes starting on page 302).

BOMB CHEESECAKE

The "bomb" refers to how awesome this cheesecake is, not to the old-school French domed cake called "bombe." This cheesecake is a blank. It's super easy to make and it's great for getting creative with. I've made literally thousands of these, adding everything from chocolate to nuts to spices and even herbs. You can even swap out the cream cheese for goat cheese. But if it's classic you're going for, don't be afraid to serve it with cheap-ass canned cherry pie filling.

I bake my cheesecakes in regular cake pans, not springform pans. There's nothing wrong with a springform pan; it's just that most people don't have one. That's okay. I have a method to get the cheesecake out that totally works and will save you a trip to the store and $30 for a new pan (see page 279).

This recipe is easy, but read the whole thing before you start. The directions may seem complicated, but they're not. It's just that the perfect cheesecake needs to be made exactly right, and all the little details in here really add up to success. —Duff

Makes one 10-inch cheesecake

1 cup plus 2 tablespoons sugar

2 cups graham cracker crumbs

1 stick (½ cup) butter, melted and hot

Kosher salt

Cooking spray

1 whole vanilla bean, scraped (you can use 2 teaspoons pure vanilla extract, but the flavor of a whole bean is extraordinary)

3 (8-ounce) packages cream cheese, at room temperature

2 extra-large eggs plus 1 egg yolk, at room temperature

2 tablespoons cornstarch

1 cup sour cream, at room temperature

1. Make sure all the ingredients are at room temperature (except the butter). Don't even try to make this cheesecake with cold ingredients. You'll fail and blame me.

2. Preheat the oven to 350°F. Place a large cake or casserole pan full of water on the lower rack. Make sure this never goes dry during the baking process. This will help keep your cheesecake from forming a skin and cracking.

3. In a medium bowl, mix 6 tablespoons of the sugar, the graham cracker crumbs, the butter, and a pinch of salt. Lay the crumb mixture in the bottom of a 10-inch cake pan and press it down very firmly and flat. Get this part right—it really affects how this cheesecake cuts later on. Using all your weight, really press down on the crust. Find something flat and heavy like a jar with a lid on it. Use the lid side to press the crust perfectly even. Also, I make the crust totally level—I don't round it up the sides of the pan. That way it doesn't break when you cut it.

4. Once your crust is perfect, lightly spray the sides of the cake pan with cooking spray. Cut a few long strips of parchment paper and line the sides of the cake pan. Spray the paper with the cooking spray and place the pan in the freezer.

5. In the bowl of a stand mixer fitted with the paddle attachment (*not the whisk!*), cream the remaining ¾ cup sugar, the vanilla seeds, cream cheese, and a pinch of salt *on medium speed* until smooth. Add the eggs, yolk, and cornstarch and slowly blend until combined, stopping and scraping the bowl at least twice. Add the sour cream and slowly mix it in, stopping and scraping the bowl twice.

6. Pull the bowl off the machine and bang it hard on the counter 10 times. Let it sit for 10 minutes. Watch the top—you'll see little air bubbles come up to the top and burst. If they don't pop by themselves, use a bamboo skewer. Those little air bubbles will kill a cheesecake. They are evil. They will expand in the oven and instead of getting a smooth cheesecake, you'll get a mealy one. Also, your cheesecake will soufflé in the oven and crack on top.

7. Slowly pour the batter onto the crust, filling it to about ¼ inch from the top. Don't let the mix get behind the paper.

8. Bake for 30 minutes, then lower the oven temperature to 315°F and bake for 45 to 50 minutes more, until the center is set. Turn off the oven and crack the door open (this is why your oven door has that spot where it will stay open a crack) and leave the cake in the oven for 90 minutes.

9. Let the cheesecake cool at room temperature for 1 hour, then freeze it for 2 hours.

GETTING CHEESECAKE OUT OF A CAKE PAN

To remove a cheesecake from a regular cake pan, run a paring knife around the edge behind the paper wrapper and make sure nothing is stuck to the sides of the cake pan. Turn on the stove and hold the bottom of the pan briefly over the flame or burner to melt anything that's making the pan stick to the bottom of the cheesecake. Lay out a lightly sprayed piece of parchment paper and slam the pan face down on it. Punch the bottom of the pan a few times and bang the edges until the cheesecake comes out on its own. Remove any paper stuck to the cheesecake. Get your hand under the parchment and under the cheesecake, flip it over onto a flat plate, and remove the top piece of parchment. Let the cheesecake thaw before serving.

GOO FOR CAKES

Cakes usually need some kind of gooey stuff, and this chapter is all about the different frostings and sauces I like. They'll be incredibly helpful and delicious as you progress into making your cakes not only something to eat, but something pretty to look at as well. I love the word "goo" because it's playful and descriptive and it shows that you can be very serious about your work, but it doesn't mean you have to take yourself so seriously.

We use these recipes at Charm City Cakes every day. That should mean something. We make the best cakes in the world, and those cakes deserve the finest goo. We think about our goo a lot. We study it and talk about it—our fascination with it is what makes our cakes so special. For example, I've been on a crusade for a long time to help the cake-consuming population understand what buttercream really means. It's not "frosting." It's not "icing." Swiss buttercream, the kind we use at Charm City Cakes, is a combination of meringue, butter, and sugar in a specific ratio using a specific method. Cheap birthday cakes that come on thin, shiny cardboard are made with "frosting."

It's funny how most quality baking involves the simplest of ingredients, made using the right ratios, and executed with diligence and caution. I think that might explain why some people are afraid to bake. A stew, for example, is pretty easy. Put a bunch of stuff in a pot and boil it for a while and chances are you'll get something that passes for food. It's much easier to make a mistake when you have so few ingredients, so I can understand the trepidation.

But don't be scared! One, you have me, and two, it's just goo. The world won't end if you have to start over.

SWISS BUTTERCREAM

This is the official Charm City Cakes buttercream. It's based on Swiss meringue and provides the correct consistency for icing cakes and decorating. Swiss buttercream is sturdier than a cold French meringue buttercream and much easier to make that a hot Italian meringue buttercream (see page 27 for more detail). It's super versatile and can be flavored and colored however you want it. You can also airbrush it, but lightly, as the high fat content will resist any substantial amount of liquid.

There are a few things to be aware of with any meringue-based buttercream:

* You can store it at room temperature for 24 hours; more than that and you need to keep it in the fridge.

* If you're not using it directly after making it, you always want to rewhip it right before use by beating it in the mixer with the whisk attachment and adding a bit of heat from a kitchen torch until it looks right.

* If you're planning on using buttercream that has been kept cold, pull it out of the fridge about 2 hours before you intend to use it, whip and heat it, and then you're ready to go.

* Sometimes you'll see people dip a spatula into hot water before icing a cake. This is wrong. If you heat the buttercream to the correct workable temperature, you won't need a warm, wet spatula.

* Swiss buttercream keeps for about a week in the fridge, but it's always good to just make what you need when using egg product.

—Duff

Makes enough to ice an 8- to 10-inch layer cake

6 extra-large egg whites, at room temperature

1¼ cups granulated sugar (not powdered; it won't work)

1 teaspoon freshly squeezed lemon juice or white vinegar

4 sticks (1 pound) butter, plus more as needed, softened

1. Put the egg whites in the bowl of a stand mixer fitted with the whisk attachment. Start the machine on medium-slow speed and whip until the eggs begin to get frothy. Turn the speed to medium.

2. Slowly add the sugar to the whipping egg whites, dropping the lemon juice in about halfway through the process.

3. When all the sugar is in, speed up the mixer and whip until stiff peaks form and the meringue is smooth and super shiny.

4. Turn the speed to medium-low and begin adding the butter. Add it bit by bit so the meringue doesn't slop over the sides of

the bowl. At this point, the meringue will fall and look ruined and broken. It's not. This is what happens and it's okay. If the meringue doesn't fall, add a little extra butter until it does.

5. Turn the speed back up to medium-high and walk away. Come back in 10 minutes. Does it look like buttercream? No? Walk away and repeat until it does. If it still doesn't look like buttercream after 30 minutes, add more butter until it does.

6. Use immediately, or cover and refrigerate for up to 1 week. Warm and rewhip the buttercream before using it if refrigerated.

AMERICAN BUTTERCREAM

Don't ever make this recipe.

Sometimes people are scared of meringue and I get that, but don't be scared. The Swiss Buttercream recipe on page 284 is awesome and it's easy. I also know that most Americans like American buttercream because that's all they have ever had. I get that, too. We're like a bunch of Pavlovian cake consumers who have been taught to like a certain thing even though there are much better things out there. This recipe is super easy, which is why you'll ignore my advice and make it anyway. That's okay. It's actually really good. —*Duff*

Makes enough for one 2-layer, 8-inch cake

4 sticks (1 pound) butter, softened

6 cups powdered sugar

1 to 2 teaspoons pure vanilla extract (or any other flavor you want, or none)

Pinch of kosher salt

¼ cup whole milk

1. In the bowl of a stand mixer fitted with the whisk attachment, combine all the ingredients. Whip the mixture on low speed for a while. When the sugar is incorporated, turn the mixer speed up and whip until the buttercream is smooth and looks right to you. If it's too cold, persuade it with a blowtorch if you have one. If it's too wet, add a bit more powdered sugar. If it's too stiff, add a bit more butter. Be sure to scrape the sides of the bowl once or twice to make sure everything is combined.

2. Use immediately or store in an airtight container at room temperature for 24 hours or in the fridge for up to 2 weeks. Rewhip cold buttercream before using it.

American Buttercream is pictured on page 288.

CREAM CHEESE FROSTING

This is the easiest cream cheese frosting—and also the best! Cream cheese frosting shouldn't contain milk or corn syrup or glucose or mayonnaise or any of that nonsense. The best, most mouth-happy cream cheese frosting has four ingredients and should take you about 5 minutes to make. —*Duff*

Makes enough for one 8-inch red velvet or carrot layer cake with a bit left over (spread it on a bagel, or eat it with a spoon)

4 cups powdered sugar

1 (8-ounce) package cream cheese, at room temperature

2 sticks (1 cup) butter, softened

1 tablespoon pure vanilla extract

Cream Cheese Frosting is pictured on page 289.

1. In the bowl of a stand mixer fitted with the paddle attachment, combine all the ingredients. Whip on low speed for a while. When the sugar is incorporated, turn the mixer speed up and beat until smooth, scraping the sides of the bowl often.

2. To spread, use it at room temperature, but store it covered in the fridge. Rewhip cold frosting before using it.

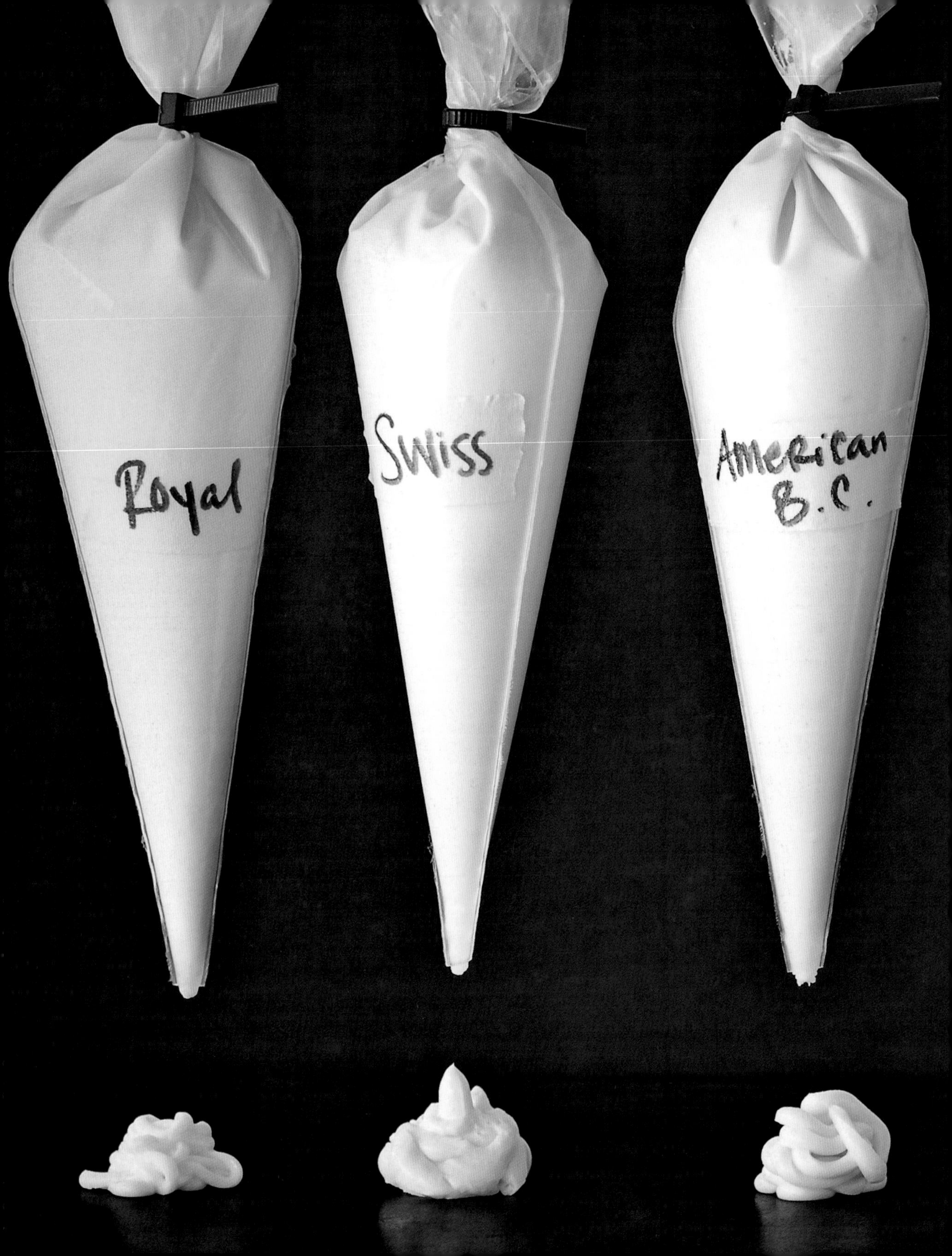
Royal
Swiss
American
B.C.

Cream Cheese

Pastry Cream

Choc Pudding

CHOCOLATE GANACHE

Here's a staple recipe. Chocolate ganache is a must for any kitchen: You can top a cake with it, you can whip it and fill a cake with it, you can heat it up and use it as a sauce, you can pour it on ice cream, you can add it to crème brûlée to make it chocolate-y. You can put ganache on anything and make it better. (Mashed potatoes? Steamed corn?) —*Duff*

Makes about 2¼ cups ganache

10 ounces dark chocolate, chopped fine*

2 tablespoons corn syrup**

2 teaspoons pure vanilla extract***

Pinch of kosher salt

1 cup heavy cream****

Chocolate Ganache is pictured on page 295.

1. Put the chocolate in a metal bowl with the corn syrup, vanilla, and salt.

2. In a small saucepan over low heat, heat the cream until it boils. Immediately pour it on the chocolate and cover the bowl with a towel for 3 minutes.

3. Gently stir the chocolate until it's shiny and smooth, then do with it what you will.

There are a couple of different ways to use ganache. You can whip it once it has cooled and set, and make a quick mousse or cake filling that sets up nice and firm in the fridge, or you can pour it over an iced cake for a smooth, glossy chocolate finish.

* For milk chocolate, use a bit less cream; for white chocolate, use even less.

** Corn syrup makes it shiny.

*** Don't use vanilla for white chocolate ganache; it's already in there.

**** For more flava, you can replace some of the cream with melted butter, equal parts by volume.

ROYAL ICING

We use royal icing for fine piping details on fondant cakes. It's also used as glue for cakes because it dries really hard and makes pieces stick together—it's the perfect binding agent for gingerbread houses.

There are many recipes out there for royal icing, and this is a solid one, but royal icing is really made by feel. Technically, it's a meringue with super skewed ratios. The way I make royal icing is to put a bunch of powdered sugar in the bowl of a stand mixer fitted with the whisk attachment and add egg whites until it looks right. It looks right when the folds that the whisk makes in the icing keep their shape. Experiment with it and find where your sweet spot is. Use pasteurized eggs because you are denaturing (cooking) the eggs with acid and sugar, but no heat. —*Duff*

Makes 2 cups; plenty for a 2- or 3-layer cake or 3 dozen cookies

4 cups powdered sugar (approximately)

3 extra-large egg whites (pasteurized)

3 drops lemon juice

-or-

4 cups powdered sugar (approximately)

3 tablespoons meringue powder

5 to 7 tablespoons water

-or-

4 cups royal icing powder (CK Products brand is my favorite)

½ cup water

Royal Icing is pictured on page 288.

1. Using a stand mixer and the whisk attachment, whip most of the powdered sugar with most of the other ingredients. Whip for 5 to 8 minutes, or until the royal icing holds its shape and is bright white (not translucent). If it is too soft, add more powdered sugar. If it is too stiff, add a bit more liquid, drop by drop. If you are using only one color, add a few drops of the color at this point and keep whipping until you have the shade you want; otherwise, proceed to step 2.

2. To store royal icing, the ideal way is to scrape it out of the bowl and into a plastic, disposable piping bag, then leave it at room temperature. Don't cut the bag until you're ready to use the royal icing, and don't overfill the bag—you want enough room to tie the back of the bag off to keep the royal icing airtight. If any air comes into contact with the royal icing, it gets hard and that part of the icing is useless. Never attempt to mix hard bits back into the royal icing—you'll ruin the whole batch. The other accepted method of storing royal icing is to scrape it into a plastic or ceramic bowl, and cover it with a wet paper towel. This method works, but it wastes both paper towels and royal icing. It's also just annoying. When you're piping small designs, you want to use very small parchment piping bags. It's easy to stick the nose of a large piping bag into a small one and extract exactly how much you need. When the icing is in a bowl, you have to use a spoon to get it out. The spoon is difficult to get into a piping bag, and you keep using spoons and wasting royal icing. Get with the times, people. Do it right and don't waste food.

CHOCOLATE PUDDING

This is an awesome filling for cakes, but only cakes that are kept cold their whole life. Don't use pudding in cakes that are decorated and are kept at room temperature. This is also a great dessert by itself with a little whipped cream, and it's awesome for filling éclairs and doughnuts.

This pudding is super chocolatey—if it's too dark for your taste, reduce the cocoa powder by a bit.

—Duff

Makes five or six 6-ounce servings

1 quart half-and-half

3 tablespoons cornstarch

1 cup sugar

1 cup unsweetened natural cocoa powder

Pinch of kosher salt

1 whole vanilla bean, scraped (you can use 2 teaspoons pure vanilla extract, but real vanilla beans taste amazing)

2 sticks (1 cup) butter, softened

Chocolate Pudding is pictured on page 289.

1. Whisk 1 cup of the half-and-half and the cornstarch in a bowl to make a slurry. Break up any lumps with your fingers.

2. In a medium saucepan over medium-high heat, combine the remaining 3 cups half-and-half, the sugar, cocoa powder, salt, and vanilla bean and scraped seeds and scald the mixture (bring it almost to a boil).

3. Put the bowl with the slurry on a damp towel to hold it in place so you can use both hands. Whisking the slurry constantly, slowly pour in all of the hot cream mixture to temper it. Pour it all back into the pot. Remove the vanilla bean pod.

4. Return the pot to the heat, whisk the tempered mixture into the pan, and stir constantly until the mixture gets thick. Add the butter and stir until it is melted and combined. The pudding should be thick and gloopy and shiny.

5. Pour the pudding into a heat-resistant container or individual ramekins and place a piece of plastic wrap directly on the surface of the pudding. If any air is between the plastic and the pudding, a thick skin will form as it cools.

6. Refrigerate the pudding for at least 3 hours. The pudding will seem too thin while it is hot, but it will get much thicker as it cools.

PASTRY CREAM

Pastry cream is a fancy custard-based French vanilla pudding; you might know it as the goo that goes under the fruit in a fresh fruit tart. It's great for filling cold cakes and almost any pastry, and can be flavored with almost anything you can think of, like liquor, spices, fruits, or nuts. This recipe is rich and buttery and so good you'll probably eat it with a spoon right out of the container.

Pastry cream is also the jump-off point for dozens of classical French creams and other recipes. I could write a whole book on custard, so do yourself a favor once you get this recipe down: Look up what else you can do with it. You might be surprised. *—Duff*

Makes about 4 cups

8 extra-large egg yolks

1 cup sugar

¼ cup plus 2 tablespoons cornstarch

1 quart whole milk

1 whole vanilla bean, scraped

½ stick (¼ cup) butter, softened

Pastry Cream is pictured on page 289.

1. In a medium bowl, whisk the yolks and ½ cup of the sugar until the mixture is light yellow. Whisk in the cornstarch and set aside.

2. In a medium saucepan over medium heat, combine the milk, the remaining ½ cup sugar, and the vanilla bean and scraped seeds and scald it (bring it almost to a boil).

3. Put the bowl with the yolk mixture on a damp towel to hold it in place so you can use both hands. In a thin, steady stream, slowly whisk all the hot milk mixture into the egg mixture, whisking constantly. Pour it all back into the pot. Remove the vanilla bean pod.

4. Put the saucepan back on the heat, pour in the hot egg mixture, and cook, stirring constantly, until it is thick. As you go, notice how the spoon feels on the bottom of the pan. If it feels smooth, keep going, and if it feels like there's a crusty layer down there, don't try to stir it in—leave it alone and turn down the heat. *Don't let it burn! Yuck!*

5. When the pastry cream is thick, take it off the heat and stir in the butter until it is melted and mixed in.

6. Store in a plastic container in the fridge. Place a piece of plastic wrap directly onto the pastry cream, pushing out any air bubbles that get trapped. This keeps a gross layer of skin from forming on the pastry cream that you have to graft off and throw away before you use it.

RASPBERRY COULIS
(OR THE COULIS OF YOUR DREAMS)

Coulis is a sauce that can be either savory or sweet (the word comes from a Latin root and basically means "to strain"). A simple preparation of fruits or vegetables, or even soup, can be blended and strained and correctly called a coulis. For desserts, coulis are usually made from raspberries and black-berries, but I've made them with apples, melons, peaches, and pineapples. Some of these—mostly berries and tree fruit*—you want to cook for a bit to activate the pectin in the fruit, but some fruits like melons don't really like the heat and you can prepare them raw.

Coulis is a great sauce for a plated piece of cake, but putting a coulis inside a cake isn't advisable, as it will soak into the cake rather quickly. I like berry coulis with white cake, but serving raspberry coulis with chocolate cake is very popular. (I personally am not a fan of raspberries and chocolate. I like chocolate to taste like chocolate and I think the acidity gets in the way, but what do I know?) It's also great for cheesecake—more refined than cherry pie filling on top. —*Duff*

Makes about 2 cups

2 cups fresh raspberries or other fruit (frozen works, too, in a pinch)

¾ cup sugar

Pinch of kosher salt

½ cup water or Chambord

1. Combine all the ingredients in a small saucepan and cook over medium heat for 5 to 8 minutes, stirring gently and constantly, until the fruit is soft and the sugar is dissolved.

2. Pour the mixture into a blender** and puree until smooth.

3. Run the contents through a fine-mesh strainer to remove all the seeds. If the sauce looks too thin, let it cool; it will thicken up. If it's still too thin after it's cool, you can reduce some of the liquid by cooking it slowly over low heat.

* FYI, if you're making a coulis with blueberries, they have a ton of pectin and the sauce will get crazy thick if you don't use more water or a blueberry liqueur.

** A blender is cool and all, but if you wanna be gangsta, get an immersion blender. They're easy to use and easier to clean. Once you own an immersion blender, you'll wonder how you ever lived without one. Like a van. When I bought my first cargo van, I couldn't believe people could actually exist without owning one.

Chocolate Ganache, page 290

Basic Sugar Glaze, page 297

Raspberry Coulis

Vanilla Crème Fraîche, page 296

VANILLA CRÈME FRAÎCHE

During my culinary travels in California, Colorado, and elsewhere, I found this great little sauce for dressing up any slice of cake or plated dessert. I saw Chef Steven Durfee make this sauce once in like fifteen seconds and it was so perfect in its simplicity and subtlety—a pure example of Steven's genius.

This works with sour cream if you must, but it's worth finding crème fraîche—it's light, delicate, and smooth and doesn't get in the way of the flavor of the pure vanilla bean. If you do end up using sour cream, cut the lemon juice in half and use a few drops of water. *—Duff*

Makes about 2¼ cups

½ cup sugar

2 tablespoons freshly squeezed lemon juice

2 cups crème fraîche

2 vanilla beans, scraped

Vanilla Crème Fraîche is pictured on page 295.

1. Put the sugar, lemon juice, and crème fraîche into a large nonreactive bowl. Personally I use plastic since I *hate* glass in my kitchen. *Hate it!*

2. Scrape the vanilla seeds into the bowl.

3. Whisk it all together. Done. Cover and refrigerate. Also, use this sauce within 36 hours—it gets weird after that and you'll turn into a gremlin.

Note: Don't make or store anything acidic in metal ever. Just don't.

BASIC SUGAR GLAZE

Here's your basic recipe for a glaze for literally almost anything. It's not so thin that it just washes off, but it's not nearly as thick as royal icing. This recipe is a base—add anything you want to this, including color! —*Duff*

Makes about 2 cups

3 cups powdered sugar

½ cup milk

Pinch of kosher salt

1 tablespoon pure vanilla
   extract

Basic Sugar Glaze is
pictured on page 295.

In a big bowl, combine all the ingredients and whisk together. Adjust the consistency by adding either milk (to thin) or powdered sugar (to thicken).

MAKING CAKES PRETTY

This is what we do. We bake delicious cakes, and then we make them pretty. The trick that I find works best is to have some kind of loose plan before you start. I usually draw a sketch of what I intend to make, and that helps me prepare all the tools and elements I'll need to get my cake looking awesome.

That being said, it's very important to listen to your cake as you're decorating. You don't have to be the cake whisperer, but as you're decorating, stop and take a step back every so often and make sure you like what you're doing. If something isn't working, you'll know, and this is where you have to stay loose. If the cake is going in a direction you don't like, don't force it. It's very difficult to undo decorations on a cake, so let the design unfold naturally.

Cake decorating is like snowboarding—you can do it the first time you try it, and you can take the rest of your life getting better at it. Make sure you have all the right tools and materials. Don't rush it. Know that it's really fun even though sometimes it can be frustrating. Now, turn off your phone, play some music, and let's make a cake.

FILLING AND STACKING A CAKE

The basics of decorating are really simple to understand, but very important to get right. All these techniques take practice, but mastering these is so worth it. They are the beginning steps in building a cake that will be exactly what you intend it to be. But you can't pipe a beautiful lace pattern on a cake if the icing is lumpy or off-center. You can't make a stunning cake if the fondant has creases in it or is bulging out. These are some of the tips, tricks, and techniques I've learned over the years—and I've made every mistake there is to make, so you can learn from them.

When you stack two or more layers of cake on top of each other with the intention of decorating them, it's important not to overfill the layers. Too much frosting and filling can cause problems, like bulging around the edges and melting off if the cake gets too warm. Conversely, you need to put enough filling into the layers so the cake is delicious. Find the balance that works and go with it.

It's important to note that when you're making decorated cakes that will be at room temperature for many hours or even days, your options for fillings are limited. If the cake is kept cold, you can use pudding, pastry cream, fresh fruit, and so on. But keep it simple for cakes that will spend hours on your counter—buttercream or chocolate frosting. You can always add sauce to a slice on a plate once the cake has been cut, like the coulis on page 294.

What happens is this: The cake and filling are very light and soft. There's a lot of air in a cake, and the filling is usually something gooey. When you put fondant on the cake after it's filled and iced, it settles as it warms up. As it settles, the buttercream covering between the layers is pushed out by gravity, and as the buttercream is pushed out, the fondant on top of it is pushed out, so you get a cake that looks ribbed.

If you're making a buttercream cake that's going to be kept cold, you can put in a lot more filling because the fats in the cake and the filling stay firm in colder temperatures and don't shift as in a warmer cake. I've also seen bakers pipe a ring of buttercream on the inside edge of each tier and then fill those tiers with all the yummy stuff. Again, for a cake that's kept cold, this is great, but for a fondant-covered cake, especially one with lots of decoration on the outside that will weigh it down, this will create huge problems. Play it safe and stick to buttercream filling for room-temp cakes. You can use shelf-stable jams and jellies, but stay away from canned pie filling if it is not refrigerated—that stuff will turn to mold quickly.

CRUMB-COATING A CAKE

Crumb-coating is applying a thin layer of buttercream to the outside of a cake and shaping it with spatulas so that the cake becomes a perfect cylinder (or whatever shape you've carved the cake into). This also keeps crumbs from soiling the clean buttercream you're finishing the cake with, or causing lumps if you're covering the cake in fondant.

To crumb-coat a typical round cake, start with nice, warm, freshly whipped buttercream. Start sloppy and get the entire cake covered in a lot of buttercream. Icing a cake is a reductive process, not an additive process. That might seem counterintuitive, but look at it like a sculpture. If I weld a bunch of pieces of metal together, that is an additive process. If I chip away at a block of stone, that is a reductive process. When you slop a whole bunch of buttercream onto a cake, you're creating the block of stone, and then you "chip away" at it to find the hidden cylinder within.

When the cake is covered, you take a bench scraper or large taping knife (see page 19) and slowly turn the cake using a cake wheel, holding your spatula like a razor and gradually reducing the amount of buttercream on the cake until you have the cylinder you want. You use a wide spatula so the buttercream climbs up the sides of the cake and goes past the top of the cake.

Next, using an offset spatula, come straight in from the sides and create the 90-degree angle where the top meets the corner. Always pull from the outside in, and wipe your blade after every pass. This will create the super-flat top of the cake and complete your cylinder.

If you're intending to cover the cake in fondant, do a slightly thicker crumb coat so that there's plenty of buttercream underneath the fondant. If you're intending for the cake to be covered in buttercream only, repeat the crumb-coat process with a ½-inch layer of buttercream after the original crumb-coat has set up in the fridge. This isn't difficult, but takes practice, so don't worry if your first attempts don't look earth-shattering.

Next, transfer your cake to a cake plate or other final surface for further decorating.

COVERING A CAKE IN ROLLED FONDANT

Covering a cake in fondant is an easy task, but one that requires practice. You're basically performing a mathematical impossibility—taking a 2-D thing and introducing a circle to it and making it 3-D. Geometry says you cannot do this. I say you can.

Note that smaller cakes are harder to cover than larger ones, because the mathematical difficulties of the operation decrease in significance with an increase in the circumference of the circle. The bigger the cake, the fewer wrinkles you have to smooth out.

First, start with a cold cake, not frozen, as this will cause condensation to build up on the outside of the cake and potentially ruin the finish of your cake. For a regular cylindrical cake that's less than 6 inches tall, you'll need to roll a circular piece about 12 inches larger than the diameter of the cake. (If the cake is taller, increase the circumference accordingly.) Roll the fondant on a large, very clean, and very smooth surface. If the surface is dirty, the fondant will pick up any crumb or color left behind. Also, if the surface is not perfectly smooth, the fondant will take the shape of every imperfection of the surface and then will in turn be imperfect, which is after all what we're trying to avoid. Also, wash your hands, as they, too, collect food coloring and food oils.

Lay a light dusting of cornstarch or powdered sugar over the surface. Cornstarch is preferred, because powdered sugar has a tendency to clump under intense pressure, as from a rolling pin, and will leave the fondant pocked and cratered once it's brushed away, while cornstarch remains granular. Remember also to dust the top of the fondant to prevent the fondant from sticking to the rolling pin. Roll the fondant out to an even ⅛ inch thick.

Drape the fondant over the rolling pin and wipe it with a dry towel or large soft paintbrush to remove any excess cornstarch. Center one edge of the fondant about 2 inches from the edge of the cake and drape it over the cake. Movingly quickly but carefully, first smooth out the top edge of the cake with the palms of your hands. This ensures two things: first, that the cake will still be firm and you'll keep that sharp, 90-degree corner, and second, that the fondant adheres to the corner and relieves the point of highest vulnerability to gravity. With your hands, slowly circle the cake, firming it gently into place.

Once you have the top inch secured and perfect, begin working your way down the cake with one hand in a side-to-side motion. Slowly move down, as working laterally will cause all the excess fondant to migrate toward the back of the cake and create wrinkles that are too large to ignore in the geometric anomaly you're attempting to produce. As one hand smooths the fondant and applies pressure to adhere it to the cake, use the other hand to gently pull, stretch, and arrange the wrinkles so they submit to the persuasion of your other hand. Continue until you've reached the bottom of the cake.

At this point, use a fondant smoother to remove any impressions left by your hands and further apply pressure to secure as much surface area of fondant to the cake as possible. Aim for 100 percent.

Using a pizza cutter, roll around the bottom edge of the cake, beveling slightly in and down at to ensure that no fondant is curving away from the cake. With a clean X-Acto knife, place the blade into the fondant and in the direction you plan to cut. With the knife flat on the table, and the blade parallel to the table, remove the bottom ⅛ inch of fondant from the cake.

You should now have a small gap to allow for settling, so the fondant doesn't crack or wrinkle over time. Poke a small hole in the top of the cake to allow air to escape from the cake. This will prevent large, unsightly bubbles from forming on the outside of the cake, but don't worry, it won't make it stale. The cake is now ready to be decorated. This is not easy—it will take you a few tries to get right. You can find videos online on how to do this (I'm sure there's one or two of me doing it out there).

ON THE TREATMENT OF CAKES

Store fondant-covered cakes at room temperature if serving within 24 hours; 48 at the absolute most. If you have to store a fondant-covered cake for longer, wrap it well in plastic wrap and freeze it. Freezing a cake is much better for its constitution than refrigerating it. When the cake is to be defrosted, unwrap it and put it out on a cake plate in front of a large fan to keep moisture from condensing on it.

Store buttercream-finished cakes in the fridge for 24 hours, or the freezer for longer.

Always serve cake at room temperature, unless the filling dictates otherwise.

ROLLED FONDANT

Rolled fondant is that smooth white covering you see on wedding cakes and lots of decorated cakes. Avoid making rolled fondant if at all possible. It is tough to get just right and there are some really good prepared ones (like mine) out on the market for retail that are so much better than the one or two old brands that used to be the only option. Nevertheless, if you're going to make a habit of decorating cakes, it's really important to know how to make rolled fondant if you're not in a position to buy any.

This is a good, solid recipe that's made from stuff you can find at any grocery store. You might need to experiment with it just a little to get the consistency right. If you live in a wet or a dry climate, it can change the firmness of the finished fondant. —*Duff*

Makes about 5 pounds, or enough for a 2-tier cake with leftovers to use in decoration

2 tablespoons powdered gelatin

4 pounds powdered sugar

2 tablespoons cornstarch

1 cup light corn syrup

2 tablespoons vegetable shortening

1. In a small saucepan, mix the gelatin in ½ cup cold water and let it soak for 5 minutes or so. Put the pan over low heat and warm it until the gelatin melts.

2. In the bowl of a stand mixer, whisk the sugar and cornstarch.

3. Add the corn syrup to the gelatin mixture and let it melt.

4. With the mixer on low speed and the dough hook attached, slowly add the liquid to the sugar mixture. Knead it with the machine until the dough forms a firm ball. Add the shortening and knead well. If the dough is too dry, add a bit of water, drop by drop. If it's too wet, add a bit of powdered sugar, teaspoon by teaspoon.

5. Scrape the fondant out of the bowl and wrap it in plastic wrap twice to be airtight. Store at room temperature in a plastic bag in a covered container. Fondant can be stored for up to a month if it's made from scratch.

Options: When you're adding the shortening is the easiest time to add color to fondant. Use the concentrated gel colors to add color, not the liquid kind. Also, if you want to add flavor, I suggest using imitation extracts, as they have no color, are very concentrated in flavor, and will have minimal impact on the texture and color of the final product. It's good manners to serve cake with fondant still attached. It's also good manners if you choose not to eat it. Fondant is almost pure sugar and everyone wants the gooey goodness underneath.

PASTILLAGE OR GUMPASTE

Pastillage and gumpaste are used to make sugar flowers and other hard structural but edible pieces of cakes. I use the words *pastillage* and *gumpaste* interchangeably, not because they're the same thing, but because they fulfill the same role in cake decorating. The difference is that gumpaste has gum tragacanth in it, which allows you to work with it longer and makes it a bit less brittle when it dries. Pastillage, on the other hand, dries out very quickly, so you need to work fast with it, and it's also more brittle.

I usually choose to use gumpaste to make sugar decorations, but if I run out, I turn to the recipe for pastillage. I could probably go into any kitchen in the world and make pastillage, whereas gum tragacanth isn't very easy to find. One thing I prefer about pastillage over gumpaste is that it's much smoother and finer and requires less sanding. Also, because it's smoother, it handles the airbrush and paintbrush better. You can treat it like gumpaste or fondant in that you can dye it with food coloring, paint it, even flavor it. Get comfortable working with pastillage, and depending on your project, you'll probably come to prefer it to gumpaste, or at least know when it will serve you better. —*Duff*

Makes about 2 pounds

1 (16-ounce) box
 powdered sugar

½ cup plus 1 tablespoon
 cornstarch (or potato
 starch if you can find
 it; it makes a whiter
 pastillage)

½ teaspoon cream of
 tartar

1 (¼-ounce) package
 powdered gelatin

2 tablespoons light corn
 syrup

1. In the bowl of a stand mixer fitted with the dough hook, mix together the sugar, cornstarch, and cream of tartar.

2. Put ¼ cup cold water in a small saucepan and sprinkle the gelatin lightly over the top. Let it stand for 3 to 5 minutes.

3. Place the pan over low heat and let the gelatin melt slowly. Add the corn syrup.

4. Using the dough hook, mix the gelatin into the sugar mixture. Make sure to scrape the sides of the bowl often, and look at the ball of dough as it forms. If it is too loose, add cornstarch little by little until it forms a smooth ball. If it's too dry and you hear the machine straining against it, add warm water a few drops at a time, until the mixture looks smooth and perfect.

5. Wrap the pastillage immediately in plastic and keep it at room temperature for a week. If you mixed this right, there shouldn't be anything to scrape off the sides of the bowl—it should be almost perfectly clean—but if for some reason there's a residue on the sides of the bowl or the dough hook, don't scrape it off and add it to your mixture. It's probably already gone hard and will just make little hard bits in your pastillage.

PROJECT 1:
PIPED HENNA CAKE

This cake is always really fun for me to make. It's the best cake to put some headphones on and get lost in a really good album while you let your mind disconnect from your hands and just let them create. Henna designs (also known as *mehndi*) are the perfect balance between ordered and organic illustration and are hugely flexible and forgiving. As long as you prepare your cake and royal icing correctly and you work clean and precise, you will make a beautiful cake. Piping royal icing on the side of a cake is very different than piping on the top and this cake will take a little practice, but you *will* get the hang of it and get better and better.

My favorite color combination for this cake is a light off-white base of smooth rolled fondant and a dark maroon royal icing. To make this color of maroon, I use about 3 parts red to 1 part brown to ½ part true black. This is very vague, I know, but you really color the icing by sight, not by recipe.

I also like to print henna designs off the computer as inspiration, or you can go to the local craft store and find a book of henna designs. They're handy to have around, as sometimes you need a bit of inspiration to keep you going.

The skill you are going to learn here is fine royal icing piping. This is one of the most difficult tasks to master, and while you will be piping right away, you can spend a lifetime getting good at this.

YOU WILL NEED

1 (6-inch) layer cake covered in off-white rolled fondant (see page 306)

1 large plastic disposable piping bag

Royal Icing (page 291), tinted as described above

Red, brown, and true black gel food coloring

iPod and headphones

10 small parchment triangles

Henna pattern images, for reference

Maroon ribbon

10-inch foam-core circle

Scissors

Double-sided tape

Honey

Large offset spatula

Tweezers

Small gold dragees

1. Set the cake on a work surface and have ready a piping bag filled with the tinted royal icing. Put on your headphones and start playing the entire Led Zeppelin catalog.

2. Start piping! Make small paper cones with the parchment triangles and fill from the big bag. You only need a little bit. You want to use small cones because you want to be able to concentrate on the fine detail, and you want to use fresh bags often as the icing warms up in your hands and gets runny. Let your mind wander and create beautiful henna patterns on the cake, referencing the henna photos often so you keep the designs fresh. Set the cake aside to dry.

3. Wrap the ribbon around the foam-core circle, cut it to fit, and adhere it with double-sided tape. Smear a small bit of honey in the center of the board to make it sticky. With an offset spatula, place the cake in the middle of the board.

4. Roll a Ping-Pong-ball-size ball of fondant into a long, thin snake and wrap it around the bottom of the cake where it meets the cake board.

5. Pipe random dots around the design of the cake and use tweezers to stick the gold dragees to the dots.

6. Take a picture of your cake and tweet it to me at @duff_goldman—I'm always looking for good pipers.

PROJECT 2:
CUTE ROSE CAKE

This is a fun yet impressive cake that's doable for adults and kids alike. It's a colorful, spring-like cake that's totally cool all year long and works for almost any occasion. You can make one color of rose for a more refined look and to get a specific message across (I think different colored roses have different meanings, right?), or you can make a whole bunch of colors for a kaleidoscopic mix. Once you've mastered how to make cute little 3-D objects with fondant, you can expand your repertoire and make little honeybees, ants, and even a teddy bear. Create this cake step by step with a clear head and you'll be blown away by how easy and fun it is to make. And whoever you make it for will be super-stoked!

The skills you'll learn by making this cake are:

- Coloring and working with rolled fondant
- Giving cakes dimension with 3-D elements
- Adhering fondant to fondant
- Rolling "snakes"—long, thin, even strings of fondant that require a very delicate touch and a bit of practice
- Airbrushing details onto flowers (a mandatory cake-decorating skill that's a whole lot easier than you think)

For this version of the cake, I'm going for red roses (I like airbrushing red roses the best, but you can try all kinds of colors), along with green leaves and stems and some silver accents. I'm going with a white background, which will make the colors pop, but this cake would look fantastic on a light green or sky blue cake as well. Think about the color of your flowers first and then choose a complementary color to use as the background. This version is perfect for Valentine's Day or anytime you need to get yourself out of the doghouse (totally works, trust me).

YOU WILL NEED

1 baseball-size ball (1 pound) white fondant (page 306)

1 billiard ball–size ball (10 ounces) white fondant (page 306)

Gel food coloring (red, black, brown, moss green, leaf green)

Plastic wrap

1 (6-inch) layer cake, crumb-coated

10-inch foam-core circle

Red or black or silver ribbon

Scissors

Double-sided tape

Honey

continued on next page

Large offset spatula

Small paintbrush

Cup of water

2½-inch circle cutter

Rolling pin

Cornstarch in a shaker

Small offset spatula

Three 12-inch cardboard
cake circles

Toothpicks

Airbrush setup (gun and
air compressor*)

Airbrush food coloring
(brown, yellow, red,
green)

Three 10-inch parchment
triangles

X-Acto knife

1 cup Royal Icing (page
291), sealed airtight in
a plastic pastry bag

Small silver dragees

8 ounces gumpaste or
pastillage (page 307)

Butterfly template
(page 342)

Scrap cardboard

* I actually have my own
brand that works great
and is very affordable and
professional. I use it in all
my stores.

1. Dye the baseball-size fondant ball red with a touch of black, brown, and a little moss green. (I like using brown in almost every "natural" thing I make, as nothing in nature is a pure color. Brown is the color of oxidization and is present almost everywhere and will make the flowers seem just a bit more real.) Wrap the ball airtight in plastic wrap.

2. Dye the billiard ball–size fondant ball green for the stems and leaves. Wrap up this ball as well.

3. Cover a 6-inch cake with white fondant (see page 302) and set it in front of a fan to dry out a bit. You're going to be adding a bit of weight to this cake, so you want the fondant to stay rigid and not buckle under the pressure of gravity.

4. Make a base for the cake using the 10-inch foam-core circle. Add a ribbon around the base, cut to fit, and secure it with double-sided tape. Spread a bit of honey on the center of the circle and use the large spatula to place the cake on the prepared base. Don't worry about the bottom edge; we'll fix that later. And if you have any wrinkles in the fondant, we'll address those later as well.

5. Let's make flowers! Get yourself a comfortable work surface and set up your equipment: your red and green fondant balls, a small paintbrush, a cup of water, a pair of scissors, a 2½-inch circle cutter, a rolling pin, cornstarch in a shaker, a small offset spatula, and a few large cardboard cake circles.

6. On a surface dusted with cornstarch, roll a small amount of red fondant out to ¼ inch thick, enough to cut 3 circles. (As you get faster at this, you can roll out enough for 6 or even 9 circles, but let's start with 3 so you have crack-free flower petals.)

7. Cut out three 2½-inch circles and dust off any excess cornstarch with a dry brush or a towel.

8. Line up the 3 circles and place a small dot of water with the paintbrush right on the edge of each circle. Overlap each circle to the one next to it so the water is sandwiched in-between the petals.

9. Turn the circles 90 degrees and gently roll them up. You aren't making a baguette, okay? Nice and gentle; use the lightest touch. Now you have a tube with petaled ends.

10. Using your thumb and two fingers, gently pinch and roll the tube until it separates into two ends. Kaboom! You just made two fun roses!

11. With scissors, cut the bottom of each rose flat and place it on the cake rounds so they dry and set up.

12. Repeat about 20 times, so that you have a few dozen little roses.

13. Now we'll take care of that pesky seam on the bottom of the cake. Take a golf ball–size piece of green fondant and roll it into a hot dog. Place it on the table and gently roll it slowly until it forms a long snake that will go all the way around the cake. Spread your fingers out so you have even pressure on the snake and don't leave any dents.

14. Brush a bit of water all the way around the cake and gently lay the snake down against the bottom edge of the cake to hide the seam. Very lightly, push the snake against the cake so it touches; the water will make it stick. Trim the ends carefully with the scissors and close the loop.

15. Next, roll out the remaining green fondant the same way and use that circle cutter to cut 3 circles out of the green fondant.

16. Then, use the cutter to make 3 leaves per circle by cutting a tangent arc from each.

17. I like to give them a twist or a curl to give them more dimension. Make as many as you like, there is no "right" number. Set these on a cake circle to dry and set up.

18. After the flowers have had a chance to set up—at least 15 minutes—it's time to airbrush them. Make a dark red with red and a bit of black airbrush color and a tiny, tiny touch of green and very sparingly airbrush the ends of the petals. This will

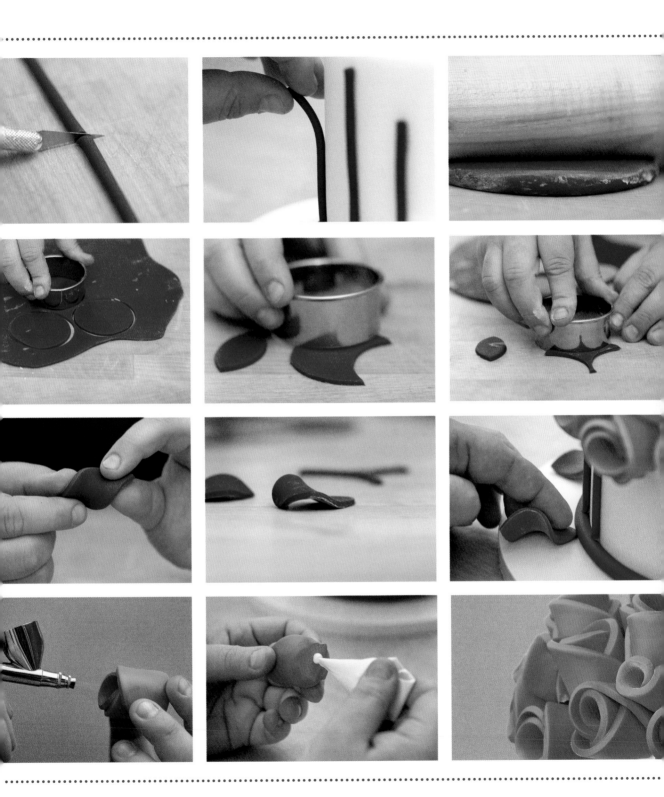

make your flowers look much more natural. Test your color and spray velocity on a piece of paper first.

19. Now it's time to adhere the roses to the cake. Use a small offset spatula to pry up the flowers if they are stuck to the cardboard. Using the scissors, cut the bottoms flat and start in the middle of the top of the cake and work your way out and down over the sides.

20. Form small cones with the parchment triangles, and fill them with royal icing. Pipe a small dot of royal icing on the flat cut bottom of the flower and place it down on the cake. Hold for a few seconds and the flower will stick to the cake.

21. When you start turning the corner and sticking flowers to the side of the cake, cut the flowers shorter so they aren't so heavy that they pull themselves off of the cake. On the sides, stick a toothpick into the cake to support the flower on the sides of the cake and let the water adhere the flower. Pull the toothpicks out right before the cake is served and after it has been delivered (if the cake is traveling).

22. Next, give the leaves the same airbrush treatment. I usually spray a tiny bit of brown randomly on the leaves, and then wash the airbrush and do the same thing with yellow. This will give the flowers a natural radiance instead of being just a flat green. Set aside to dry.

23. Roll out another long, thin snake of green for the stems. Paint straight lines of water up the sides of the cake from the bottom snake to the flowers. Cut pieces of the green stem snake to go up the sides of the cake and try to get the ends right up against the flowers. It will look silly if the flowers are floating above decapitated stems. Here, make sure to place a snake anywhere you have a fold in the fondant. The snake will cover up that imperfection. There won't be a stem for every flower; just make a few to give the impression.

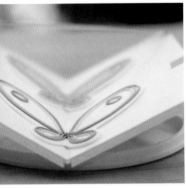

24. Place the leaves into any space available in the flowers, using a small dot of royal icing to adhere them to the cake. Also, a leaf or two at the bottom of the stem will hide where the stem meets the ground.

25. To add some sparkle, pipe little dots of royal icing randomly on the open white parts of the cake and stick on tiny silver dragees with the tweezers.

26. For a butterfly, fold a piece of cardboard at a 20-degree angle and tape it to a flat base that will support it and hold its shape. Copy the template on page 342 and cut it out. Trace the butterfly shape onto gumpaste or pastillage, using the X-Acto knife to mark the outline, then cut it out, center it on the cardboard mold, and let it dry uncovered for 24 hours.

27. The next day, gently clean the edges for any loose bits of gumpaste, then make a few colors out of royal icing and get creative with the decorating. When the royal icing is dry, adhere the butterfly with a few large dots of royal icing, wherever you think it looks good.

GREAT JOB! YOU'RE ABOUT TO MAKE SOMEONE VERY HAPPY!

PROJECT 3:
TIE-DYE PEACE APPLIQUÉ CAKE

This is one of my favorite cakes to make with kids and beginners because the elements are very simple, but they create a very colorful, dramatic cake that anyone, from twelve-year-olds to pros, can be proud of. It's also really fun because you get to play with all kinds of color and it always turns out really cool. Set up some stations in your house and have a decorating party with this cake. I chose a peace symbol for this cake, but the sky's the limit—decorate this cake however you want.

The skills learned here are:
- Working with colored fondant
- Cutting precise shapes with an X-Acto knife
- Learning how to treat delicate rolled fondant pieces very gently. That is a skill that will take you very, very far in cake decorating.

YOU WILL NEED

Cornstarch

Rolling pin

2 golf ball–sized balls (5 ounces) white fondant (page 306)

A clean, flat cutting board or self-healing cutting mat

4½-inch circle cutter

8-inch cardboard circle

Flower cutters in various sizes

1 cup Royal Icing (page 291)

Small parchment triangles

Gel food coloring

4 to 5 tennis ball–sized balls (5 ounces) white fondant (page 306) in your choice of colors

1 (6-inch) layer cake, iced and cold

Pizza cutter

Fondant smoother

10-inch foam-core circle

Ribbon (any color you like)

Scissors

Double-sided tape

Honey

Small paintbrush

Cup of water

X-Acto knife with a new, clean blade

4½-inch peace sign template (page 343)

Small offset spatula

Tweezers

Small silver dragees

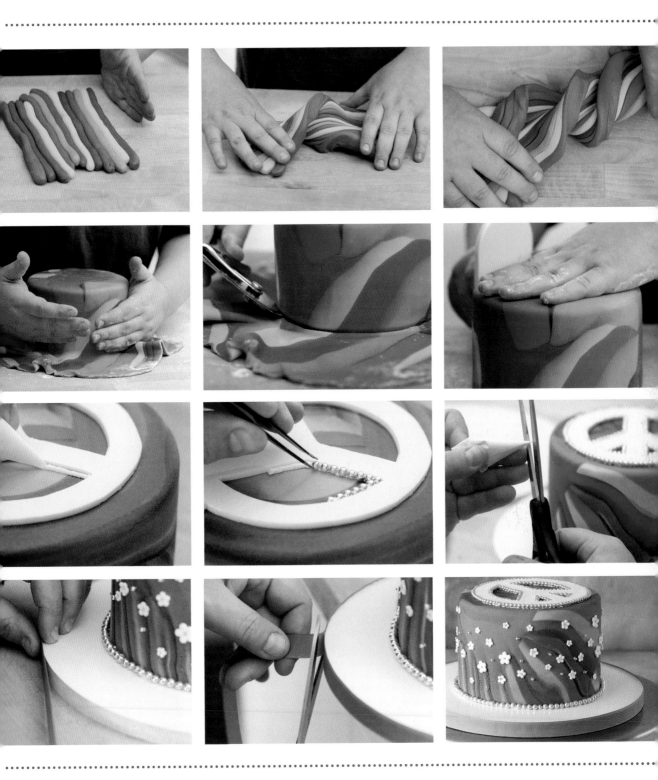

1. On a surface dusted with cornstarch, roll out a small piece of white fondant to about ¼ inch thick and cut out a 4½-inch circle with the circle cutter. Set it aside on a piece of cardboard and let it dry for at least 30 minutes.

2. Roll out the remaining white fondant to about ⅛ inch thick and cut out 20 to 30 little flowers in a few different sizes. Place them on the cardboard.

3. Make small cones from the parchment triangles. Tint some of the royal icing yellow with gel food coloring. Fill 1 or 2 cones with the yellow icing. Fill 1 or 2 more with white icing.

4. Pipe a small dot of yellow royal icing in the middle of each flower. Let them dry for 30 minutes.

5. Pick 2 or 4 or 5 colors (again, your cake, your call) for the fondant. On a cornstarch-dusted surface, roll them into fat snakes. When all the colors are together, they should be about the size of a softball.

6. Push the snakes together and twirl them into a circle. Press the circle down with your hands to push out any air and make the snakes adhere to each other.

7. Roll this colorful circle out to ¼ inch thick and cover your cake. Eyeball how big you need to roll out the fondant (I use the rolling pin as a visual measurement). Center the rolled-out fondant and start smoothing it over the cake using clean, dry hands. Start at the top corner of the cake and continuously work your way around the cake and down. Don't finish one side and then move to the other; that will make your life difficult.

8. Trim the bottom edge with a pizza cutter and then, using a fondant smoother, smooth out any fingerprints or other imperfections.

9. Make a base for the cake using the 10-inch foam-core circle. Add a ribbon around the base, cut to fit, and secure it with double-sided tape. Rub a small amount of honey on the foam-core circle to make it sticky and center the cake on the circle.

10. Use a golf ball–size piece of fondant (any color you wish) and roll a long snake to go around the bottom edge of the whole cake. Paint a stripe of water around the base and gently push the snake up against the cake to adhere it.

11. Copy the peace sign template on page 343 and cut it out. Use the X-Acto knife to cut the peace sign pattern into the 4½-inch white fondant circle. It should be hard enough now to cut cleanly without distorting or tearing it. Remove the extra fondant within the symbol. Wet a small spot on the top of the cake and gently place the peace sign on the cake. The water will adhere the peace sign to the cake.

12. Next, pipe small clusters of dots of white royal icing randomly around the cake and use an offset spatula to place the flowers onto the cake (the royal icing is the glue).

13. Pipe an outline of white royal icing where the cake meets the board, 1 inch at a time, and then use the tweezers to outline the entire thing with small silver dragees. Repeat for the peace sign, outlining the entire circle and the contours inside of it.

14. Groovy. You now have a hippie cake.

UNIVERSAL CONVERSION CHART

OVEN TEMPERATURE EQUIVALENTS

250°F = 120°C

275°F = 135°C

300°F = 150°C

325°F = 160°C

350°F = 180°C

375°F = 190°C

400°F = 200°C

425°F = 220°C

450°F = 230°C

475°F = 240°C

500°F = 260°C

MEASUREMENT EQUIVALENTS

Measurements should always be level unless directed otherwise.

⅛ teaspoon = 0.5 mL

¼ teaspoon = 1 mL

½ teaspoon = 2 mL

1 teaspoon = 5 mL

1 tablespoon = 3 teaspoons = ½ fluid ounce = 15 mL

2 tablespoons = ⅛ cup = 1 fluid ounce = 30 mL

4 tablespoons = ¼ cup = 2 fluid ounces = 60 mL

5⅓ tablespoons = ⅓ cup = 3 fluid ounces = 80 mL

8 tablespoons = ½ cup = 4 fluid ounces = 120 mL

10⅔ tablespoons = ⅔ cup = 5 fluid ounces = 160 mL

12 tablespoons = ¾ cup = 6 fluid ounces = 180 mL

16 tablespoons = 1 cup = 8 fluid ounces = 240 mL

ACKNOWLEDGMENTS

FROM DUFF

I had this really terrible art instructor once at the Corcoran Art School in D.C. He had really bad breath that I swear you could see. He told me I would do well in life to never pursue a career in the arts. Me, being the stubborn bastard that I am, took that as a challenge. Cheers, mate.

My big brother, Willie, has been my biggest fan and my worst critic my whole life. Willie has been my life coach from day 1, literally. Thanks, bro, and remember, you will always be older than me.

I can't skate backward very well. I know: I played ice hockey in college and I couldn't skate backward. My best friend in the world is Art Umlauf, and he was the goalie on my team. He would grab my hands in full goalie gear and drag me backward around the ice until I learned. He could have made fun of me (and he did, but not for that—it involved a slice of cold pizza), but instead he took the time and helped me out. He hasn't stopped to this day. Thanks, Art. You probably have forgotten that small kindness, but I never have.

In Baltimore, there is a man who is the world's most lovable jerk. His name is Kevin. He is, most definitely, a jerk. He is also one of the warmest, most giving people I know. I'm not thanking him here; he doesn't deserve it and he is a jerk. Kevin realized that I was stretched too thin when I first opened Charm City Cakes and was running it by myself out of my apartment and also trying to be a full-time musician and comedy stage performer. Kevin then informed me that I had hired a guy who lived in the same warehouse that he did. His name was Geof Manthorne. I knew Geof from college, but not that well; we were both musicians in a small community. Geof is the best cake decorator in the world now; I fully stand behind that. He has been there for almost fifteen years, keeping me from doing anything too stupid, and even when I do stupid things, he is right beside me getting me out of trouble. Thanks, Geof, for everything.

I've been cooking since I was fourteen years old. I started cooking so I could make enough money to buy spray paint for murals I would paint on underpasses and subway cars. At every kitchen I've ever worked in, I've met several people who have taught me about food, cooking, joy, and how to love this business. My homie Mel at the Hyannis McDonald's on Rte. 132 taught me that it was okay to have fun at work. If you ever meet me, ask me about Mel—I've got a funny story for you.

Cindy Wolf was the first fine-dining chef I ever worked for. She almost didn't hire me because all I had on my resume was fast food, pizza joints, and greasy spoons. She took a chance and hired me, and in doing that, she shaped the rest of my life. Cindy taught me how to bake, and she also taught me how to love food and cooking with real sincerity. If there's any chef I have tried to emulate in my career, it's Cindy. She's tough, but warm. She's a teacher. She loves her craft deep down. She cherishes her cooks and wants to see everybody succeed. She's also the toughest and strongest chef I know.

I worked for Stephen Durfee while I was in culinary school, and that guy did two important things for me: He taught me how to think critically and abstractly about technique and flavor, and he also grabbed me by the back of the neck and dragged me into realizing how deep I could dig inside myself.

I've met so many chefs and I've made hundreds of friends during my journey in food, and I owe them all something. You know who you are and you know what you have done for me—thank you.

And Sara, thanks for being an amazing baker. You remind me why I love to bake. I hope you love your book and you keep it forever and you show it to your grandkids. My grandma was an artist and she was in a book of retrospective of artists from the 1950s and I thought that was coolest thing ever. Your grandkids will think the same thing. I also hope you know how awesome I think you are.

ACKNOWLEDGMENTS

FROM SARA

I would like to sincerely thank all my friends and family who supported me throughout this process. Special thanks to my parents, for being so encouraging, and thank you, Mom, for being my first baking teacher and partner. Thank you to my bestie, Erica, for experimenting with me in the kitchen and always making everything fun. Thank you to Cotty, for continuing to inspire me with the love of baking, and for letting Erica and me trash the kitchen so many times. Thank you to Alex, for dealing with my craziness in the kitchen and helping me out so much during all of this, and a big thank you to Brett, for having my back no matter what. Biggest thank you has to go to Duff, for believing that little ol' me could be a part of this with him. I owe him so much, and am very excited to continue to learn from him. Love you all, and thank you so much.

INDEX

NOTE: Page references in *italics* refer to full-page photos of recipes.

Butterfly template for Cute Rose Cake, page 313

Peace Sign template for Tie-Dye Peace Appliqué Cake, page 321